⌐ SO-ANF-325

"Tony Hillerman's Native American detective Joe Leaphorn has long allowed the average mystery reader to do something extraordinary: join the tribe, and join the tribe at a time of great peril. With *Darkness Bids the Dead Goodbye*, Gary McKinney takes the reader deep into another sort of tribe altogether: the diehard followers of the Grateful Dead. Can divorced, semi-evolved, sensory-deprivation-tank-floating, ex-pot-smoking County Sheriff Gavin Pruitt find those responsible for an extraordinarily brutal murder? It'll take a miracle, but of course for a Deadhead Sheriff, miracles are all in a day's work. An incredibly entertaining tale."
—Philip Baruth, *The Millennium Shows*, *The Brothers Boswell*

"The interesting thing about Gary McKinney's Gavin Pruitt mysteries is that they're fiction wrapped around truth. Strange but true: Sheriff Gavin Pruitt really is both a Deadhead and a cop. And wrapping your mind around that conundrum makes for great reading."
—Dennis McNally, *A Long Strange Trip: The Inside History of the Grateful Dead*

"A thoughtful, thought-provoking mystery that "furthurs" Sheriff Gavin Pruitt's Deadhead and sleuthing careers in a wonderfully wrought novel that will delight Deadheads and mystery readers alike. McKinney's handling of Deadhead arcana is spot on, and his genuine appreciation for the richness of the Grateful Dead phenomenon as a setting for his exploration of the darkness in the human psyche helps make this a powerful sequel, and worthy successor, to *Slipknot*."
—Nicholas Meriwether, archivist, the Grateful Dead collection at UC, Santa Cruz; editor, *All Graceful Instruments: Contexts of the Grateful Dead Phenomenon*

"Gary McKinney laces his mystery writing with a heavy dose of Grateful Dead ethos. The result is his "Sheriff Gavin Pruitt Mystery" series, which combines labyrinthine plot twists with flashbacks to Dead shows. *Darkness Bids the Dead Goodbye* unfolds like a great rock concert that you'll wish would never end."
—Peter Conners, *Growing Up Dead: The Hallucinated Confessions of a Teenage Deadhead*

"*Darkness Bids the Dead Goodbye* sizzles with small town intrigue and tension from the moment the victim is assassinated on the shore of a muddy coastal estuary to the final pages when Gavin Pruitt—'60s Grateful Dead freak turned rural Pacific Northwest county sheriff—stares into the icy hot eyes of the murderer. Riveting chase scenes, SWAT teams, and an unpredictable cast of townspeople and co-workers have the Deadhead Sheriff beginning to wonder if his sky was yellow and his sun was blue. McKinney's sequel to his breakout novel *Slipknot* rides the swift currents of corruption, betrayal, and intrigue through the strangest of places and less than saintly circumstances. It's as though we are being taken to hell in a bucket—but at least we're enjoying the ride."
—Scott MacFarlane, *The Hippie Narrative: A Literary Perspective on the Counterculture*

"McKinney is a long time Deadhead, as is his protagonist, a small town sheriff in the northwest. It's a well-crafted murder mystery full of plot twists, a car chase, crooked cops, and other surprises. It's a good read, not just for Deadheads."
—George Walker, Merry Prankster, Further Driver, and author, *Trouble Ahead, Trouble Behind*

"In *Darkness Bids the Dead Goodbye*, McKinney unfolds this murder mystery like a tie-dye shirt preserved in a dime bag recovered from time warp, the mysteries of who killed Wilma Gillespie woven together with the mysteries of how we all got so old we have started burying the icons of our youth? And what is left for us? Plenty—if you take a ride with Sheriff Pruit in his cruiser. The narrative captures a compelling mix of small town folksiness and underworld grit, vivid characters in all their idiosyncratic neuroses and fragile humanity—criminals and victims, cops honest and corrupt, witnesses helpful and not, along with nosey neighbors and enigmatic ex-lovers."
—Larry Strauss, *Now's the Time*, and columnist for the Huffington Post

DARKNESS BIDS THE DEAD GOODBYE

DARKNESS BIDS THE DEAD GOODBYE

A SHERIFF GAVIN PRUITT MYSTERY

GARY MCKINNEY

This is a work of fiction. Names, characters, places, and incidents are products of the author's imagination or are used fictitiously and are not to be construed as real. Any resemblance to actual events, locales, organizations, or persons, living or dead, is entirely coincidental.

Copyright © 2011 by Gary McKinney.

All rights reserved. Printed in the United States of America. No part of this publication may be reproduced, stored in a retrieval system, or transmitted in any form or by any means, electronic, mechanical, photocopying, recording, or otherwise, without prior written permission.

Special thanks to Ice Nine Publishing for allowing the use of Grateful Dead lyrics.

Illustration: Thomas Yeates © 2011
Cover design: Karen Parker © 2011

ISBN: 0-9723706-9-2
Library of Congress Control Number: Pending

Kearney Street Books
Darkness Bids the Dead Goodbye
Second KSB printing (January, 2012).

Printed in the United States of America

Kearney Street Books
PO Box 2021
Bellingham, WA 98227
360-738-1355
www.kearneystreetbooks.com

Thanks to Sgt. Dave Richards of the Bellingham Police Department. Any errors in police policies and/or procedures are the author's competely. Thanks to Alan Trist of Ice Nine Publishing. Thanks to Robert Lopresti for the insights. Thanks to Laura Crest. Thanks to Paul Piper for the close read. Special thanks to Chas Hoppe. I hope all writers find an editor as good as he is. Thanks to Meredith Cary, friend, mentor, and guiding light. RD oversaw this project, as he does all the projects for those of us who knew him. Dedicated, of course, to my family: Karen, Morgan, and Fallon. Please note that Elkhorn is a figment of the author's imagination.

PROLOGUE:
THURSDAY, MAY 25ᵀᴴ, 1995

THE PATH WOUND through spring foliage, the ground underfoot soft as a damp carpet. Dusk to evening transition, the gurgling song of marsh wrens surrendering to the rubbery-throated barks of tree frogs. Full night would bring the bird-like cries of boreal toads, sweet and lonesome—as evocative as the whistle of a flycatcher.

The slough neared, the yellow blooms of skunk cabbage glowing iridescently in the gloom, their stink mingling with the fetor of low-tide, a primordial mud and blossom stench irresistible to scavenging flies and beetles—especially with the heat generated by the skunk cabbage flowers. Recent warm days had brought out swarms of gnats, easy to miss in the post-sunset gloaming. If she'd been walking for pleasure she'd have watched out for them, waved them out of her way. But with her mind racing, she got a mouthful and coughed, stumbled and got a poke in the back.

"Just keep going."

"Why are you doing this?"

"You know why."

The ground buckled up suddenly, and she slipped, grasping a fistful of huckleberry bush stems, thin and yielding. She fell to a knee.

The gloved hand on her shoulder, pinching. "Get up."

"Stop this. Just stop it."

"Just move."

Forward to the edge of the fresh water tidal basin she'd relished standing near the last few months, the reason she'd taken the rental in the first place. The forest of hemlock and cedar transposing to red alder and willow, transposing again to sedges and bulrushes, sweet grass and cinquefoil—and, of course, the bright yellow leaves of skunk cabbage.

"Kneel down. Right there."

The last flicker of dusk gave up its fight with sunset. A three-quarter moon softly lit the slough, where the sharp fingers of the Willapa River's South Fork cut the reeds and grasses into isle-like tufts, surrounded at mid-tide by black muddy channels. She'd seen bittern and great blue heron fish here, and listened to cedar waxwings and yellow warblers.

"Please," she begged. "Don't murder me."

PART ONE:
MAY, 1995

CHAPTER ONE

THE FRAGRANCE FROM hibachis and Coleman stoves cooking everything from sweet onions to buffalo burgers mingled with the redolence of marijuana and wafted over the parking lot east of the Seattle Center towards Memorial Stadium in aromatic clouds. For Gavin Pruitt, Willapa County Sheriff, it was an immediate contact high—about as close to smoking pot as he got anymore.

Molly, Pruitt's long-time love and brand new wife, said, "What's this?"

"The smell?"

She raised her famous eyebrow, the one that always spoke volumes. "I *know* the smell, Gavin. I mean this place."

Pruitt chuckled. "They call it Shakedown Street."

Olivia, Pruitt's nineteen-year-old daughter, said, "What a scene."

Molly said, "There's probably as many people here as there are in Elkhorn."

"Many more, I'm sure." Pruitt figured this gathering alone was double the 5,000 residents of Elkhorn. The concert itself would be well over 20,000. You could lose Elkhorn here. More importantly, he smiled, you could lose yourself.

He turned to his daughter. "Some of these people will spend an entire tour following the band."

Olivia said, "How can they go to so many concerts by one band? People don't go to all the Bryan Adams shows, or Hootie and the Blowfish. You go to somebody's concert, then somebody else's concert, not twenty concerts in a row."

"It's a lifestyle," Pruitt said. "And music. Every concert you hear something new, new songs, new arrangements of old songs—some made up on the spot. You just never know what's going to happen." He closed his eyes and took a deep breath, relished the very human scent of the scene. "And that is so cool."

Molly said, "And you're sure we've got tickets?"

Pruitt looked at Molly and tried to share all that was in his heart: her beauty, his daughter's, the magic of the place and time. He could feel himself beaming like an idiot, could see, too, that Molly was getting it. "Biscuit's got 'em," he said. "We'll meet him here."

"Where?" Olivia said. She didn't seem to be getting it at all. Which was fine. Everyone in their own time. "I mean, look at this. How could you find anything?"

"We just find each other."

"That's all he said, that you'd find each other?"

Pruitt shrugged. "It's what we've done since the seventies. He gets the tickets and calls me and says be at such-and-so place on such-and-so date." He glanced over her shoulder. "Speaking of finding someone, there's Christopher. When did he get lost?"

All three turned in the direction of Olivia's boyfriend, easy to spot at six-foot-three and a head full of shoulder-length blond dreadlocks.

Olivia shook her head. "He got high." Turning to her father, she said, "Sorry, Daddy."

Pruitt shrugged. "I didn't see him get high."

Molly laughed. "Don't ask, don't tell."

"I don't ask Biscuit any questions either." Making quotes with his fingers, Pruitt said, "He just goes to the 'bathroom'."

"Are those bagpipes?" Molly said. "Bagpipes?"

With the phalanx of drum circles and street musicians—one long-haired young man singing in a helium-induced falsetto—the sound of Shakedown Street was an aural mélange as heady as the aroma and sights: horse-mounted Seattle police eyeing a man in a psychedelically-painted top hat; T-shirt vendors hawking tie-dyes of every imaginable hue; a woman in a loose, full-length skirt dancing on the roof of a Vanagon camper. Pruitt wondered if the music she danced to was something specific or just the coalescence of the wild rumpus surrounding her.

Christopher shambled up. Olivia gave him a look. "What?" he said.

"I can't do that. I thought we agreed."

He shrugged. "Ran into a friend."

Christopher was visibly shrinking under Olivia's slow burn. Pruitt recalled a similar scene that had played out between Olivia's mother and himself in 1969, at his first Dead concert, the Eagle's Ballroom in Seattle. Although she wasn't pregnant yet, Claudia, his first wife, was still straight—was curious about, but still mistrustful of weed. She did not like the idea of Pruitt being on a different "trip" than she was. Not good karma, by her figuring. But he'd run into friends in the bathroom and taken a couple of hits. When he arrived back at Claudia's side, she'd given him that same withering look, had used the same disapproving tone of voice.

The flashback wasn't giving him much confidence in Olivia and Christopher's future together. A nineteen-year-old pregnant dropout and a boy not much older hanging on to a college career by his fingernails? Six months ago, when he'd first met Christopher, this would have been the last thing he would have expected.

He knew he was in no position to judge. He and Claudia hadn't lasted long after Olivia's birth, a couple of rocky years and kaput. He'd wanted to follow the Dead; she'd wanted a home. Yet somehow they had managed to do right by Olivia. Joint custody a hundred-and-fifty miles apart hadn't been easy, but they'd done it. Pruitt cherished his summers with his daughter. Even in his most avid touring days, following the Dead from city to city, he didn't tour during his custody periods. Until he joined the Sheriff's Department, he'd never had much money, either. A fact lost on Olivia. Like any kid, all she wanted was a good dad.

When he peered again into Shakedown Street's clamorous multitude, there in the middle of it was his best friend.

"Hey, hey," Pruitt said. "The man himself."

"That's Biscuit?" asked Molly. "The straight-looking guy?"

Pruitt laughed. "He lives in Boise. Sells insurance. Hey! Biscuit! Over here!"

Biscuit caught sight of Pruitt and waved with gangly arms and hands so broad and flat they could have been mistaken for semaphore flags.

"Daddy, he's gotta be six-foot-four!"

"Six-nine, but who's counting."

With such exaggerated arms and legs, Biscuit in motion reminded Pruitt of a giraffe: it took a moment for the synapses shot from the brain to arrive at the feet. His gait even defined his personality: gentle, caring. He walked like he was trying to avoid leaving a footprint—even in sand. Loping toward the Pruitt clan, a huge grin creased his face. "They're both pregnant!" he yelled over the din of music and hawkers, pointing at the two women who stood one on either side of Pruitt. "That is so cool!"

Olivia looked appalled at Biscuit's social impropriety— her condition pointed out for all to see, for god's sake!—but Molly started laughing. "You said he was a straight talker, Gav. You didn't tell me he'd shout the obvious out loud."

Biscuit had never met Molly, and had last seen Olivia when she was about three. So now to witness the two lovely, expecting women in their maternal glow—his friend's new wife, his friend's child—frankly, it seemed to overwhelm Biscuit's sense of cosmic oneness and wonder. He forgot to look where he was stepping with his gentle, but still giraffe-

sized feet, and heaved right into a beer vendor. Bottles of
Sam Adams and Budweiser scattered into one of Shakedown
Street's makeshift aisles. Glass broke. Beer suds roiled up
white on the black tarmac.

The vendor screeched, arms up wing-like in disbelief.
"Hey, man! What the hell!"

Pruitt muttered, "Crap," and, as quickly as he could
without knocking into a vendor himself, jogged over toward
the uproar between the beer man and his old friend.

"Sorry, sorry . . . so sorry." Biscuit's huge hands wagged
like palm fronds trying to cool the heat.

"That's, like, three-quarters of my business gone, man!"

"I'm so sorry. Really, brother. I've got money. Let me pay
you for it."

"Let me pay for it, too," Pruitt said, pulling up quietly
to the vendor's side, who besides beer smelled like patchouli
and three days without a shower.

"But I knocked him over, Gav."

"Yeah, because I distracted you."

"When you called," Biscuit said, grinning in spite of
himself, "you didn't tell what the surprise was, but I knew as
soon as I saw them."

"I shoulda said something, buddy. Sorry."

"Hey, man, it's my *beer*, man," said the vendor. "It's what I
do. The money's just maya. I meet people. I make *friends* doing
this. I get *miracled* doing this, man. You haven't got tickets for
me, do you?"

Biscuit let his hands drop. "I don't, man. I wish I did. Let
me buy all your stock. You'll at least have some money."

The beer vendor reared back and roared at the sky.
"Goddamnit! This sucks!"

"Trouble here, fellas?" It was a Seattle bike patrol officer,
short-sleeved blue shirt with epaulets and black pocket flaps,
a full duty belt heavy around his waist. He was straddling the
crossbar of his mountain bike. His partner had dismounted
and stood with keen interest just behind. Both wore mirrored
sunglasses—the Robocop look.

"An accident," Pruitt said.

"My freakin' beer!" The vendor pulled his worn, wool knit cap off his head and threw it to the ground in frustration, right in a puddle of suds. "Ah, man." He picked it up again, dripping now, and gazed at it morosely. "My hat, man. My freaking hat."

"We're going to pay him for it," Biscuit explained to the officers, hands still waggling at his sides.

Robocop lenses assessed the vendor. "Taking this a little hard, aren't we, son?"

"It's my lifestyle, man!" the vendor beseeched, nearly in tears. "Doesn't anybody *get* that?"

"You want us to buy you another supply of beer?" Biscuit asked.

"More beer?" the vendor said. "You'd buy me more beer?"

"More beer for this guy?" said Robocop.

"We'll make it right," Pruitt said.

Robocop's partner said, "He appears intoxicated. On the verge of disorderly."

Pruitt gazed up at Queen Anne Hill, its spiky, red-and-white radio towers like the antennae of some amorphous, humped beast looming over Shakedown Street and this absurd confrontation. He said, "Officer," and then badged the bike cop standing nearest. It was the last thing he'd wanted to do, but he did it: reached into the top of his shirt and pulled it out, his badge in a holder on a chain. "I can handle this. You guys can get on to more important things."

Both the cops leaned in. "Sheriff?" said the front-standing cop. "You're shittin' me." He removed his sunglasses and spoke in a stage whisper: "You undercover?"

"No. Just here to enjoy the music."

"You're a pig?" said the vendor. "A freakin' pig, man?"

Turning to the vendor, Pruitt spoke quietly. "Chill out, brother. Strangers stoppin' strangers, right? Just to shake their hand? You know what I'm saying?"

The vendor opened his mouth but no words came out. Pruitt's quoting "Scarlet Begonias" finally got the man's attention. He gazed misty-eyed at Pruitt a moment longer, then turned and mopped his brow with his beer-soaked wool cap. "Wow," he said. "Wow."

Biscuit stuck out his big paw to the vendor. "We're going to make this right, brother. Whatever you need."

The vendor regarded the paw, then Biscuit, Biscuit laying the biggest set of puppy eyes Pruitt had ever seen on the guy. "Okay, man," the vendor said. "Okay."

When Biscuit hugged him, the tears that had been standing on the vendor's lids fell. "It's been a weird day," he confessed.

Pruitt turned back to the bike cops. "We all right?"

"You're not undercover?"

"I'm a Deadhead, officer." It was cop-to-cop now, eyeball-to-eyeball. Pulling the badge put them there; Pruitt knew it, the cop knew it. "Have been since 1968. What can I tell you?"

"You can tell me how you reconcile being a part of all this law breaking. This degeneracy."

Pruitt's gaze didn't waver. "These people look like criminals to you?"

The bike cop had been standing just on the relaxed side of "atten-hut," but now straightened his back fully. "They're breaking laws left and right."

"They're doing nothing to hurt anything or anybody other than themselves—if that."

The cop pointed a finger at him. "A law's a law."

Pruitt ignored the finger, continued holding the man's eyes, hard cop eyes, just as Pruitt knew his were now, too. "You don't look like a rookie. But something about this is making you sound like one."

Another beat and the bike cop hooked his glasses back over his ears. Welcome back, Robocop. "You have a good day, Sheriff."

He gripped his handle bars, preparing to ride off. "I'll do that officer. Thanks for your help."

CHAPTER TWO

THREE DAYS LATER the concert still flashed in Pruitt's mind. That flock of Canadian geese, for instance, rising up behind the stage during "Stella Blue," soaring around the stadium like nature's Blue Angels.

The image came to him as he gazed out the window in his office at the Willapa County Courthouse complex. His vista was narrow—framed to the north by the main courthouse building and to the south by a copse of beech and red alder— but Pruitt could nonetheless see the distant clear-cut hills, the tideflats at their feet, and the dark olive-green Willapa River snaking through the valley on its brisk rush toward the bay. Unfurling spring buds were turning the second growth Douglas firs that abutted the clear cuts into nature's viridescent bunting, but it was the sky that drew his attention. Peacock blue and tracked with altocumulus clouds broken into a mad pattern of mazes.

Wow, what a great sky. And it had been a great sky at the concert, too, and "Stella Blue" was one of his favorite songs. Molly sat under his arm, swaying with him. Biscuit grinned from ear to ear. Olivia smiled, her head resting on Christopher's shoulder, one of his dreadlocks wrapped around her finger, his indiscretion with the pot forgiven. What a moment. His wife, his daughter, his best friend, a child, not to mention a grandchild, on the way.

And "Stella Blue," a song so sweet. Sad, too, but in that complete way of yin and yang, life as sad as it could be sweet. Jerry singing, "There's nothing you can hold for very long." And, yes, Pruitt got that. And maybe he couldn't hold on to the moment like he could the cup of tea in his hand, nor could he make time stand still, but the memory was sweet, and right now that was good enough.

Then his phone rang, snapping him out of his reverie, his day about to begin. He stole a quick sip from his Steal Your Face mug, green tea purchased on Shakedown Street from an herb vendor. A little honey in it. He was a Ready Freddie.

"Pruitt."

"Just got a call from Ing." His dispatcher, Madeline Box. "He wants you to meet him out in Nalpe." She gave him the address.

"Why?"

"He wouldn't say."

"Wouldn't say?"

"I know. It's odd. But he was insistent. And he said not to call him on the radio, either."

Odd, indeed. Ing Yen, his most trusted deputy—a Laotian immigrant who as a teenager had fled the aftermath of the Vietnam War and the Hmong's reputation as American collaborators. A strange request, but he must have had a good reason for it.

•••

The sky overarching the Nalpe slough was the same mottled maze of white and peacock blue upon which he'd been meditating back at the office. Wonderment, however, had been replaced with wretchedness and outrage. Pruitt had known that some sort of police business was inevitably going to sour his memories of "Stella Blue" and "Franklin's Tower"—but this? This he could never have imagined—here in this primal marsh with the stink of skunk cabbage wafting with the breeze, where he stood on bare ground that had a palpable give to it, as if a few good bounces would push it down into the water table lurking underneath.

The clearing wasn't much, a quick slope to the edge of the slough, hedged by willow and alder—reeds and sedges tiptoeing into the slough itself. It would have been easy to miss the body. Although not exactly Saint Stephen's seashore washed by suds and foam, this was still the backwash of a tidal plain, and if the moon's centripetal force was particularly strong, the river this far upstream could still taste faintly like the ocean.

"Who found her?" Pruitt asked Yen.

"Couple boys fishing," Yen said in his English/Laotian patois.

They stood together looking at the scene, not exactly shoulder to shoulder, as Yen stood barely five-four and Pruitt nearly six-one.

"Do the boys know what they saw?"

"Don't think so. Just knew it wasn't right."

"They know who it was?"

"No."

"What do you think they'll tell their parents?"

"Saw dead body?"

Pruitt took off his hat and ran his hand through his hair. "I figure we got until about the middle of the afternoon before the rumors are rampant."

"Sound about right."

Pruitt put his hat back on and gazed up the winding path. "The boys walk down here this way?"

"Yep."

"So did we."

"Yep."

"So the path is next to useless for evidence." He gazed again at the slough. "But we've got the scene and we've got the house."

"Path maybe. Never know."

"You're sure it's Wilma?"

A stupid question. Maybe because he hadn't got as close to the body as Yen had, seen what Yen had seen, his mind was fighting him, unable, or unready, to accept the truth. What was he even seeing? A lump of muddy clothes? A shallow swamp hillock? An animal that had crawled off to die? It had been a few days—three? four? Scavenging animals had already begun taking their toll on the exposed parts of her body.

Finally, Yen said, "She had that charm bracelet. You know?"

Pruitt did. "Cross, Star of David, Islamic crescent?"

"Still on wrist."

The image of Wilma Gillespie's charm bracelet—but more so the image of it dangling from her lovely wrist—broke Pruitt into a sweat, prickles rising along his shoulders and arms.

The horror rush was how he thought of it, when the nightmarish finally manifests itself physically. His vision tunneled and dimmed. Fighting it only made it worse, so Pruitt stood calmly. Let it pass through him.

The first time he had seen the bloody aftermath of a car accident—bodies ripped open, turned nearly inside out—he tried to suppress the sensation. Which only caused him to vomit. Arthur Hujack, the former sheriff, and Pruitt's mentor, had given him advice. "As soon as you can, get a deep breath, a slow one. Find a place in your mind that'll help get your brain back in gear. Like 'Cop,' or 'Job,' or whatever. I've seen guys carry paper bags with them to a traffic accident or crime scene. Sit down and do that whole breathing thing. Nothin' wrong with it. But what're you going to do, issue paper bags as part of a kit? Thing is, you'll find something that works for you. And the other thing is, you'll never get over it. You better never get over it. You do and it's time to see a shrink."

As Yen waited, Pruitt took his long, slow breaths. Finally, he said, "Do you think this might be some sort of accident? Some hunter taking a wild shot?"

"Homicide either way, but somebody shoot her and run away? Don't call cops? Not impossible." Yen held up his hands like he was a director framing a shot. "But see how she's lying on ground?"

Pruitt took a closer look. "She's fallen over her knees."

"If somebody shoot her by mistake," Yen said, "some hunter or kid think he's shooting deer, she won't fall that way. Take by surprise, rifle bullet knock her off her feet. Be all sprawled out. Can't say for absolute, but I bet she was kneeling when shot. Bullet come from behind, impact took her forward."

Pruitt's skin settled down, the rush passing. He felt Yen's assessment was accurate. This was no accident. She'd been murdered. "I think we'd better give Lee Wilson a call."

Yen scowled. "You don't think we can handle this?"

Pruitt realized he had just slighted his best deputy. It wasn't "we" Ing meant, but himself. In the horror of the moment, Pruitt had forgotten Yen's designs on becoming Willapa County's next lead investigator, stepping into Wilson's formidable shoes. That his deputy was the right person for the job was not the issue. Since Wilson's departure—technically his leave of absence—Yen had been assigned the toughest burglaries, break-ins, and traffic accidents. But this . . . .

"Ing," he said, "I'll have you assist Lee for the duration. Shadow him every step of the way. Plus it's high time we got you up to the Academy for those classes you're supposed to take, get you properly certified."

Pruitt looked at him. "But this is heavy, man. And I think we need Lee."

•••

Technologically, the Willapa County Sheriff's Department was underfunded—according to some of Pruitt's colleagues, woefully. Just recently, Pruitt's friend Sheriff Gary Bowman of nearby Lewis County had procured and issued cellular phones to his officers. He was jealous of Bowman's budget. For that matter, he was jealous of the budgets in just about every other county in the state. Yet even if they had the money for the luxury of cellular phones, the coverage in Willapa County was spotty. Nearer the major routes like Interstate 5, Bowman's jurisdiction, the coverage was fine and the usefulness of such devices unquestioned.

Coverage was also decent at the eastern edge of Willapa County, but the best Pruitt could do for his deputies working that sector were a couple of Motorola bag phones—cheap, bulky things that nevertheless got the job done. Neither he nor Yen, however, had one of those with them.

Such technology would have been a welcome asset right now. Just as Yen had not wanted to announce a murder over the police band—thus giving those civilians listening in a heads-up—Pruitt did not want to patch his radio through to Lee Wilson. Using the phone in Wilma's house wasn't an option either. Too much risk that they'd disturb possible evidence.

So Pruitt strode to the nearest neighbor's, about a hundred yards away. Millie Johnson's was a small, bleak place with a crab grass yard and unweeded flower beds. The only incongruity to its visual squalor was the crimson-bloomed rhododendrons on either side of the front door: crisp, vibrant, full of life. Kind of like Millie, a feisty septuagenarian widow, who was glad to see him. He was surprised at her tidy living room. No patina of dust, no clutter of memorabilia attesting to a long life.

"Phone's on the side table." Millie was a slight woman with erect posture—no osteoporosis stoop. Her hands were dabbled with liver spots, and her knuckles shone through the skin, but they showed no sign of arthritis. She looked great. The gleam in her eye reminded him of Ruth Gordon in the movie *Harold and Maude*, one of his favorites.

"I'll cover this long distance call," he assured her.

"Not stingy with my money," she said. "Consider it a donation to the police fund." She headed for the kitchen. "Coffee?"

"Sure, Millie. Can I take one up to Deputy Yen, too?"

"You sure can, Sheriff."

He began to pick up the receiver, but hesitated. "Millie, did you hear anything unusual a couple of days ago?"

"Like what?"

"I dunno. Shots, maybe?"

Millie appeared again in the door well. "I hear shots around here all the time. Kids shooting at whatever they think they can hit. But I'm too far away from anyone to notice any arguing. That's why I like it here."

"Anything at all that made you stop and take pause for a moment?"

She thought. "Well, there was a car parked in that alder patch across from Wilma's. I wouldn't have thought anything of it if you hadn't asked."

"Do you remember what night?"

"Maybe Thursday?"

"Do you remember the color? Was it a sedan or a truck?"

"A car. Not a truck. Maybe blue." She gazed at the ceiling a moment. "I just can't say for sure."

"Strike you as suspicious?"

She shrugged. "No, not really. People park there sometimes to get access to the hill. They hunt up there occasionally."

"You see anybody in the car?"

Tapping her temple, she said, "Eyes aren't what they used to be, Sheriff."

Pruitt smiled. "Millie, that's about the only part of you that's showing any age."

"Cut it out, now. I know how old I am."

"As old as you feel, right?"

She snapped her hand at him, a curious but affable gesture. "I'm doing okay."

"So you were taking a walk that night?"

"Yes. Sometimes I like to take my constitutional around sunset. Especially if it's been a bright day. My eyes don't like the brightness. Those kind of days, I wait until sunset."

"You don't worry about walking on the shoulder at night?"

"I always wear that." She pointed to a bright yellow jacket hanging on a peg near the door.

"Gotcha. See that a mile away. So the evening we're talking about, you saw this car as you were walking by it?"

"No. I saw it from the road. I was heading in the other direction."

"Was it still there when you got back from your walk?"

"Didn't think to look, Sheriff."

"And you didn't notice anybody other than Wilma parked at her house?"

She shrugged. "Like I said, I didn't go that direction. Can't see Wilma's from here, even at the front of my property. Not with that little bend in the road."

"Okay. Thanks, Millie."

She gave him a look, then glanced into the kitchen. "Cream or sugar?"

Pruitt almost had to ask what she was talking about. "Just black would be great."

When Millie disappeared from the door well, Pruitt took the note pad he kept in his breast pocket and found the Police Academy's number. He got the secretary first, then was patched through to Lee himself. After a quick "How you doing?" Pruitt gave his ex-Chief Deputy for Investigations a summary, carefully explaining Yen's description of the body position. "You too busy to come down and take this over?"

"Wilma?" Lee asked. "You gotta be shittin' me. Wilma? And you guys think she was murdered?"

Pruitt rubbed the bridge of his nose. "I can't believe it, either."

"Gaawwd," was all Lee could say back.

Like Yen had done for him, Pruitt gave Lee a moment to deal with the shock. Wilma was the City of Elkhorn Police Department's office manager. Not a cop, but part of the cop family. Chief Dan Louderback's best hire ever.

Wilson finally broke the silence. "It's nine AM," he said. "I got a test I was supposed to give at ten, but I can get someone to do that for me. If I go Code 3, I can get down there in an hour."

Burien to Elkhorn in an hour? That concerned Pruitt. High-speed driving had never been Wilson's strong suit. "Lee," he said, "she's been dead a few days at least, and Yen and I are sitting tight on this. Take a couple of hours, my friend."

•••

When Millie brought out the mugs of coffee, she looked stricken.

"I'm sorry you had to find out that way, Millie."

"It's a small house."

"I'm going to make a formal announcement later today. But we need to keep this between us until then."

As Millie handed him the mugs, he noticed her hands shaking.

"Millie, let's go have a sit, okay?"

"Yeah."

Pruitt reached to help her, but her back was already turned. Once on the couch, she took a ragged breath.

"You and Wilma see each other much?"

"Girl was all about herbal tea." There was a box of tissues on the side table and she took one and blew her nose. "Wilma was new out here, but we hit it off. If she saw me on one of my constitutionals, she'd wave me over for tea. Always herbal tea."

Pruitt placed the mugs on the coffee table, then sat next to her.

Millie said, "You think she was murdered? That's why you're calling Lee?"

"We don't know for sure, but that's our first impression. That's why it's important to keep this between us right now. If it turns out to be something else, an accident or whatever . . . "

Weakly, Millie gave him a zipped-lip gesture.

Pruitt took her hand. The skin was smooth. He could feel the strength in them. "You want me to call someone?"

She patted his hand back. "No, no. I'll just sit here for a few minutes."

"I'll get the mugs right back to you."

"Oh, don't worry about the dang mugs," she said, "They're nothin' special and I got a cupboard full of 'em."

Before heading back to the crime scene, Pruitt stood at the spot Millie had likely stood when she'd noticed the parked car on the day that may have been the day Wilma had died. The thicket she had referred to was triangular in shape, thicker at Wilma's end of the road, narrower at Millie's. From Millie's angle he could see it would have been easy to spot a vehicle parked there, even at dusk, even with her imperfect vision. The alder was thin, the huckleberry only as high as a man's waist. If someone's intent had been surveillance of Wilma's place, especially late in the day with the shadows getting long, it would have been a good place to do so. A grown-over branch off Weaver Road, maybe a couple of dozen yards deep, petering out at a slope leading to a sparsely wooded hill. There were hundreds of such paths and turn-offs in the county—maybe thousands. The car's presence, however, didn't necessarily translate into anything sinister. There probably was something to hunt up the hill—or at least on the other side of it. Somebody could have been looking to poach a deer. Or maybe someone just wanted to traipse through the woods on a nice spring day.

•••

Pruitt and Yen drank Millie's coffee next to their cruisers on the apron of crushed gravel that served as a carport to the rental home Wilma had been living in the last eight or nine months.

"We got a boatload of things that need doing."

"One," Ing said, "is get evidence van. Two is interview ex-husband."

"Technically, Mark's not her ex. They're separated."

"That's just technicality." Yen flashed one of his rare smiles. Here and gone, just like that.

"Yeah, yeah. Good one."

"Husband murdered, wife number one suspect. Wife murdered, husband number one suspect. 'Til we know otherwise."

"Have Bobby bring the evidence van out. He can go back to the office in your cruiser."

"You going to tell your family?"

"Hell, yeah. Absolutely."

Yen ticked his nose. "Very unprofessional."

"I know." Pruitt took a sip of of Millie's coffee, which was faintly bitter, but not unpleasantly so. "You, too, if you want, Ing. This is Wilma, for god's sake. Olivia and Molly knew her. It's like losing someone in your family."

"My family, too. Wilma very good to us when we first move here. Maybe first to come around and . . . What do you call it? Bring welcome wagon? Brought fat oranges. Homemade soap that smelled to us like America."

"I especially don't want Olivia getting a phone call about it."

"Olivia? She on edge, 'cause of baby?"

"That and Christopher. He's been a little less than fatherly to this point."

Yen ticked his nose again. "Christopher pretty young. Pretty smart, too. I've heard dreadlocks called antenna to world. Maybe make him even smarter."

Pruitt smiled. "I've actually heard him say that very same thing about his dreads. And he is a good kid."

Yen said, "How you handle husband?"

Pruitt thought a moment. "We go with your assessment, that she was murdered. Rattle his cage and see what kind of squawking comes out of his beak."

Yen nodded. "Yeah. I like it."

"But if it was an accident? As unlikely as that seems?"

"Apologize. What they say here: easier for forgiveness than permission?"

"Much easier." Pruitt tossed the dregs of his coffee onto the crushed gravel.

"But first," he said, "I'm going to return these mugs. I want to check in on Millie again."

CHAPTER THREE

MARK GILLESPIE, WILMA'S not-quite ex, worked at the Saginaw Lumber Mill, a sprawling operation situated in a wide U-shaped bend in the Willapa River, where laser-guided saws milled slender second- and third-growth Douglas firs into two-by-fours. Gillespie managed the yard, the logs coming in, the lumber going out. His office was a modest-sized storage shed with windows, a space heater, and a half-dozen clipboards dangling from screw hangers twisted into the exposed framework. Seated on a metal stool, he was perusing the paperwork on one of the battered clipboards when Pruitt knocked lightly on the doorjamb.

Gillespie frowned. "Sheriff?"

He was a pale-skinned man with blondish red hair whose face had gone ruddy from a combination of time spent outside and the natural inclination of his Scots-Irish heritage. Though he was not known as a drinker, gin blossoms had already appeared on his cheeks and nose and gave him the appearance of one. A Seattle Mariners baseball cap was pushed back on his head.

As Pruitt explained why he was there, Gillespie's eyes began to lose focus, then he fainted, falling from his stool by degrees, a marionette cut from its strings one by one. His knees thumped to the plywood floor. He tipped backwards over them—looking eerily like Wilma's death fall in reverse—the stool toppling, his head striking hard.

Pruitt rushed in and pried Gillespie's legs out from under him, trying to be gentle, hoping he hadn't over-extended the man's hamstrings. Then he checked the back of Gillespie's head for blood. Fortunately, there wasn't any. A welt, however, had already formed. On the makeshift desk—a plank across metal sawhorses—sat a thermos with a Mariners logo, a cellular phone, and a couple bottles of water.

Pruitt grabbed one of the bottles, cracked it, sprinkled a little on his hands, then patted the coolness across Gillespie's ruddy cheeks. After a moment or two, he came around. Once his eyes began flickering open, Pruitt held his head up and helped him get a swallow.

"Take it easy, man," he told him.

Gillespie tried to reach the back of his head, but couldn't. "That really hurts." Slowly his eyes refocused. "How?" he asked. "A car accident? What?"

"We think she was murdered."

"What? No. No way. Who could possibly—"

"You ready to come up?" Pruitt reached to place a hand behind his shoulders.

"Yeah. I think so." Together they got him to a sitting position, his legs splayed in front. "When?"

Pruitt kept his hand on Gillespie's shoulder. He didn't want to say when. For one thing, he didn't know. The decomp would make time-of-death tricky. For another, he wanted to see if Mark could tell him. "Just stay there a moment. Take it easy," Pruitt advised. "When's the last time you saw her?"

"Wilma?" Gillespie was now able to reach the back of his head. "We haven't been seeing each other much. You know, the separation and all."

"You saw her last when?"

Rubbing his neck, Gillespie said, "Had some papers to sign Monday."

"Monday last? Divorce papers?"

"Oh, boy, this hurts."

His eyes had glazed over. Physical and mental trauma. Part of Pruitt hated himself for trying to take advantage of the man's vulnerability. He also knew it was too good an opportunity for the truth to pass up. "So last Monday you talked about the divorce?"

"Yeah, a week ago." Gingerly, he touched the welt. "Not about the divorce, some property stuff. Bank stuff. She wanted to buy the place she was renting. Out there by Nalpe. I was going to cash out her share of our house. That was going to be her down payment."

"Can we go up and take a look around your place?"

Although his hand remained at the back of his head, Gillespie stopped rubbing and squeezed his eyes shut. "You think *I* did it?"

"Just following protocol, Mark. Police procedures."

"Help me to my feet."

Pruitt did so.

Gillespie said, "I gotta think about that, Sheriff."

"Why, Mark?"

He lifted the metal stool from the floor and set it back on its feet, placed his open palm on the seat to steady himself. "I don't like the fact you think I could do something like that."

"Like what exactly?"

For a moment he looked confused. "Hurt Wilma. What else?"

Pruitt let that pass. "Good way to get clear of all that is let us look around."

Gillespie held up a hand. "Okay. Okay."

"Thanks," Pruitt said. He let another beat pass. "There's some paperwork involved. Pretty simple, a Consent to Search Form. Strictly red tape. Take about two minutes."

"Yeah. Fine."

"And you'll need to come with me. Up to the house."

He touched the back of head again, winced. "Right. I'll get my truck."

Pruitt looked at him. "I don't think you should drive."

"I can drive."

"Mark, you just fainted, man. Come with me, we'll take care of you."

•••

Pruitt's first thought was to grab a Consent to Search Form from the Elkhorn Police Department, save himself a trip all the way across town. Their office was nearby and Pruitt's office had a good relationship with them. His second thought was that taking Mark Gillespie there would be perverse, considering Wilma worked there. *Had worked*, Pruitt corrected himself, swallowing down that horror feeling again.

A blast of perversity, however, might be just the thing to further this investigation along. If Gillespie had indeed killed his wife, Pruitt would love to get this closed and over with—start moving on to grief. Plus he had to tell Dan Louderback, Wilma's boss, what had happened, before he heard about it from someone else. Just enough people—the boys, their families, Millie—had just enough information to send rumors spreading and distorting swiftly and in equal measure.

When Pruitt started to bundle him into the back of the cruiser, Gillespie said, "What? Am I under arrest?"

"Just formality."

"I don't like the way it looks. Like I've done something wrong. I'd rather take my chances and follow you in my rig." He glanced at his truck, parked alongside the storage shed / office. A white Chevy S-10 with a Seattle Mariners bumper sticker.

"Okay, Mark. I understand. Hop in the front."

Although hardly standard operating procedure, allowing a citizen to ride shotgun wasn't prohibited. Pro forma may have made him a person of interest, but at this point Gillespie was far from under arrest. Besides, Pruitt had known him for years, an acquaintance he'd seen minimally every year at the law enforcement Labor Day picnic. Most importantly, Pruitt wanted to keep tight reins on him for as long as he could without appearing obvious about it.

With Wilma's estranged husband sitting next to him, Pruitt drove slowly, keeping Gillespie in his peripheral vision, looking for unusual body language. Too much and he was dramatizing, too little and he was freezing—both indicators of truth hiding, if not out-and-out lying. But outside of a long sigh, the man just slumped in a stunned state of silence.

To get him talking, Pruitt said, "I see you got one those new cellular phones. How do you like it?"

Gillespie patted his coat pocket where he'd placed it. "Yeah, I don't even know why I keep it with me around here. There's no service you can count on."

"Right. What's the point?"

"I got it for the road. Going to the games."

"Mariners? There at the Kingdome?"

"Yeah, you get out of town a ways and the service is fine. If there's an emergency, I can call 911. Or if I'm going to be late, I can call home."

"Call Wilma?"

"Yeah." He choked. "I mean . . ." He touched his forehead. "Jeez."

"Sorry, man. I didn't mean to . . . you know." Pruitt pulled up to the curb in front of the Elkhorn Civic Building, a stucco-sided, featureless structure sitting atop a raised cement foundation to avoid the semi-annual flooding. The mayor's office was there, and a town council meeting room, plus the suite that comprised the police department. "I'll go in and grab the forms."

Gillespie sighed. "Fine."

"You want to come in with me?"

"No. No, I don't want to do that."

Pruitt held onto the car wheel. "It may take a minute. I've got to tell the chief about this."

It looked like he was fighting back tears.

"You don't mind waiting?"

He held up his hands. "I'm good."

Again, if Pruitt were playing by the book, he would not have left Gillespie to his own devices in a police cruiser. But procedures were different in a small county, not as strict, not as formalized. What was important to Pruitt this early in the investigation was seeing the man's reactions, trying to get a read. Besides, what would he do, vandalize the cruiser? Run the half mile back to his truck? If that was the worst scenario, at least Pruitt would know who killed Wilma. And re-apprehending him would be easy.

There was, of course, no receptionist to greet him, since that would have been Wilma's job. But the sound of the door opening drew Elkhorn's police chief, Dan Louderback, out from his office. "Gavin?" he said.

Pruitt told him what had happened.

Louderback fell into Wilma's chair. It almost looked like he was pushed. His gaze rose to the ceiling. Tears glazed his eyes. "I knew something was off."

"What was off?"

"She would've called if she had car trouble. Even if she was only going to be a few minutes late, she'd call."

Pruitt gave Louderback a moment. "Anything going on with her that could explain this?"

Still with his gaze on the ceiling, the police chief worked his lips with his fingers. A nervous tic Pruitt had noticed lately, maybe the last few weeks.

Sounding perturbed, Louderback said, "Explain it?"

"Anything troubling her, Dan? Any talk of someone stalking her? I know this is tough, but help me, man. Let's be cops here."

Dan glared at Pruitt, hurt by the accusation that he was being unprofessional. Pruitt, however, refused to feel bad for pushing him. There had been rumors of a love affair, and whether true or not, Dan and Wilma had worked together for years, and as colleagues in a small office they would know things about each other that even their significant others would not.

"She seemed more intense the last few months," he said. "Figured it was her and Mark, this separation and all."

"Speaking of Mark . . . " Pruitt explained what he needed, the forms. "Who's on right now?"

"Jerry."

Jerry Louderback was both Dan's younger brother and one of his officers.

"Can I borrow him for a hour or two? My crew's spread out all over right now, and I need somebody to baby-sit Mark while we search his house."

"Sure. He's just checking for speeders by the bridge." Louderback worried his brow. "You think Mark did it?"

"Do *you* think he did it?"

His fingers went back to his lips. "I don't know. It wasn't my first thought."

"Your first thought being?"

"Regular crime? A burglary gone bad?"

"Mark mentioned he'd seen her last week. Getting some money from the house? This break up, how was it going?"

Louderback stood. Normally they would be looking eye-to-eye, but Louderback was uncharacteristically slumping.

"They were negotiating."

"Smoothly?"

"Relatively. They'd always kept their money separate. It was Mark's money paid the mortgage all these years. He didn't think she should get half."

"She wanted half, then?"

"No. She thought he was right. They were just trying to settle on a figure, that's all. Lookit," he said. "I gotta go to my office. Can you take care of this?"

•••

Using the police band radio that Wilma herself would normally have been attending, Pruitt called Jerry Louderback and asked him to come back to headquarters. While he waited, he found the paperwork he needed and took the form out to Gillespie on a clipboard. When Gillespie rolled the window down, Pruitt handed it to him. "Go ahead and fill this out. We'll go in just a minute."

Walking back to the offices, a breeze wafted over him, suffused with the aroma of oyster stew. Not far to the west was Bendick & Son's, a seafood processing plant. On cooking days, when the wind was right, the whole town could smell like buttery soup.

While he waited for Jerry, Pruitt used Wilma's desk phone to call his office and request that Raphael "Raphe" Jones meet him at Mark Gillespie's house. He noticed that Elkhorn PD had a computer. He wondered how long they'd had it, if they'd beat the county to the punch. In January, some unexpected money had allowed his office to purchase their first. In an arrangement with the state that allowed officers to retain their local commissions and seniority, Willapa County continued to pay Lee Wilson's salary, even as he worked at the Police Academy—with the state reimbursing them. In the six-week window before a new deputy was hired, the windfall had allowed the department to purchase what his staff told him was a PC. It had arrived in a box designed like a Holstein cow—white with black spots. That was about the extent of Pruitt's understanding of computers, that they came in cow-colored boxes.

Then Jerry arrived. Just inside the door, Pruitt told him about Wilma. Jerry burst into tears. Pruitt hugged him. Jerry gripped his arms. "Oh, my God," was all he said.

Pruitt patted his back.

After a few moments, Jerry let his grip fall. "Okay, Gav. Okay."

Pruitt looked him over. "You losing weight, Jer?"

He wiped his eyes. "Yeah, some."

"So you took the health club up on that deal I cut with them? Twenty percent off for law enforcement personnel?"

Pruitt was hoping the chit-chat would help Jerry pull himself back together.

"Naw," he said. "Just running before my shift."

"Well, good for you, man. Now you just gotta cut back on the cigarettes."

"Tryin'," he said. "Tryin'."

He was looking a little better already. Color coming back. "How's Dan?"

"He's in his office." But when Jerry made a move to go to his brother, Pruitt took him by the elbow. "I need you to come with me right now. You can hook up with Dan later."

He told Jerry what was up. "Follow me up to Mark's, okay?"

•••

Wilma and Mark Gillespie had purchased a rambler when they'd married. It perched on a gently-rising hillside at the corner of Gravel Pit Road and Jackson Street in the Riverview district. Pruitt, too, now lived in the district after marrying and moving in with Molly. Other districts within the Elkhorn city limits included Downtown, East Elkhorn, Sawlog Slough, and Riverdale, Pruitt's former neighborhood. At one point, each district had its own elementary school, but budget cuts had pared the number down to two, one each in East Elkhorn and Sawlog Slough, essentially dividing the town into east and west sections.

Pruitt and Deputy Jones were about equidistant from the Gillespie's house and everyone arrived at nearly the same time. The parking apron was wide and easily accommodated the three vehicles. As he unbuckled his safety belt, Pruitt said, "Gonna have Jerry sit with you, Mark."

Gillespie said, "I need to use the bathroom."

"How bad?"

He squeezed his eyes shut a moment. "You want me to sit out here while you do your search?"

Pruitt wanted to read some drama into his gesture, but it just didn't register that way. "I do, Mark. It'll be easier for everyone."

He sighed. "I guess it's not that bad. I'm just . . . You know. Feeling stressed."

"I understand. It's a formality, so it won't take long."

Pruitt got out of the cruiser and signaled Jerry Louderback to swap places with him.

"If I keep the door open, can I have a smoke?" Jerry asked.

Gillespie leaned across the center console to look up at them. "You got a cigarette?"

Jerry pulled out a soft-pack of Marlboros, regarded Pruitt expectantly.

Pruitt almost said something about Jerry telling him less than fifteen minutes ago that he was cutting back. He noticed, too, that Jerry's eczema seemed to be getting a little worse, creeping up his neck just above his shirt collar. Smoking was just so bad for a body in so many ways.

But this was not the time for a health lecture. "Fine with me," he said. "But roll the windows down."

Then he joined Raphe Jones by her cruiser, which was far enough away from Jerry and Mark for privacy, as long as they kept their voices down. "So you got the gist of this?"

Grim-faced, Jones nodded. She had been Pruitt's second hire after Ing Yen. The two of them in combination had earned him the short-lived moniker of Equal-Opportunity Pruitt—short-lived because both Jones and Yen had figured out quickly how things worked in a small town, had found that balance between friendliness and distance necessary to do their jobs capably without coming across as arrogant.

As usual, Jones had her brown, blond-streaked hair tied back in a French twist and wore enough make-up to keep the rumors of gayness at bay without it bothering her if she had to break a sweat. After a stint in the Navy, she earned a degree in sociology from Washington State University and moved back to her hometown of Longview to consider her first post-college move. She'd answered an ad Pruitt had placed in a half-dozen Southwest Washington newspapers—from Aberdeen to Long Beach—and he couldn't believe his luck to have found someone of her caliber interested. While county protocols hadn't exactly allowed him to hire her on the spot, bureaucratically that's what he'd done.

"You getting anything off him?" she asked.

Careful not to use any gesture that might indicate to Gillespie that he was their topic of conversation, Pruitt said, "Not really."

"That line between stress and lying can be a fine one."

"He could have prepared for it, but . . . "

Jones said, "Yeah," then, "What are we looking for?"

They stood gazing at the two-car garage that connected to the main body of the house and dominated the entrance to the home. Architecturally, it was more like the back, but nobody came in through the "front." The design was fairly common on the hills around town, taking advantage of river and valley panoramas.

Pruitt said, "Smoking gun would be nice."

Jones chuckled in spite of herself. "That's so old."

Pruitt acknowledged as much. "Maybe some muddy boots that we could trace to the slough?"

"Everybody's got muddy boots in their homes this time of year. How long have they been separated?"

"Going on a year, I think."

"Her presence is going to be all over this house."

"That may be something. If he wasn't letting go, expecting her back."

Jones said, "This place is deceptively average looking."

Pruitt, too, noticed the expertly-poured foundation. Even the parking apron concrete was flawless, nary a crack nor blemish. The roof was shakes, heavies. With ¾-inch butts, they were the most expensive. A high-end heat exchanger sat on a raised slab next to the roadside of the house. Air conditioning was an uncommon luxury in Willapa County. The really hot days were so few that most home owners didn't bother with more than a fan and an opened door. On a quick glance, the house seemed ordinary, but some serious money had been invested on it. "Both of them worked," he said. "No kids."

"Unusual for the husband to keep the house and the wife to move out."

Pruitt told her about Wilma wanting to get cash for her equity, about her plans to buy the home she was renting in Nalpe.

As he talked, Jones continued staring at the house. When he was done, she looked at him and said, "How're we getting in?"

Pruitt held up a set of keys. "Got 'em from Mark."

•••

Inside, Pruitt said, "Let's do a quick prelim, fifteen minutes, then do a briefing. I don't want Mark waltzing in here to use the bathroom, I don't want him out there fretting, don't want him changing his mind. If we think there's more to be done, then fine, we'll take it from there."

•••

The prelim revealed nothing that either raised or lowered Pruitt and Jones' suspicion of Mark Gillespie. Both, however, were impressed with the layout and the amenities: separate bathrooms off either side of the master bedroom, walk-in closets for each. Grand by anyone's standards, conspicuous on two middle-class incomes. There would have to be an investigation into their financials.

In Wilma's bathroom a few items remained, but only, as Jones noted, peripherals—out-of-fashion lipstick and a few out-of-date prescriptions. All the necessities were gone. A few key pieces of furniture were also gone: the bed and probably a chest of drawers from the guest room that appeared to be serving now as an office. A couple of chairs had likely been taken from the living room and as yet replaced. All the remaining furniture was top of the line. The two local furniture stores stocked nothing of this quality. They'd shopped out of town. Portland, maybe, or Seattle.

Jones said, "It's just the opposite of what I expected."

"Wilma everywhere?"

"Yep. But it's like she never lived here at all. Usually husbands leave the decorating to the wife. They might get a room of their own, like a den. More likely, they fix up a basement or garage. The man lair. But this is, like, Mark's house. Jeez, all this Mariners stuff. Bobbleheads, banners. Got that one room painted navy blue and teal, for criminy sakes. Like a shrine. Drive me nuts, stuff like that."

They'd convened in the kitchen to compare notes. Because the home had been built at the apex of a long hillside rise, the view out the window was spectacular: glinting river, verdant wetlands, distant green hills. If located in a city even as large Olympia, it was a million-dollar view. Located in Elkhorn, it was worth much less—yet a valuable property regardless.

Pruitt said, "She didn't move out *that* long ago. This has been his house for a while."

"Control freak? She can't handle it anymore?"

"She hung in there. They've been married, what, over ten years?"

"And no kids, either. Like you said."

"Not even thinking about it, apparently. A two-bedroom house very intentionally designed for two adults."

"I suppose they could have adapted the spare bedroom, that office, into a nursery."

Pruitt looked at her. "Think they fought over it? Some tension building up?"

"No domestic calls. I checked before I drove up."

"No spats in pubic, either. At least none I've ever heard of."

"I suppose they just grew apart?"

"Plus you've got those rumors, about Wilma and Dan having an affair."

"Just rumors." Jones raised her eyebrows. "Unless you know something."

Pruitt shook his head. "Just two good-looking people working in the same office."

"Small towns like their gossip. Especially those two, tall and elegant. Like Jackie and JFK. Camelot in Elkhorn."

"There's something bothering me."

Jones pulled the edges of her mouth down. *What?*

"If they don't have kids, and they're not planning on having kids, why are there baby wipes in the side bathroom there?"

Jones shrugged. "You don't have to have kids to have a use for baby wipes. Wipe your hands. My dad, when he got older, kept a box near the toilet. Used them for . . . you know."

"Cleaning up?"

"Yeah."

"Still."

"You want to take 'em?"

Pruitt thought a moment. "We're not taking anything else. It's going to look pretty weird on the Seizure List if all we've got on it is some baby wipes. If Mark is the one, and if they are evidence, that's going to tip him off."

Jones gave his notion some thought. "I got two work-arounds. One, we scoop up a bunch of immaterial cleaning supplies—paper towels, old rags, whatever—and say we're collecting effects that may have been used at the crime scene."

Pruitt shrugged. "Good logic, but I can't say I'm in love with it. The crime scene is a long ways from here, and outside to boot."

"Can't say I am either. So how about two, we collect a sample of the wipes—four or five of them, just put 'em in a plastic bag and haul 'em away with us—and note them in the Seizure List."

"But that gets back to what I'm concerned about. It's gonna stand out like a sore thumb."

"No, like a dirty thumb. Or in this case, dirty hands. One of us touched something, right? During the search? I mean, we're poking around under the kitchen sink, under the bathroom sink—behind the toilet, for that matter. So we grabbed a couple of baby wipes and cleaned up with them.

Didn't want to spoil those perfectly displayed hand towels in there."

Pruitt held up a palm. "We're gloved."

Jones smiled. "Mark doesn't know that. We didn't glove up until we got in here. Strip 'em off and shove 'em in our pockets. He'll never know."

Pruitt nodded. "And we tell him that anything we take from the premise has to be noted, even if it's not evidence. If one of us had blown their nose on a Kleenex, we'd have to list it. All about formality."

"Exactly."

"It's a bit of a risk."

Jones said, "The thing is, is the risk worth it? I mean, really, they're probably not even relevant. We're just going on a hunch."

"Right." He thought about it. "Screw it. I say listen to your gut. You got that form with you?"

CHAPTER FOUR

BACK OUT ON the parking apron of the Gillespie home, Pruitt squared everyone away. He thanked Jerry Louderback and let him get back to his brother, Dan. He dispatched Raphe Jones to the office with their evidence, however flimsy. Then he rejoined Mark Gillespie in his cruiser. Handed him the Seizure Form on the clipboard. "Read it, sign it, date it, and we're done. Thanks."

As he was pulling back out onto Jackson, Gillespie said, "You took some baby wipes?"

Pruitt gave him the story. "These formalities have to be adhered to. Your protection, our protection. Keeps everything above board."

He signed.

"Just pull your copy off. It's the bottom one."

After he did so, Gillespie held up the clipboard with the remaining copies of the form. "Where do you want this?"

"Just toss it in the backseat, man. Thanks. You want me to drop you off at your truck?"

"Yeah, I guess."

"You mind if we stop by Elkhorn PD, just for a minute?"

Although there was no particular investigative reason to put off letting Gillespie go, Pruitt clung to the notion that the longer he kept close to the person of interest, kept talking to him, the better chance there was that something useful would pop up out of his mouth or, if he were trying to hide the truth, some tells would surface, some odd gestures or a turn-of-phrase being used like a touchstone to help him keep his story straight.

"Sure. Whatever."

Pruitt kept just under the speed limit. "So how have things been for you since this break up?"

Gillespie shrugged. "Not that much different. Home by myself instead of home together."

"You guys go to a lot games?"

"Naw. Wilma wasn't a fan."

"So you had to go by yourself?"

"Guys from work. A few of us went in on a deuce."

"Season tickets?"

"Yeah. Split up, it's not so bad."

"She was all right with you taking off to games?"

He shrugged again. "It worked out to about three or four days a month."

Pruitt had reached the bottom of Jackson Street. Off the hill, the view was gone, just a small neighborhood now. Actually his neighborhood, if he'd kept going straight.

He made a left on Fowler.

"Is that how it's been without her, a little lonely?"

"Yeah, I guess. We were never big on the night life."

From what Pruitt knew, this was true. Wilma performed a lot of charity work, but she was rarely seen in the bars— maybe the Elk's Club after a meeting, but one drink and gone. He and Jones had noted the liquor cabinet at the Gillespie's house was a meager one. Kalua, apricot brandy, a bottle of cheap whiskey—none more than half empty. Hardly a drinking family's stash.

"Maybe all the more reason for the loneliness?"

"That's not how I thought of it."

"I went through a divorce. It was hard."

"Well, yeah. You're with someone a long time."

Fowler ended at West Port Drive—technically a part of Highway 101. Across the street was a shopping center that included Everybody's Store, the largest grocer in town, and Olivia's part time employer. Pruitt made a right.

"So getting back together wasn't in the cards? With Wilma wanting to buy the rental?"

"No. Didn't look like it was in the cards."

"Women, man. You just never know what's going on in their heads, do you? Why this? Why that?"

"I guess not."

"Just leaving you that way."

Gillespie turned to look directly at him. Not wide-eyed, just irritated. "C'mon, man. Why're you doing this?"

"What? Having a conversation?"

"No, the cop stuff. I just found out my wife is dead."

"She was your soon-to-be ex-wife, Mark."

He turned away. "Whatever. You know what I'm talking about."

They crossed over the South Fork Bridge. Pruitt wondered if there was a tact with Gillespie that might loosen up the control he appeared to have over his tone, his gestures, his responses. That kind of control, the man was either seriously guilty and well rehearsed, or utterly innocent and simply acting naturally. At this point, Pruitt couldn't tell one from the other.

"You just seem to be taking things pretty well."

Gillespie snorted—more exasperated than angry. "You don't know what I'm feeling. We see each other, what, once a year at that picnic? You don't really know me. I don't really know you. You're a cop thinks I had something to do with this. That's it. What do you expect?"

As they pulled up to the curb in front of the Elkhorn Police Department, Gillespie said, "You know, you can just drop me here."

"Here?"

"I think I could use the walk."

"You want to call your boss from here? Let him know you're out for the day?"

Gillespie stood from the cruiser and shook himself out. "I'll see him when I get back."

Talking over the top of the cruiser now, Pruitt said, "Can you not tell him about Wilma?"

He got a confused look. "People saw me leave with you. What'll I tell them?"

"Just say you can't talk about it. I'm trying to keep the rumors down."

"Yeah. Whatever." Weakly he raised a hand. "Sorry. That came out rude, and I'm not trying to be. I get it. I know you're just doing your job. Thanks, Sheriff."

"I'll keep you up-to-date."

Watching him trudge towards the mill—his Mariners jacket with a logo on the back as big as an archery target— Pruitt was a little disappointed that he had gotten nothing of real use out of the man. Of course, that would be presuming there was something useful to get. Maybe there just wasn't. He thought Gillespie looked more than a little shaky on his feet. Probably the walk would do him good.

As long as he was there, Pruitt considered checking in on the Police Chief again, but he also noted his brother's cruiser parked nearby. A couple of other Elkhorn PD officer's cars were parked out front, too. Dan, or Jerry, had made some calls apparently. All the more reason to get his ass in gear. He figured there was less than an hour before everyone in town knew what was going on.

He jumped back in his vehicle and headed towards Riverdale. Driving by Everybody's Store had reminded him of Olivia. He needed to see her, break the news. He needed to tell Molly, too, but she was the stronger of the two right now: older, wiser, more stable. If somehow word of Wilma's death reached her ahead of him, she could handle it better than Olivia. His daughter's current state of mind was volatile.

Maybe it was hormones, but more than likely it was the tenuous nature of her life right now. Nineteen-and-a-half and pregnant by a boyfriend who had yet to show her that he was a man in anything but a biological way. He wasn't a bad kid, just freaked out, just as Olivia was freaked out.

Are you going to marry him? Pruitt had asked. Not right away was her reply. And what could he say. He hadn't married her mother right away either. The big ol' cosmic wheel turns, brother, and you can no more slow it down than you can go back over its tracks.

On the other hand, if these were the life circumstances his family had to deal with, at least everyone had a roof over their head. He'd married Molly and moved in with her in January and immediately began considering renting his place when Olivia broke the news—both about her pregnancy and dropping out of school. The house became hers, of course. She and Christopher hadn't many options. With Christopher so close to his degree, it was sensible to figure out a way to keep him in college. They considered moving out of their dorms and into a nearby apartment, but Christopher was on scholarship and his finances were hanging by a thread. With first and last and a deposit due up front, it was an expensive proposition.

The compromise was to split their life. Christopher moved into an inexpensive off-campus room-and-board, driving down to Elkhorn after his last class on Friday, driving back up to Tacoma on Monday morning. The main problem with the arrangement was the four days away, when Olivia's imagination ran wild. What was he really doing up there? Smoking grass? Seeing other women? *Imperfection*, Pruitt thought. From where would the drama in our lives come without it?

He parked behind Olivia's Rabbit—her high school graduation present—which was nestled in the narrow parking spot that ran alongside the garage, which had never served Pruitt as protection for his car, but rather two other purposes. Half was his drum studio. Pruitt's degree from the University of Washington had been in music—percussion emphasis— and he gave free lessons to anybody who wanted them, mostly the kids playing in the Elkhorn High School marching and concert bands. But with the marching and concert seasons over, the teaching had pretty much dried up. And he missed it, but not as much as he missed his isolation tank, which took up the other half of the structure. For whatever reasons he hadn't used it in a week. Thinking about a float didn't make his mouth water so much as his muscles tingle. The tank's cedar-lined chamber beckoned him with the promise of meditative silence and repose.

Wouldn't happen today.

He spied Olivia catching a glance of him from the window above the kitchen sink. *My god*, Pruitt thought, *she's become a homemaker*. Not at all what he'd envisioned for her. He'd been thinking professional woman, or champion of important causes, the environment or world hunger. CEO of a non-profit. That she'd lasted exactly one semester at the University of Puget Sound still didn't sit well with him, but his dreams for her were not her dreams. His urge to protect and guide Olivia was powerful, but he also understood that the whole point of parenting was not to corral a child but rather to open the corral gate and point out a few directions to run—safe ones if at all possible.

Stepping through slats of the picket fence, Cleo, his tortoise-shell tabby, angled slyly toward him, over for a look-see and pet of the head.

"That's all a kitten needs," he said to her. "Food, love, and water."

Cleo's good fortune had been that with Olivia moving in, she hadn't had to move with Pruitt to Molly's, where Angus, Molly's aging black cocker spaniel, ruled—if in no other way than out of pure cantankerousness.

Then something on the wind caught Cleo's attention and she scampered off. Undoing the back gate, Pruitt got only one foot up on the back steps when Olivia was opening the kitchen door for him. "Pop-cop," she said. "What are you doing here this time of day?"

"Playing cop right now, honey. Let's go in."

•••

Lately, Olivia wept at the drop of a hat, so Pruitt was especially thankful that he'd been the one to tell her about Wilma. After a good cry, she went to the bathroom to wash her face. While she was gone, he put on the kettle. The kitchen had been Pruitt's favorite spot in the house. White walls and sky-blue moldings, the side panels of the breakfast nook painted with geese standing amongst white flowers. Lace curtains lined the window above the sink, and a series of canisters marked Sugar, Flour, and Coffee sat on the counter. He noted the addition of a black microwave, glaringly modern against the otherwise traditional decor. Must have come back from college with Olivia.

When she appeared in the kitchen again, Pruitt got snared in one of those moments when his child looked like someone else. Olivia aglow with her pregnancy and a singular natural beauty that he could hardly believe he'd had something to do with. She had his ex-wife's figure and height, but her face and skin echoed Pruitt's mother. The whole biological aspect of parenthood just gave a person pause sometimes. *There he goes now, here she starts*. The words from "Cassidy" had never seeped deeper into his heart.

"Daddy?" she said. "What?"

"Sorry, honey, you just look lovely today."

She smiled. "Thanks, Pop-cop." She went to sit at the kitchen table. When the kettle started to sing, she pointed toward the cabinet next to the sink. "I bought some Red Zinger yesterday. After my shift."

Olivia had come by her job at Everybody's the summer between her sophomore and junior years in high school. They were glad to have her on a more regular basis.

Pruitt pulled the Red Zinger from the cabinet and took a double bag out.

"Angela's over at Bill's, you know."

Pruitt's back stiffened. "I thought she was moving back to Chicago?"

"No. Just went to get her things."

Pruitt dropped the bags in the tea pot, its blue-flowered pattern keeping consistent with the rest of the kitchen. "Not for a second did I ever think she was serious about Bill."

"Angela's been great. Mom's doing the best she can, but she's got her job and Dick . . . her step-kids. But Angela's been there for me. I had tea with her practically everyday before she went to Chicago. I'm glad she's back. I'm glad she's with Bill."

As he poured the boiling water into the pot, Pruitt said, "My feelings are a little more complicated."

Last fall, after an absence of nearly twenty years, Angela Caracitto, Pruitt's ex-lover from his college days, had appeared in his office wearing a red bustier under a studded black leather jacket. She sported knee-high Doc Martin boots and full-blown goth make-up—black lipstick and black-and-red eye shadow. He'd never forget what she'd said to him: "Bet I'm the last person on earth you expected."

But prick-teasing Pruitt had been just the tip of her iceberg. Her real intention had been to dog his investigation into to the murder of John Carpenter, another of her lovers, an environmentalist hung dead off a spar pole at a logging operation in Pruitt's jurisdiction. She promptly insinuated herself into Pruitt's life, taking up with his next-door neighbor, Bill Logan, a retired longshoreman. Of course first she'd nearly given poor Bill a heart attack by showing up at Pruitt's for a painting party in a pair of overalls—only overalls. When Bill offered her a deviled ham sandwich from a stack of them on a plate, Angela helped herself and in the process flashed him a nipple. "Oops," she'd said, tucking it back in like a pet mouse. Then she'd ogled him lasciviously and that was it for Bill. He didn't care why she was interested in him, just that she was. Pruitt, on the other hand, had been furious with her—at least up until she'd saved his life by shooting Carpenter's murderer as he was about to shoot Pruitt. For that he owed her. But with the case over, and Carpenter avenged, Pruitt figured it was sayonara Bill. Yet, against all odds, a romance blossomed.

Olivia said, "Have you *seen* Bill lately?"

Herbal tea didn't take long to steep, so Pruitt drew cups from the cupboard. "Maybe not."

"You know Angela: studs, tattoos, pierced everything?"

"Don't tell me Bill got an ear pierced?" The thought of Bill with anything *other* than an ear pierced made him queasy. He quashed the image.

Olivia flashed a smile. "You know how Bill always was. Carhartt's? Some old threadbare Pendleton shirt? Now he's all duded up. A Western shirt, red and khaki plaid no less. Cuff and button snaps."

"She's been buying him clothes?"

"Or showing him what to buy." She chuckled. "He looks good, actually. A lot younger. You know, I think he's only about sixty. But he didn't look it before, after his wife died. Then Angela comes along."

"She's a good person." Pruitt poured the rosé-colored tea into the cups. "When she isn't on a political jag. Or interfering with police business."

Olivia ducked her head. "I hate to say this, but she and Wilma had something going on."

His stomach clenched. "Please. I don't want to hear that."

"The middle of March sometime. Wilma drove up and went into the house with a black case. Christopher thought it was a laptop computer."

"Like a portable computer?"

"Yeah. They call them laptops."

"Jeez, the department just got its first regular computer. One that sits on a table."

"Those are called desktops."

"Well, I guess that only makes sense. Anyway, Joyce is only just figuring that one out. Much less have a—what did you call it? Laptop computer?"

"Then she's back again in April. Just before Angela took off for Chicago. Same deal. That same black case and stayed late. I remember it was late because I'd fallen asleep on the couch and Wilma's car starting up woke me. It was, like, after midnight."

"You ask Angela about it?"

"No. I didn't want to pry. You know Angela. She's open, but she's not open about just anything. You know?"

"I do." He caught himself wringing his hands, took hold of his tea cup to stop it. "You think she's home now?"

Olivia glanced at the blue-and-white cat clock on the wall above the door leading into the living room. "11:45? She might be up, I guess."

•••

Not one to put things off, Pruitt finished his tea, stepped out and crossed the yard, straddled the low fence separating the two properties, and knocked on Bill Logan's back door. Anxious. Trying not to wring his hands any more. Where the hell had he picked *that* up? Although if anything were to get his hands wringing, it would be dealing with Angela, a provocateur who stood out not so much like a sore thumb as one garlanded and festooned. Throw a punk, a hippie, and a biker into a blender, hit swirl, then pour out Angela. Leather skirts with long fringe, wrist bands with spiked studs—even a dog collar she wore on occasion. Not a necklace made to look like a dog collar, either, but an *actual* dog collar. "They're cheap in a pet store," she'd told him. *No, duh*, he'd thought to himself at the time. What kind of crazy fashion concoction would she be in now?

But it was Logan who answered the door. "Gavin! Good to see you."

Pruitt was impressed. Bill did look good. A sunny smile. A nice shirt, pressed jeans.

"Is that Gav?" asked a voice behind him. "How cool!"

In spite of the warm welcome, Pruitt remained wary. Maybe she wouldn't have clothes on at all, public nudity being one of her favorite shock-in-trades. He was hearing her in his head already: "This is my house. I can wear what I want." Then the big grin. "Or nothin' at all!"

And then there she was and he was more shocked than he would have thought possible. By how normal she looked, sitting at the small kitchen table in the corner, restaurant-styled salt and pepper shakers, a bottle of ketchup, and a covered sugar bowl arranged neatly in the middle. A mug of coffee steamed in front of her. She wore fluffy pink bunny slippers, cotton pajamas, and a worn terry-cloth bathrobe. Without the black mascara, bright red lipstick, and diamond-studded nose ring, Angela looked practically everyday. He assumed it was a ruse, something to throw him off guard.

He told them about Wilma.

Bill said, "Oh, dear." He rushed to Angela's side, leaned over and placed his head next to hers. "Oh, dear," he said again.

Angela placed her hand on his arm. "It's okay, baby. It'll be okay."

Pruitt wasn't sure who was comforting who. It was a "Reuben and Cérise" moment, one lover being heroic for the other, but this time without clear roles. Which moved him, unexpectedly. Maybe there was something real between these mismatched souls.

Bill kissed the side of Angela's head. She held the sleeve of his shirt. Pruitt had to wipe a tear away.

He took a deep breath. Time to wade in. "Is that a cup of Bill's famous Thunderclap?" Logan was notorious for his blend of drip coffee with shots of espresso and Amaretto.

Angela patted Bill's arm one last time. "I'm good, honey."

Bill straightened, but moved only a step away. If needed, he was prepared to swoop his love down to her again.

She raised her head. "Naw. Those Thunderclaps are too strong for me."

Angela had never been an easy read, but there was no doubt she was shaken now. He felt for her. Shock was harsh, but often also brought out the truth. "What were you and Wilma getting together for?"

"You know. Girl stuff. Clothes, make-up." She gave Bill a wan smile. "Men."

"Bull."

She turned a look on Pruitt. He'd expected anger, but he got something else. Something he'd never seen before. He'd hurt her. "There's nothing wrong with me having a friend, Gavin."

That he'd hurt her made him feel bad and powerful at once. Which was disconcerting. But neither was it time for sorting out his conflicted feelings for his ex-lover. In for a dime. "Why would Wilma bring her computer over if you were talking about 'girl' stuff?"

"We're modern girls." A wave of impassiveness spread over her eyes, as palpable as a breeze. "C'mon, get with it. We take notes. Compare things."

So it *was* a computer, one of those laptops, and that was good to know. But why did Wilma have one, and why was she bringing it to Angela's?

Her impulse to mask her thinking, however, didn't surprise him. She'd been a master manipulator from the day he'd met her. At an anti-war demonstration in 1969 she'd thrown a hunk of brick at a police cordon because it looked like the crowd was ready to disperse. Pruitt had sworn she'd pulled it from her purse, though she contended she'd just found it on the ground, that it was a spontaneous act. A contention Pruitt could not disprove but also did not believe. She'd been a spectacular lover, but an unnerving companion.

"Men," he said. "And make-up."

She wouldn't look at him.

Getting harsh, at least in the morning with this awful news, wasn't working. He softened up. "We want the same thing, Angela. We want to find out who did this to our friend. Don't fight me this time. Please, tell me what you know."

"Honestly, there's nothing. Wilma had a book idea is all. I read some of it."

"What kind of book?"

"A romance. One of those bodice rippers?" She took a sip of coffee. Then it looked like she wiped a tear from her eye—although she was so quick about it he wasn't sure. "Of all things."

"I didn't know Wilma wrote."

"It wasn't bad, actually. I've got publishing contacts in Chicago."

•••

Was Angela's story plausible? Absolutely. Out on the back steps, saying goodbye, Bill Logan had told him that when he'd been back in Chicago with her—going to night clubs, Bill's fondness for blues and jazz something else Pruitt had not known about him—he'd heard Angela make a call to someone that sounded like a publisher to him. Yet a plausible explanation from Angela could just as easily been a clever cover-up.

Back in his cruiser, he checked the time. He needed to see Molly, but decided to drop by Elkhorn PD one last time. He was curious if Dan Louderback knew about the laptop. Besides, it was on the way.

•••

A knot of off-duty officers had gathered in EPD reception. The Police Chief's door was closed, so Pruitt commiserated with them. Sergeant Arlie Petit and Officer Kyle Spoor sat on either end of Wilma's desk, each with a leg extended, a leg up. Bookends. Officer John Gailey stood close by. They asked if Pruitt had anything yet, to which he answered no. It was all cordial formality. They knew he wouldn't share information at this point in the investigation unless he needed something from them—which he didn't, not yet.

Then Arlie, military-cut hair and a body shaped like a Russian nesting doll, started the reminiscing. "She never missed a day. Don't know how she did it."

"She used to leave pastries for the night shift," noted Kyle, who also had military-cut hair, plus a close-cropped goatee.

"Fresh, too," John added. He was the elder of the Elkhorn PD force. His goatee and short hair had gone gray years ago. "She'd go down and pick them up at Everybody's at four."

"I want whoever did this," Arlie, one bookend, said. "Want 'em bad."

"You need anything, Sheriff," Kyle, the other, said, "we're there, man."

"Appreciate it, guys," Pruitt said, clapping the nearest, John, on the shoulder. "I'm going to have a chat with the boss."

•••

He knocked and entered when Dan acknowledged. His colleague stood at the window overlooking the empty lot behind the building. Across Blake Street was the Elkhorn Fire Station where volunteers were washing one of the department's three rigs, white suds streaming across black tarmac into a storm drain.

An open bottle of Johnny Walker Black and a water glass with an inch of it stood on the desk blotter.

"Is Wilma's laptop computer here?" Pruitt asked him.

Not turning to look at him, Louderback said, "No."

"So she had one?"

Louderback turned. "Sure. She was all over that computer stuff. Took some classes over at the community college."

"That why you got one for the office?"

"Absolutely. I don't even know how to turn one of those things on."

Pruitt could relate. "They're expensive, aren't they? Those laptops?"

"Yeah. I think she paid nearly four-grand. A Mac, she called it. Powerbook?" He shook his head. "I'm not sure."

"That's a lot of money."

"Well, she was good with her money."

Something Pruitt had learned about today.

"What'd she do with it?"

"Her laptop?" Louderback made a "beats me" gesture. "I think she might have been writing something. If it got slow, she'd be pounding away at it."

He raised the bottle of whiskey by the neck. "You want a shot of this?"

His colleague's eyes were glassy. Pruitt was curious how many pops he'd had.

"No, Dan. Thanks. I've got a few other things to take care of here today."

The police chief raised the two-fingers of amber-colored whiskey to his lips. It glittered momentarily in the sunlight before disappearing down his throat. "I'm having another. Sorry if I'm coming across unprofessional, but right now I really don't give a crap."

•••

On the way out he said goodbye to Arlie, Kyle, and John. Promised to keep them up to date via their chief. "Dan will know as soon as I know."

He kept to himself how disappointed he was in their boss. Yet he was also trying not to be too judgmental. He hadn't known Wilma as well as Dan had—affair or no affair.

It was also time to get moving, to try to stay ahead of the rumor wave, which was probably reaching tsunami size by now. He needed to see Molly.

•••

His wife worked as the office manager for Jeannie Rae and Joannie Taylor.

Wife, Pruitt reflected. The word tickled him, their marriage still so new. It brought a smile to his face.

Taylor & Taylor Bookkeeping owned a two-story building located on the river side of West Port Drive, also known as Highway 101. The business took up two-thirds of the main floor. They leased the other third to a sewing machine repair business. On the top floor were three one-bedroom apartments. Jeannie and Joannie, confirmed bachelorettes, lived in the apartments on either end, with the middle one rented out.

The apartments had been built to take full advantage of their spectacular location. The bathrooms and bedrooms were on the street side, while the kitchen and living areas, with their floor-to-ceiling picture windows, faced the Willapa River's tideflats and estuaries.

Pruitt parked and entered through the double glass doors, announced by the old-fashioned shopkeeper's brass door bell. Taylor & Taylor was a wide-open, shambling office space spread out behind an antique service counter Joannie had found at a shop somewhere near Cathlamet. Scattered about a rat-maze of aisles and dead-ends were five work stations. To Pruitt it looked chaotic, but Molly assured him that everything had its place and everybody's financial records, including their own, were not only scrupulously neat, but safe. The Taylors kept backups at a rental unit on the other side of town, and were even beginning to make the change to computer accounting. Pruitt noticed that three of the five work stations had computers, although not Molly's.

Seeing him, Molly rose in greeting. He got nods from everyone else and, from Jeannie Rae, a terse "Sheriff." She didn't look up. Gruffness was a cover for her kind heart.

At nearly six months along, Molly still walked rather than waddled. She was, however, well into her pregnancy wardrobe, which consisted of three outfits, all based on soft trousers with stretchy waistbands. She wore flat shoes and a mix-and-match collection of tops: a short-sleeve with a lacy V-neck, a three-quarter sleeve smock, and a long-sleeved baby-doll shirt, wine red with thin white stripes—his favorite. When he saw her in that one he could have eaten her up. Pruitt had no idea how other men felt about sex and pregnancy, but watching Molly change physically, practically radiating, turned him on. While they weren't making love any more than they once had, they certainly weren't making any less either.

"C'mon and step outside for a moment."

She made a face at his unusual request, but rose and said nothing. She pulled the gate open separating the reception area from the work space.

Once out the door, he offered his arm. She smiled and took it, and they strolled to the picnic table on the river side of the building. On nice days, the Taylors and their employees ate lunch here, Jeannie or Joannie often supplying casseroles they would have started in their crock pots in the morning.

He hugged Molly, kissed her, and told her about Wilma. He held her as she wept quietly in his arms. Then amidst the ambient rush of the river and the softly gusting breeze, he was weeping with her. Temple to temple. Another "Rueben and Cerise" moment.

•••

His arm wrapped around Molly, Pruitt watched the dark olive-green Willapa flow swiftly by. While not exactly a black river, it was certainly muddy enough to serve as an apt metaphor for the ephemeral quality of life. The sky was patchy with clouds, and fingers of sunlight haphazardly illuminated the slough and the distant dark outlines of homes along Highway 105 to the north. Mingled on the breeze were the aromas of oyster stew and salty river water.

"All right, Gav." She pulled away and took his measure, her walnut-colored eyes, as they often did, reminding him of "Brown-Eyed Women," not simply because of the obvious reference, but also because of the lyrics' thunder and rain imagery. He and Molly had made love the first time at a borrowed beach house in Tokeland, a winter storm raging at the window panes. They had come so far since then, yet the memory was as tactile as if it had been yesterday.

"Can I can tell everyone in the office?"

"I suppose, at this point, it can't hurt anything."

She nodded. "Olivia knows?"

"Yeah, I just went over there." He almost mentioned his conversation with Angela, but stopped himself. There was no love lost between Molly and Angela. He'd tell her about all that later, after this first shock wore off. "I'm going to have to eat sometime today. You want me to come get you?"

"I don't think I'm going to be able to eat."

"I don't really feel like it, either, but if I don't I'll get jittery."

"You've got a lot to do today. I brought something. You better get at it, mister."

One last hug and it was time to break the news of Wilma's death to the *Elkhorn Echo*.

CHAPTER FIVE

AFTER A QUICK visit to the *Echo*, Pruitt radioed Joyce Cody, his office manager, and asked if she'd heard from Ing Yen and Lee Wilson. He didn't care about people listening to the police band anymore. He figured his window of opportunity for keeping Wilma's murder quiet was about over.

"Ing called. Said it would probably be close to quitting time before they'd have some preliminaries."

So with the wheels of the investigation spinning, and nothing else critical for him to do until he heard from his deputies, Pruitt decided his next stop would be to update a completely different case, a task that earlier had looked like the worst of his day.

•••

Some fifteen years ago, fresh off her internship, Dr. Marion Johnson, or simply Dr. Marion, as everyone knew her, set up her practice in a leased space in the Torchlight Restaurant building. But she tired quickly of the street-level location and the Willapa River's perennial flooding, which ruined the carpets and stank up the baseboards on a regular basis. The carpets got replaced and the baseboards were cleaned, but it was getting ridiculous. The problem was the downtown district had been built on reclaimed wetlands.

At the dawn of the 20th century, Elkhorn was a stilt town, businesses perched five or six feet above the sloughs and tideflats. Then the Army Corps of Engineers built a dike, drained the sloughs, pounded creosote-dipped pilings into the ground for stability, and filled the whole thing in with dirt. For the most part, their efforts had proven successful—though with notable exceptions. When the tides got high, for instance, the tips of the aging pilings raised a series of bumps along the pavement of Fourth and Fifth Streets. Flooding, too, bedeviled the businesses north of Third at least biannually.

So Marion built on Sixth Street, three blocks off the flood zone. Yet even there, she cautiously did what smart people did when building in the downtown district, which was add another three feet of clearance with a raised cement foundation.

Pruitt pulled up in front of her office. Not fancy, it was nevertheless pleasant: natural wood siding, large windows, a spacious lot. Rhododendrons figured predominantly in the landscaping, surrounding the front and sides of the structure. Although their blooms were fleeting, their leaves hid the concrete year-round. Flower barrels—an explosion of begonias, pansies, and bleeding hearts—flanked the door.

Marion handled the physical aspects of Willapa County child abuse cases, Pruitt the law enforcement end. The two of them worked closely with a caseworker from Child Protective Services, and County Prosecutor Carl Pulkkinen, who worked the legal side. Today the issue was the disposition of the two pre-teen children whose parents were methamphetamine addicts. The husband had recently been convicted, the wife was possibly incompetent to retain custody.

There was no practical reason for Pruitt to meet with Marion face-to-face—the issue could have been handled by phone or paperwork—but Marion was his good friend, and in spite of the fact that too often he saw her to discuss troubling matters, it was always good to see her gray-streaked raven hair, high cheekbones, hazel eyes, and straight, strong nose.

"I was just on the phone with your office and heard about Wilma," she said as he entered her office. "It's unbelievable."

Rather than say anything, Pruitt held his arms out. She was already standing and circled her desk. They hugged. She was a tall woman, nearly six feet and they placed their cheeks next to each other's.

"It's awful," she said.

In another time's forgotten place, Marion might have been the love of Pruitt's life. As it was, they had to settle for being best friends—not that he felt he was settling. A true and faithful friend is a blessing unto itself. Nevertheless, how they'd run in the same circles for so long yet never connected remained a mystery to them.

They were both University of Washington grads in 1973, although they hadn't met on campus or in the U-District. They were both Deadheads, but somehow had never run into each other at a show. They actually hadn't met until ending up, many years later, in Elkhorn: Pruitt to return home, settle down, and eventually become a cop; Marion to set up her practice and become a public figure in her own right. Elkhorn was small enough a place that the social elite were not the rich and famous but simply trained professionals.

She broke their embrace. "You want a glass of water or something?"

"Naw. I'm good."

She gave him a last pat on the shoulder and returned to her chair. "You're thinking Mark?"

He sat. "First thought, but so far he's not acting guilty, not behaving inappropriately. He fainted when I told him. That's hard to fake."

"Not impossible," she said, "but, like you say . . . "

Pruitt sighed.

"How was the concert?"

He chuckled. "It was great. A beautiful sky. The light at sunset was magical. Fabulous music."

"I wish I'd been there."

For a moment, he just enjoyed her presence.

On the wall behind her was her famous T-shirt. The one a boyfriend had hand-designed for her in 1967, when they were both seniors in high school. He had real talent as an artist and was possibly trying to use it to convince her not to go to college at a different school than he was. Or maybe he'd been saying an elaborate goodbye. To this day, she wasn't sure of his intentions. With the passage of time, however, it hardly mattered. The final product was gorgeous. He'd used rapidiograph pens and colored inks, plus sewn-on beads, to create a one-in-a-million homage to the Grateful Dead. She'd worn it once, she'd told Pruitt, then stashed it. Rediscovered when she'd moved to Elkhorn, she'd had it framed. Surrounding it were her medical degrees and awards, utterly drab by comparison.

"Someday," he said, "you're going to have to break that out and wear it again."

She smiled. "It would have to be a very special occasion."

"I'll bet it still fits."

"The kayaking," she continued smiling, "keeps a girl trim."

She held up a folder. "I've got the urinalysis and blood work for these kids. Checked their lungs, of course. They're healthy."

He didn't really feel like getting down to business, and almost said so. But Marion always had a full appointment queue. "They weren't exposed?"

"Can't say they were or weren't. Just that nothing is showing up in the tests. The mother claims she was careful. Insisted on no open chemicals when they were in the house."

She acknowledged Pruitt's skeptical look. "It happens. Said she had friends look after them when they were cooking. And you should have seen the house. Spotless. The caseworker told me it looked like she took a toothbrush to the linoleum. Said she couldn't keep her own house half as clean.

"You know how it is," she continued. "The drug is the drug, but the users are all different. Different reasons to use, different behaviors when high. Yes, it's bad to be stoned around your kids. No, she did not take care of their psychological needs as well as she should have. But did she do anything to seriously jeopardize their physical health? The tests say she did not."

"Well, thank god. Does that mean they'll be going back to her?"

"Probably. Psychologist report on her is inconclusive. No obvious signs of psychoses, or other mental conditions. She's clearly addicted right now, but also appears genuinely ready to enter a program."

"Kids will go into foster care while she's rehabbing?"

"She's signed off on that. But expects them back when it's over. Pending how she does in rehab and an updated psych report."

Pruitt sighed. "I was hoping some family members could step up for them. Does she have a sober brother or sister, parents maybe?"

"A sister who lives in Montana." She shook her head. "Apparently not interested."

•••

As he left Dr. Marion's, Pruitt's stomach started growling. He checked his watch, saw it was going on three. He'd been right about what he'd said to Molly. In spite of what he'd seen that morning, in spite of the thought that he might never eat again, there was that old biology at work. He needed fuel.

He drove back through downtown, past the Elkhorn Theatre—which advertised on its billboard upcoming summer shows. Mickey Rooney in July, then the Coast Guard Concert Band in August. Pruitt wondered what the heck Rooney, at his age, would do on stage. Probably show old clips and reminisce. But would he sing and dance? The guy had to be pushing eighty. But maybe he *could* still do the old soft-shoe. Although Pruitt wasn't big on dancing, he'd sure love to still be playing basketball into his retirement. One guy he played with during Thursday night rat-ball, Ernie, was seventy-two and still throwing down threes.

Conor Williamson, waiting for one of Elkhorn's half-dozen traffic lights to change, waved to him. Williamson sold insurance two blocks east on Duryea Street, kitty-corner from the Post Office, and directly across the street from Elkhorn's Library, a neo-Tudor that had been added to the National Register of Historic Places in 1979. Elkhorn's pride and joy.

He parked next to Clyde Johnston's dental clinic on Third Street, waved to Jenny Hulbert, the receptionist, who could see him from her window, then walked down the alley, slipped into The Torchlight by the back door and took the first open table. When Chuen Hsia, the owner, acknowledged him, Pruitt raised three fingers. Chuen nodded and put the order into his wife, Loy, then brought tea over, pouring the first cup ceremoniously as he spoke. "Is it true about Wilma?"

Pruitt almost said, *Jeez, that didn't take long.* "It's horrible," is what he said out loud.

"Michelle was just in," Chuen explained, referring to Michelle Parnell, senior editor at the *Elkhorn Echo*. "You just missed her."

He knew, of course, that once he'd stopped by the *Echo* the news would spread fast. The *Echo* was a weekly and word of mouth would be the only way they could scoop the coverage by the *Riverton Daily World*, whom Pruitt would call later. The *Echo's* readers would at least have the satisfaction of picking up tomorrow afternoon's paper and saying to themselves: *I already knew that.*

Chuen said, "So, nobody's sure what happened?"

"Won't know until the investigators get done at the scene." Then, before his host could leave, Pruitt said, "Wilma was a regular, right?"

"Monday and Wednesday. Always with Dan. 11:45, just ahead of the crowd. She liked the crab Louie, 1,000 island dressing on the side."

"You ever see her carrying a black case?"

"Like a purse?"

"Probably not much bigger."

Chuen shrugged. "Can't say so."

"She ever in here with Angela, the wild one?"

"Nose ring woman? Living with Bill Logan? Maybe once or twice."

"Thanks, Chuen."

When his lunch arrived he once again thanked the culinary gods for Chuen and Loy Hsia. Not only were they good people, ten years ago they'd saved The Torchlight. The previous owners had been one dimensional in their approach to restauranteering: great food amidst a ramshackle atmosphere and shoddy bookkeeping. When the Hsias took over they cleaned, remodeled, and got in the black in less than six months, putting the wary locals at ease by retaining the excellent local seafood dishes that everybody loved—oyster stew, clam fritters, salmon baked in lemon sauce—while introducing their own Chinese specialties, for which Pruitt had a particular fondness. His usual vegetarian plate looked delicious as ever. Egg foo young, baked tofu in sweet-and-sour sauce, and a mound of steamed white rice. He splashed Tabasco over the eggs, soy sauce over the rice.

•••

After lunch Pruitt took a quick spin by the Saginaw Mill to see if Mark Gillespie had indeed gone home. Any other behavior would have been odd, and Pruitt was very interested in any sort of odd behavior from Gillespie. But it seemed he'd done as he said he was going to do, get his truck and take some time. But since it was on his way back to the office anyhow—or at least not too far out of the way—Pruitt cruised by Gillespie's house. Sure enough, his white, late-model Chevy S-10 with the Mariners bumper sticker was parked on that perfectly poured concrete driveway. When he got back to the office the first thing he was going to do was get a warrant for those financials.

CHAPTER SIX

PULLING INTO THE Willapa County Courthouse complex, Pruitt knew there would be news. Back in it's usual spot was the department's evidence van, the one Lee Wilson had painstakingly outfitted during the course of his tenure as deputy. If it had to do with forensics—from barrier tape to portable UV lights—you could find it in the pigeon holes, shelving, and drawers Wilson had personally installed.

Wilson and Ing Yen were waiting for him in the Swamp, the narrow room of desks where the administrative assistants and Pruitt's office manager, Joyce, worked. And his staff was indeed hard at it—though probably working harder on listening in than actually working.

Flanking the Swamp were private offices, a conference room, and a kiosk-sized dispatch center crammed with communication electronics, some of which were pretty long in the tooth—the story of a small county's life.

"We got a lot," Wilson said as soon as he saw Pruitt, "but we ain't got much."

Pruitt almost said, *Good to see you, too, buddy*, but held his tongue. Pleasantries had never been Wilson's forte. If it didn't have to do with crime scene investigation, the man was practically oblivious. Pruitt had learned to live with Wilson's terseness. In some ways it was refreshing. Not that they hadn't had their share of bad blood. Of that, there'd been plenty. The most notable had been the aftermath of Arthur Hujack's retirement when they'd run head-to-head for the position of Willapa County Sheriff. Pruitt had won, of course, and by a significant margin.

One moment in particular had sealed Wilson's fate. At a public forum, the candidates were asked if they would preserve the tradition of acting as Santa Claus at the annual Chamber of Commerce Children's Christmas Party. Pruitt had no intention of donning a Santa costume and fake white beard, but had some understanding of how to be political. "Well, I wouldn't want to tarnish Art's legacy," he'd said, "by pretending I could be as good at it as he was." Wilson, on the other hand, had simply said, "No fucking way." Predictably, the voters announced something similar to Wilson on election day.

For months afterwards, Wilson's frost towards Pruitt was transparent. It hadn't thawed until the previous fall's investigation into the murder of John Carpenter, Angela's friend. The case had made national news, and when it was finally solved, Pruitt had singled out Wilson for specific praise. Then came the deal sealer, Pruitt's glowing recommendation of Wilson's skills as a forensics investigator to the Washington State Criminal Justice Training Center. Since Wilson had already had an offer to teach there, the letter had been nothing more than red tape. But seeing his boss's sincere words written down in black-and-white had moved him. Pruitt knew this because Wilson had thanked him personally. It had been an easy letter to write. Wilson wasn't much of diplomat, but he was superb at forensics, and, like many with a gift for a technical skill, was never happier than when he was sharing that knowledge with a rapt audience.

Pruitt said, "Why don't you two come in my office." As he was closing his door, he scanned the faces of his staff, saw a lot of disappointment that he wouldn't allow Lee to speak in front of them.

"What have we got?"

Wilson, a rangy man with a sharp nose and darting eyes, was fastidious about his uniform and noticed a thin ring of soil on the hem of his pants. "Jesus, this freaking mud around here." He looked back up. "That mud was the problem at the scene. It's the reason for what we haven't got. Those tides? They've been high and strong down river, and strong enough up river that anything like shoe prints got erased. Probably dragged any other physical evidence out into the slough, too. And that gravel skirt in front of the house? Impossible to find tire tracks. Besides, even if there were tracks, and if they were from Mark's truck . . . "

"He'd been there a few times, right? Nobody's heard that this separation has been contentious."

"Exactly."

"Had the house been burglarized?"

"Neat as a pin. Nothing obviously missing."

"You find a computer? What they call a laptop?"

Wilson shook his head. "No. Nothing like that."

"Then you're right, we haven't got much, do we?"

Wilson leaned against Pruitt's desk. "Actually, we're pretty sure we got the murder weapon."

"You're kidding me?"

"Not really good news," said Ing Yen.

Pruitt could see how anxious his deputy was to pitch in, to display both to his boss and his mentor that he was worthy of the promotion he'd been promised. And which he would get. Although Wilson was officially an adjunct instructor whose contract would expire in two years, nobody expected him to return to Willapa County. Some large force would snap him up, put him in charge of a serious CSI unit. So it was important to get Yen up to speed.

"Found it easy," Yen added.

"That's not good news?"

"Killer wasn't trying to hide it," Wilson said.

"Because they didn't care," Yen followed.

Pruitt got it. "We won't be able to trace it, will we?"

"A .22," Wilson said. "Ruger MKIII. Short barrel model."

He glanced at his pants cuff. "Common as mud, man. Reliable. Grip and trigger taped. So no prints."

"Serial number filed?" Pruitt asked.

"More than that," Yen said. "Ground off."

"Acid won't raise it, then?"

"Maybe," Wilson said, "but don't count on it."

Then both Yen and Wilson were looking at him.

"What?"

Wilson said, "It was a hit."

"Oh, man." Pruitt blew out a slow stream of air. "Oh, man. That is hard to get my mind around."

"Weird, yes," Yen said, "but that's where evidence points at this time."

Wilson gave Yen another approving glance. Apparently the role of instructor was one he embraced. When he'd worked for Pruitt, he'd never shown this sort of kindness to anyone—civilians *or* officers.

Finally, Pruitt moved around his desk to take a seat, and in the process bid his officers do the same. "This gun, it's not going to get us the killer, but it's the only evidence we've got, so we've got to hold back the details about it: caliber, make and model. Just in case something comes up later. Yen, I want you to secure it. I want it locked in a box, I want the key to that box in my hand, then I want the box locked in the vault."

"You mean when it gets back from lab, right?"

"Right. We need the ballistics to make sure it was the murder weapon. And let's see if they can raise the serial number." He held up a hand before Lee Wilson could jump in. "I know it's a long shot, but what the heck, right?"

"But I want that report to come directly to me," he said. "Or to you, Ing—no one else. I don't want it released to the press. If Michelle over at the *Echo* comes nosing around, I'll have a chat with her. Let her know why I'm not releasing the details. It's going to be the three of us and the three of us only that know anything about that gun."

Wilson nodded. "Smart thing to do."

Pruitt told Wilson about the baby wipes they'd taken from Mark Gillespie's house. "Would there be any residue if they'd been used to wipe the gun down?"

He thought a moment. "First thing is why would they wipe it down if they've already got it taped?" He held up a hand. "But, okay. Let's say the shooter's being extra careful. Those wipes would leave some residue. The problem is even if they find some residue, you can buy that stuff anywhere. It could link the gun to Mark, but it also to anybody that's ever bought that brand of baby wipes. As evidence, it's not just circumstantial, it's weak. If you link the gun to him, that's different. It's still circumstantial, but a lot stronger. But obviously, the way this was carried out, the chances of linking that gun to anybody are just about zero."

Pruitt sighed. "So let me get this right. You're saying this was, like, a mafia thing?"

"Professional doesn't necessarily have to mean mafia," Wilson said. "But, yeah, it was a hit. Whoever killed her had her kneel, then shot her from behind at a sure angle. Then again in the back, a heart shot, then dropped the gun and walked away."

"No foliage disturbed," Yen said. "No frantic running away."

"A .22 is a pretty quiet gun, too," Pruitt noted.

Wilson summed it up. "A pretty quiet execution is what it was."

PART TWO:
JULY, 1995

CHAPTER SEVEN

PRUITT AND DUANE Wildhaber had been floating the South Fork of the Willapa River since they were twelve years old. Even when Pruitt had been away at college, or following a Grateful Dead tour, he always managed to get back to Elkhorn for a river float with his old friend. In thirty-five years, the only summer float they had missed was in the late sixties, when Wildhaber had been in the army, serving in Vietnam.

"The Han was our kind of river ," Wildhaber said, as they unhooked the bungee cords holding the inner tubes. "Easy going, just like we like it. We could've rode that puppy right down to China Beach, man, which was beautiful. Sometimes the water looked turquoise there."

"Must have made an impression on you, Duane," Pruitt said, "'cause you always talk about the Han right about now." He hefted an inner tube—one of the tall ones they purchased from a tractor store in Riverton—out of the back of Wildhaber's pickup. It was a pretty fancy affair for a truck, with a cab as comfortable as a car, a CD player and leather seats.

"It was one of the normal things I used to think about. Tubing on a river, having a beer on a beach. The rest of it was so weird, I needed something like that."

When Wildhaber had been drafted, he had entered the army with a mane of black hair he'd inherited from his mother, who was half Chinook Indian. Within a year of returning from his tour of duty, his hair had turned shock white. He still had it, though, which he was grateful for. "I'm sure stress turned its color," he would say, "but at least it didn't make it fall out."

Pruitt stripped off his purple University of Washington "Dawg" sweatshirt. "I take it you never had the chance to tube it then."

Wildhaber chuckled, though not with real humor. "Yeah, we tubed it all right."

Pruitt tossed the sweatshirt into the cab. He was clad in the local tubing outfit: T-shirt, cut-offs, and a pair of old sneakers. His T-shirt was vintage Dead. The kid from the *Live in Europe* album smashing a cone of ice cream into his forehead. There were days Pruitt related to that notion more than any other.

He attached his car key to a safety pin on his shorts. His car was parked down river, at their terminus. After the float, they would stash the tubes there, drive back in his car to Wildhaber's truck, then pick up the tubes on their way home. The only other must-have accessory was a six-pack cooler. Wildhaber's was a hard plastic one with a red top that he chained to his tube with a dog leash and let trail in the current, cold and close by.

"Disappointing deal," Pruitt said, "the whole thing over there."

Wildhaber shrugged. "I try to look at it as a part of life. You don't get everything you want."

"You just do your best, let fate decide the rest."

His friend smiled. "Gav, did you just throw down some Dead on me?"

Pruitt smiled back. "Sorry, man. I did. 'Built to Last.'"

"I like that. Built to last as long as we can, right?"

Pruitt slathered on sunscreen. Once finished, he tossed the bottle to Wildhaber, who squeezed a dollop on his palm, then began his own slathering.

Wildhaber said, "Speaking of things that didn't go right. Nothing more on Wilma's murder?"

Pruitt shook his head. "It went so cold so fast. I mean there was nothing. Nada. Zilch."

"Everybody thought it was Mark." Wildhaber tossed the bottle of sunscreen back in his truck. "Too bad about the alibi."

Pruitt shouldered his tube, which, at five-feet in diameter, was a comfortable toting size. "Well, nobody was more disappointed that he was at a Mariner's game than me."

The question of an alibi hadn't come up during the initial investigation because they hadn't known the time of death. When they did finally get the TOD, and they asked Gillespie where he'd been, the man had shrugged and showed them a ticket stub mounted in a stamp collector's album. Under each he had jotted down the game score, plus notes on who had homered, or pitched well. To add insult to injury, other aspects of the case had not lined up either. Wilma's laptop computer, for instance, had never been found, and while it had been over six weeks, gun ballistics had not yet returned. The state crime lab was just that swamped. When it came to Gillespie, all they had was a lot of suspicion wrapped up in a baseball game.

After making sure his truck was locked, Wildhaber said, "All right, man. Let's hit that river."

He led them down a worn path that had been used by tubers for as far back as tubing had become a pastime. Of course, tubers would wear it down even further as the weather kept improving. In Southwest Washington, July—and not June—ushered summer in. June was about rain, which could make things dismal, but also accounted for the explosion of foliage along the trail: hardhack and Oregon grape, willow and alder, huckleberry and salmonberry—leaves, branches, and vines, all in profusion. And the lushness was appreciated. Thank you, June. Thank you, rain. But most especially now, thank you, July. All the signs pointed to some blessed heat.

"That was one helluva funeral," Wildhaber said. "Wilma's."

At five-five, Pruitt's buddy had to hold his tube up with a raised arm to keep it from dragging on the ground.

"I'm not trying to sound crass here," he said, "but do you remember that blue skirt she wore sometimes? The tight one?"

Pruitt said, "Good lord, yes."

"When she wore that, I'd have followed her into the Valley of Death. And I'll bet I could have easily found another six hundred to go with me. Willingly. Smiles on their faces, man."

"Amen, brother."

"And the weird thing?" Wildhaber said. "I'm not even sure she knew how great she looked in it."

The crisp smell of the river was finally reaching Pruitt's nose. He wanted to savor it, but Wildhaber had gotten on a roll.

"Louderback," he said. "What an ass. Drunk like that? Funerals are sad, but getting drunk? C'mon. And now, you run into that guy, you can smell the Sen-sen on him a block away. But that's the thing about hard booze, man, you drink enough of it, people can smell it, I don't care if you chase it with a bottle of Listerine. It just seeps through your pores."

"I'm worried about him," Pruitt admitted.

"There had to have been something going on between them."

"Everybody's always thought so. And believe me, we looked. But if they were having an affair, they covered their tracks well."

Then the thick foliage cleared and they were at their castoff off point. This far up, the South Fork was more a creek than a river, shallow and rocky. But creek or river, it had that lovely crisp smell.

Wasting no time, Wildhaber strode out shin-deep into the current. "You ready, Gav?"

Catching up, Pruitt said, "Let's go, man!" And they flopped their tubes on the water, flopped their tails into the tubes, and pushed off with dangling legs as well as they could, entering the flowing channel that veered right.

"Water's freaking, cold, man!" Wildhaber exclaimed. What he always yelled at the beginning of the trip.

"And so will be the beer!" Pruitt yelled back. His practiced rejoinder.

Wildhaber laughed, deep and throaty, and the float was on.

Although it wasn't a true float quite yet. The draft for the first half mile was so shallow that in a some places they would portage across the gravely bottom—hence the necessity of the old sneakers. This far up, too, the water was translucent, with only the shadows of overhanging trees and submerged logs offering cover to minnows, crawfish, and dragonfly nymphs.

Twenty minutes passed before the river deepened and portaging became unnecessary. At the same bend as every year, Wildhaber opened his cooler for a couple of Rainiers—Vitamin R's, as everybody called them. Crappy beer, really, but so much a part of their youth that between nostalgia and icy coldness it tasted just fine.

"C'mon and get it!" he teased.

Clumsily, Pruitt paddled near enough for the handoff.

"Thank you, sir. A gentleman and a scholar."

Another part of their summer floating ritual was raising their drinks in mock salute to everything they saw. Not exactly the kind of behavior an elected official might engage in. For that matter, neither was the tubing. But in Pruitt's current space and time, forgotten or otherwise, he didn't care. At least not anymore than he cared about his hippie past, his Deadhead present, or his soon-to-be-a-grandfather and father-again future. Yes, he was an elected civil servant, but he was also a human being walking the earth, trying to leach as much goodness from life as he could. And there was nothing better in life than a long, slow float down a clean, clear river.

Soon they were passing through the Willapa Harbor Golf Course. Its wooden swinging bridges crossed the South Fork at three spots, connecting the various fairways. Here scores of balls a week splashed into the water. Passing over those stretches, the riverbed was littered with them, looking like the dimpled eggs of some pre-historic fish.

At the second swinging bridge, they caught sight of their first toastees, a foursome about halfway across.

Wildhaber held his beer can high. "Good round?"

And who should turn to gaze at them but Pat Crowley, head of the local GOP, who had vowed since Pruitt's election to get him unseated. Crowley's day job was overseer of Saginaw logging operations. During the Carpenter investigation last fall, he'd been in Pruitt's face relentlessly. The environmentalist had been killed at a Saginaw logging operation and every conversation they'd had during that time, whether Crowley was admitting to it or not, was about spin. Simply put, the man was one-dimensional, short-sighted, and a pain in the ass. Crowley cast him a menacing glare.

In his friendliest voice, Pruitt raised his can and yelled, "You get over?"

Disarmed by Pruitt's grin, Crowley called back, "In one!" He was almost giddy, and well should have been. The seventh hole was a notorious handicap killer. About 185 yards from the tee, the South Fork bisected the fairway. Only the boldest of weekend duffers even tried to get over. Most babied up to the river's slope, then ironed it to the green.

"Good for you!" Pruitt continued smiling at his nemesis, but just loud enough for Wildhaber to hear, said, "Who says I don't know how to play politics."

"Crowley's usually got a stick up his ass."

"Or a sand wedge."

Which got Wildhaber cackling wickedly.

A quarter mile past the golf course, where Beaver Creek and the South Fork converged, the river's depth actually became truly river-like, averaging between three to six feet. Now the journey morphed into a mellow, beer-sipping drift. Pruitt and Wildhaber would next raise their cans of Vitamin R to salute cows and barns, the occasional dairy farmer astride a tractor, and sometimes even a deer or elk, down from the hills to forage among the soft summer grasses and sedges.

At this point, they didn't talk much, either. As the sun rose higher in the sky and warmed the day and tubes, both would snooze a little—the South Fork was that serene. They might bump into an overhanging tree limb, but so lightly as to hardly disturb a nap.

Up ahead past the farmlands were marshlands and tidal flats. These murkier waters were at the head of the tide, where the river began to pick up speed, especially on the backwash, and where they would heave to, just before Morris Lagoon. Only a quarter of a mile further on, the Willapa began ripping and rolling toward the sea at a rate far too dangerous for tubing. The river's tidal pull was one of the strongest in the Northwest.

So this was the mellow time, maybe two hours' worth. If there was ever a time when Pruitt felt safe in nature's arms, this was it. The idea was more than a little sentimental, but he couldn't help himself. Here he felt tranquil in a wholly singular way. His eyes closed gently.

A kingfisher chittered. Out on a pasture, a robin convention was in full discourse, so many voices as to lull the ear into hearing but one rising and falling chatter. But it was the high, clear notes of a cedar waxwing that got Pruitt thinking about May's Grateful Dead concert.

Canvas sails had been hung at the back of the stage. In the cooling late afternoon breeze, they riffled in congress with the row of tall pine trees standing behind Memorial Coliseum. At some point, Jerry had kicked in the MIDI system on his guitar, a trick of technology that allowed him to transcend mere steel strings and magnetic pick-ups. With MIDI he could enter entirely unreal sonic realms. And enter them he did that day, eliciting visions of white-bellied orcas rising from the canvassing of the stage, ribbons of blue wildflowers next, a cornucopia of juniper berries, pine cones, and the fresh green shoots of evergreens following that. Pruitt heard Jerry mimic birds, zephyrs and, eventually, a trumpet. The mechanics of brass and guitar were so utterly disparate that it was impossible not to scan the stage furtively, looking for the guest musician—Branford Marsalis had been a not-infrequent guest in recent years, why not his brother, Wynton? It was, after all, the Grateful Dead here, the band for which anything could, and often did, happen. But it was Jerry, all Jerry. Somehow he heard trumpet in his mind and played trumpet with his fingers, emulating not only the sound, but the logical and joyous phrasing that came with breath and lips and brass.

"Jesus-freaking-Christ!" yelled Wildhaber.

Jerked from his daydream, Pruitt could only stupidly call back, "What! What!"

"Barbed wire! Look out!"

Pruitt twisted on his tube in time to see Wildhaber, who'd been a few yards ahead, plunging into the water, trying to avoid the fence strung dead across the South Fork's banks, south to north. His ride was not so lucky. Barbs shredded, compressed air liberated. As Wildhaber swam against the current towards the muddy north bank his tube deflated in a gaseous rubber stink.

Sliding into the river, Pruitt located the mooring rope and tried to pull his tube to safety. But the current had gotten stronger in the last quarter mile. Factoring in the surface tension between water and rubber, the task looked impossible. He finally decided to save his skin and just let it go. A second pop and Pruitt's tube, too, transformed from a fat, tight doughnut into a flaccid loop of fabric tugging against the sparkling talons of the fence.

Although clumsy swimming with sneakers, Pruitt reached the bank and pulled up next to Wildhaber.

"Who the hell strung that fence up there!" Wildhaber was still panting. "Look at it, practically brand new. I'll bet it hasn't been up more than a couple of months. That can't be legal."

After a couple of catch-up breaths, Pruitt said, "Sure as hell can't be."

"I mean, I know what he's trying to do. If you put your last fence post at the bank, a cow might try to go around it, get to that fresh grass on the other side. Cow can't judge how quick the drop-off is. Or how fast that river's running. So he just runs the damned wire right across. Keep those cows in, that's for sure. The son-of-a-bitch."

"You know who's farm this is?"

"Pretty sure it's Larry Skaggs' place. It's a stunt he'd sure as hell pull. He's a freakin' poacher, too. Not the kind that needs to put meat on the table, either, just an asshole that likes to kill things."

"We'll find out soon enough, I guess. We're going to have to hike out of here, so it might as well be across his pasture. We'll have to swim back over to the south bank."

"We lost the beer, too, man. I'm not risking those barbs to try and save it."

"Just a six of Vitamin R, man."

"Well, just a two, actually."

Pruitt looked at his old friend. "A two? I only had one."

"I was saving 'em for you." He grinned. "Nice and cold."

Then the breeze changed course and Pruitt caught a foul scent. Turned his head toward it.

Wildhaber, too, raised his nose. "Jesus. What the hell's that?"

"It's coming from over there." Pruitt stood and began traipsing across a long-untended field. Thigh-high thistles nicked at his legs. "Watch it, man," he said to Wildhaber, trailing him.

A hidden embankment popped up a few yards later. It looked like a short, shallow finger had insinuated itself into the field. Pruitt reached the rim of the bank and immediately had to cover his mouth and nose. "Good god," he mumbled through his hand.

The stink of the fish kill this close was gagging. It wasn't the numbers of fish causing the stench—because there were only a few dozen of them—but the state of their decomposition, bloated and floating on the oddly-stained water, grayish and scummy. Mostly minnows and bullheads, there were also a couple of smelt. Nearby, half in the water and half on the narrow bank, was a dead heron.

Wildhaber pulled up next to Pruitt, took a look and also covered his mouth and nose. "Man, that's nasty."

"Why does this seem to stink worse than just dead fish?"

"Warm weather?"

"I don't think so."

"I don't think so either."

"Something poisoned them."

Pointing, Wildhaber said, "Whatever it was, it got in the river."

Pruitt said, "It'd be all watered down by now."

"I don't care. The South Fork's clean, man. It's gotta stay that way. I'd string whoever did this up by their thumbs, then gut 'em."

They looked up from the shallow death pool and scanned the perimeter of the forgotten meadow. A treeline of mixed deciduous and evergreens was only a couple of dozen yards off. Pruitt nodded towards it. "Let's take a peek."

"Anything to get out of these damn thistles."

Entering the copse of beech, cascara, Doug fir, and young maples, they hadn't gone thirty feet when Wildhaber pushed down on Pruitt's arm and went into a crouch. Pruitt joined him, then peered where Wildhaber pointed. In a narrow clearing sat a dirt-smudged, single-wide mobile home leaning slightly askew on cinder blocks.

No sign of activity, no vehicles that they could see at this angle, they proceeded in their crouched position, Wildhaber wordlessly signaling that he would flash to the right, and that Pruitt should flash to the left.

Going left brought Pruitt to the back of the mobile home, where he noted a pile of debris: five-gallon cans with red labels haphazardly stacked one upon another, plastic buckets of various sizes, cardboard boxes, and what looked like large pill bottles. He knew then what this was, and wished he had his sidearm. Pruitt also worried that Wildhaber wasn't seeing what he was and might not have recognized it as a meth house. On the other hand, his friend had reconnoitered plenty in his days as a soldier and as a hunter, and was also a cautious man. Besides, the place looked abandoned.

Other than a narrow gap at the high noon point of the arc, the mixed-tree grove encircled the meadow. It soon became obvious that this encampment existed completely off the grid. A portable toilet sat crookedly at the bedroom end of the trailer. Although a rental unit, which ostensibly would have a paper trail, Pruitt assumed it had been stolen and would not help in tracking down the operators of the lab. A 55-gallon drum had been welded to a makeshift scaffolding, which in turn had been welded to the roof. Plastic tubing ran from the drum to the house—the water source. As the main entrance of the mobile home came into view, Pruitt noted a gas-powered electric generator was nailed to a wooden pallet and placed just outside the window of the living room. A thick, eight-gauge orange extension cord ran into the house through a broken pane.

A bird called. For a moment Pruitt thought it was another waxwing, but the cry was a little off. He caught a slight movement. The sound had come from the fringe of woods at about two o'clock. And he realized he hadn't heard a bird calling, but a bird caller, Wildhaber, trying to get his attention.

The pair continued moving cautiously towards each other until both arrived at that high noon position, the gap in the arc of trees forming a pathway that separated them by a couple of yards.

"I don't think anybody's there," Wildhaber whispered across the divide.

"I don't think so, either, but I don't think we should go any closer. We need to get a hazmat team. When they cook, they get chloride gas, ammonia gas. Who knows what else."

•••

They stuck to the fringe of forest that followed the path until they were out of sight of the mobile home, then began walking alongside each other in the ruts on either side of the overgrown center. The birds were calling, the grasses were high, a breeze was riffling the thick canopy of leaves. An eerie normalcy, Pruitt thought, considering what they'd just found.

The barbed wire fence incident had occurred a couple of hundred yards past the convergence of the South Fork and Beaver Creek. They weren't too far from Bloomhardt Road, probably just a half-mile or so off the outskirts of East Elkhorn. Unincorporated Willapa County, Pruitt's jurisdiction, although from here on out this would become a group law enforcement effort. Once Pruitt and his officers determined that the lab was abandoned, the nearest hazmat team, stationed in the Centralia Fire Department, would assess the scene and, working with the Department of Ecology, remove any remaining equipment and bulk chemicals. Investigative information would be shared with the state's Methamphetamine Task Force, and the degree and extent of the contamination to the property would be evaluated by the Willapa County Health Department. Finding residual pollution from the chemicals and biohazards was the norm: needles, feces, blood. Given the relatively remote location of the lab, the county would, eventually, have the mobile home towed away and destroyed, then post No Trespassing signs, place a chain gate across the path, and let nature return the clearing to its original condition.

But first things first: contact the hazmat team.

He and Wildhaber trekked over a rise as the path wound between the higher hills. At the road intersection, it would have been hard to pick out the path, and even if someone had noticed it they wouldn't have given it much thought. The actual tire ruts were minimal, and the drooping grasses hid it even further. Pruitt was rather alarmed at how relatively close to a significant population the meth lab existed. Of course, small quantities of meth, what tweakers might cook for themselves, could be produced in your next-door neighbor's kitchen. But he and Wildhaber had just stumbled across a more substantial operation. It wouldn't surprise him to find out that hundreds of thousands of dollars were involved back there in the woods.

Wildhaber stretched his arms over his head, then dropped them. "Where to now, bwana?"

"Hitch a ride, looks like."

Teasing, his friend said, "Too bad Crowley isn't here to witness this latest breach of police protocol. I bet he'd love to have a photo of you and me with our thumbs out here on Bloomhardt."

"You know he would," Pruitt replied. "Hey, there's somebody now. To hell with this hitch-hiking business, I'm going to flag 'em down. I've got a ball game to get to."

CHAPTER EIGHT

THE ECONOMY IN Elkhorn could be summed up as fishing and logging, the culture as shopping and sports. Pruitt was an ambivalent shopper, but he loved his sports, and he was very proud of the Elkhorn Athletic Complex, where so much of the town's culture found its expression. The complex was located along the north bank of the Willapa River, in the Riverdale District. Tonight the breeze carried the smell of freshly-sawn Douglas Fir logs from the Saginaw Mill directly across the river. The fields were home to Little League and Babe Ruth baseball, as well as the Elkhorn High School Sea Eagles football team. A track circled the football field. Lights on 125-foot poles circled the entirety of the facility. When Pruitt had lived in Riverdale, he would sometimes come here to jog. The city made sure it was always open for use. Elkhorn taxpayers could imagine no better way to spend their money.

And while rugged individualism permeated the town's ethos, sports gave them common ground. Attendance at events was excellent—although playing sports was equally important. Pruitt himself still played pickup and town-team basketball. But in the cycle of popular athletics, baseball ruled the summer. Tonight one of the short fields hosted coed softball, the other Little League, and the long field Babe Ruth.

Over near the covered stands, a ragtag group of young men and women were playing a pickup game of flag football

The Sheriff's Department sponsored a Little League team, the Five-O's, and Pruitt enjoyed taking in the games. At the Lion's Club concession stand, he handed Bretta Montgomery five bucks for Molly's bratwurst and a couple of bottled ice teas.

As he was the only customer at the window, Bretta said, "So sad about Wilma. She used to work here with me sometimes, you know."

"Yes, I *do* remember."

"She used to work football games, too, but not last fall, for some reason."

Pruitt nodded. "You guys talk, when you worked the games?"

Bretta may have been big, but her face was slim as a model's. She had an expressive mouth and gentle eyes. "When it got slow, sure. You know what was funny about Wilma?"

Pruitt said, "I don't."

"She was beautiful, but women weren't jealous of her."

"That's weird?"

"For women it is. C'mon, Sheriff, you know that. Especially in a small town."

"You liked her, then."

"I did. But I never felt like I *knew* her knew her, you know?"

"I think I do."

Bretta raised a hand. "Sorry. I'm going on."

"Not at all. I'm glad to talk about it."

Pruitt had given her the opening she felt she needed to really say what was on her mind, her disappointment in him. "I really want you to find out who did this," she said. "Everybody does."

•••

Returning to his seat, Pruitt felt as if the eyes of everyone in the stands were on him, wondering when the heck he'd make an arrest. He knew, of course, that they were watching the game, not him. It was his own frustration coming into play. That he hadn't been able to solve this crime.

After her remark, Bretta had apologized, but Pruitt told her not to worry about it. Yes, she had made him feel self-conscious, criticizing him, but in his position as a public servant, criticism was expected. He didn't want Bretta feeling bad about expressing herself. It had just caught him a little off guard.

He sat down between Molly and Bobby Charneski, one of his deputies. He handed Molly her brat and tea, then turned to Bobby, whose boy Ranger had just smacked a rope into the gap between left and center and was rounding first, heading in for an easy double. Ranger had the best hitting stroke Pruitt had ever seen in a kid so young.

"Jeez, Bobby, that swing of his. Looks effortless."

Bobby tried not wallow in pride. A lot of dads would have, and why not? But Bobby's younger son, Jeremy, was sitting right next to him. In his fist, Jeremy gripped one of those handheld video games, although he wasn't playing it. Rather he gazed intently at his older brother, who was now scooping up a little dirt to rub on his hands, out there at second base.

Bobby was paying attention to a Charneski family dynamic. Being careful not to overpraise Ranger in front of Jeremy. Trying to keep in mind that every child has his or her own life path. In the office, Pruitt had heard Bobby talk about the two boys being gifted with different talents. It was impressive to see him keeping all of this in mind as everyone around him chattered on about Ranger's talent, one of the other dads leaning forward to slap Bobby's back. "Your boy's gonna get us to state, Bobby. Then who knows."

Yet proud of his older son he was. Leaning in close to Pruitt so that Jeremy wouldn't overhear, Bobby said, "He's only twelve."

"You teach him how to play ball like that?"

"No way, boss. That's coming from Judy's side of the family. Her brothers are the athletes."

"Well, she was, too. Back in her day. Didn't they place in the state basketball tourney when she was a junior?"

"They did. Third. She averaged nearly twenty a game."

"You played football, didn't you?"

He shrugged. "Just a big body for the line."

Big, indeed, Pruitt was thinking. Big-boned. The kind of body that could quickly go to fat if neglected, which Pruitt could see was becoming the case, that previously flat stomach pushing at his shirt. Pruitt preferred his crew fit. Like it or not, fit cops made constituents feel more protected; moreover, fit cops did their jobs more efficiently. It wasn't about being able to chase a suspect over hill and dale, it was about mental acuity. In Pruitt's experience, a fit cop was a better thinker, a better decision maker.

The regulations that guided public service would not, however, allow him to dictate a required level of fitness he felt appropriate. The best he could do was lead by example, encouraging diet and exercise programs. He had even worked out a deal for discount vouchers at the local fitness club. It had worked for E.L., the Under Sheriff, who had shed forty pounds in the last couple of years. And it had been working for Bobby, too, up until recently.

After Ranger stole third, and then home, for Pete's sake— no mean feat in Little League, where base runners were not allowed to take a lead—the rest of the inning fizzled away.

During the side change, Bobby said, "Don't know if you heard, but Judy's going back to work."

Pruitt said, "Oh? Is that why she's not here tonight?"

"Yeah. She's cooking at the Dairy Queen." He made a scoffing sound. "Your recent hires get the prime shifts."

"Part time?"

"Yeah. We were hoping to keep her at home, but . . . "

Pruitt said, "I suppose it would have helped if we'd gotten a cost of living raise this year. Sorry about that."

GARY McKINNEY • 99

"Hey, boss. That ain't your fault. Besides, the boys are both in school. After a couple of months, they promised her they'd give her the weekday lunch shift."

Molly peeked about Pruitt to look at Bobby. "What's Lindy going to do? She's not retiring, is she? She can't be more than fifty."

Lindy Wrona currently worked the day shift at Dairy Queen.

Bobby smiled. "You won't believe it. She got a job cooking for Amtrak. She's goes out for ten days, then has two weeks home. Her kids are grown and she and Riley want to travel more."

Molly said, "Riley's about ready to retire, isn't he?"

Bobby chuckled. "I've heard of cooks on ships, but . . . "

"Yeah. Good for Lindy."

When the inning changed again, Pruitt said, "Hey, here's another kid that hits pretty good."

"Yen's boy," Bobby said. "The smart thing he's learned this year is patience."

Pruitt said, "Last year he'd swing at anything." He turned to Molly. "Yen told him, 'You're little, but you're strong. Wait for your pitch. If you walk, you walk. Helps the team.' The kid just wanted to smack that ball so bad."

What Pruitt didn't dare say out loud, especially in an open, public place—even if it was true—was how sports were also slowly easing the fear many locals had that their previously all-white town was being taken over by immigrants. Hispanics and Laotians had moved in initially to plant trees, work the fishing docks, and take the menial jobs at the mill. With the children of those immigrants now playing ball, and playing well—like Yen's boy, maybe the second or third best player in the league—that fear, at least in some circles, was slowly dissipating.

CHAPTER NINE

THE HAZMAT SQUAD couldn't make it to the site until Thursday. Not only had the Fourth of July holiday interrupted the week, they were just that busy. At times it seemed to Pruitt that "labs" were proliferating like an algorithm gone mad. He'd been in law enforcement long enough that he did not believe in drug "epidemics." What he did believe in were drug crazes: the drug du jour crack, then ecstasy, now meth. In five years it would be something else—maybe prescription drugs again—but right now meth crimes, direct or tangential, were taking up a lot of his time.

Frankly, because tweakers were often intemperate with the way they handled the chemicals involved, his officers were put in two kinds of jeopardy—regular crime and the potential exposure to nasty fumes—so the craze couldn't fade quickly enough for his liking.

As a very personal case in point, the last place he expected to find himself as a cop was clad in a Level C hazmat suit— white Tyvek coveralls, rubber booties, a gas mask, and latex gloves with taped sleeves. But here he was with Deputy Raphe Jones dressed just so, getting ready to enter a mobile home potentially rife with deadly compounds. The demands on law enforcement were ever-changing, but Pruitt was having a hard time imagining it getting any stranger than this.

Yet strange or not, this was procedure. The hazmat team was culled from the ranks of fire fighters, not policemen, so after outfitting Pruitt and Jones, they had to wait for the house to be declared unoccupied. Once that was established, the team itself would follow in their Level A suits, which appeared outwardly similar to Level C suits, but were also vapor-tight, and with SCBA's—self-contained breathing apparatus—strapped to their backs.

And unoccupied it was. It took only moments to see that. Surprisingly—or maybe not, as tweakers tended to be obsessive-compulsive types—it was quite neat. To Pruitt's untrained eye, this lab looked professional—at least compared to what he'd seen in the past. Most of which didn't look like labs at all, just exceptionally messy kitchens. The cookers at this site may have tossed the spent cans, boxes, and bottles of chemicals and materials in a heap outside, even poisoned the finger of slough where Pruitt and Wildhaber had first found the fish kill, but inside they had been meticulous. This was probably a good sign for the hazmat team, as the level of toxicity would be less than that of an amateur's work. As Pruitt had suspected, this was clearly much more than a local tweaker out to provide some crank for himself and his friends.

But a cursory look was all that was necessary. Pruitt and Raphe wanted out as quickly as the hazmat team wanted them out—maybe more so. Burglaries, evictions, and traffic violations were the staples of a county sheriff's office, not this scary chemicals-and-vapors stuff. They were glad to turn things over to the captain and two technicians from the Centralia Fire Department.

"The gloves and tape go in the red container." The captain's voice through the mask was eerie. "Your suits go in the yellow one, and the masks leave on that pull-down shelf."

Back at the hazmat team's mobile unit—a Ford F-550 chassis with a custom box outfitted with drawers for equipment and clothing—they began stripping off the gloves and coveralls.

Raphe said, "I've got no interest in ever going into the kind of work they do."

"Amen."

Once rid of their protective shells, they took refuge under the shade cast by a stand of cascara mingled among the beech, maple, and alder that predominated the rest of the forest surrounding the clearing.

Jones pulled a pack of gum from her pocket and offered Pruitt a stick, which he took gratefully. The mask hadn't been strapped to his face for more than fifteen minutes and yet it had made his mouth taste funny.

"You know I've heard some of our constituents bitch about you appearing soft on drugs, but they wouldn't think that if they saw you now."

"Just because I don't see the point of busting everyone with a joint."

Jones pushed two sticks of the gum in her mouth. "We definitely got better things to do."

"It's the lump-it-into-one category thing I don't get," Pruitt said. "Pot smokers? We have more trouble with drunks. Make it legal and let's make money off it. Maybe help people with real problems: booze, heroin . . . " He pointed in the direction of the mobile home. "This stuff."

Jones chewed her gum hard, really grabbing the flavor out of it. "Why don't we just give the tweakers what they want, too?"

Pruitt thought about that a moment. "People who smoke a joint every day might not be spending their money wisely, but they're not putting their neighbors at risk with all these chemicals."

"If they can get it cheap and legal, no more home cooking."

"Yeah, maybe." Pruitt made a scoffing sound. "They'd probably want something stronger than they could buy, even if it was cheap and legal."

Jones nodded. "Some people are just going to be users. It doesn't matter what you do." Then she was looking over Pruitt's shoulder. "What have we here?"

The hazmat captain was walking towards them carrying some sort of case.

Pruitt said, "What do you suppose that is?"

Jones said, "My first take is it's a laptop computer."

His voice still alien from within, the hazmat captain said, "We found this under a pile of empty Sudafed boxes in the bedroom."

"Somebody shot it," Jones said. "The screen's blown all to hell."

"Wilma Gillespie had a laptop," Pruitt said. "This couldn't be that one, could it?"

"Don't know whose it is," Jones said, "but whoever shot it was an idiot. All they did was ruin the screen, not the CPU. I'll bet that hard drive is still intact."

"Hard drive?"

"Where all the data is. We pop that out, plug it into a different computer, we'll find out whose it is."

Pruitt didn't really understand what Jones was talking about, but he appreciated the fact that she was up-to-date on computer technology. By default, she was teaching his staff how to use the department's new PC.

"Have you got a computer tech?" the hazmat captain asked.

Pruitt gave Jones a glance, who looked at him expectantly. He trusted she could do the work, but— "Not officially," he had to admit.

The hazmat captain said, "Well, we've got somebody pretty good. Why don't I log this in as shared evidence. As soon as our guy has whatever's on here in some kind of form us mortals can read, I'll have Sheriff Bowman call you."

Pruitt raised his eyebrows to Jones, who nodded, reluctantly, that it was the right thing to do.

Chapter Ten

"YOU REALLY THINK it's Wilma's?" Molly asked him. "Or just hoping?"

"Hoping." He gestured. "I mean, what are the chances?"

"Guess you'll know soon enough."

They were having morning coffee—or in Molly's case, morning herbal tea—at the small table in the kitchen of Molly's house, both getting ready for work. He hoped she couldn't read minds because she'd have a fit if she knew he still thought of the house—the kitchen, the yard, everything—as hers. She'd been trying so hard to reinvent it as theirs. But truth-be-told, he still hadn't made that leap. He was utterly committed to Molly, but remained wary of the house. She had begun living there with her first husband, Steve—who, along with Molly's mother and father, had died in a car accident some five years back. And although she had shared the house with Steve, in the years since his death it had taken on her identity fully. So strongly had she marked the home Pruitt hadn't had time to assume ownership of even the spare room, the one Molly had designated as his "den."

Yet however tenuous his current relationship with the house, he knew once the baby arrived it would become home to them both—home to them all. In the meantime, he was plenty comfortable, glad to finally have Molly to wake up to every morning without that nagging feeling of guilt they had endured while unmarried—living in sin, as Mrs. Guglomo, Molly's next-door neighbor, would say, venom dripping from every word. All that time spent keeping an eye on the two of them, making sure Molly was preparing for work at her own house in the morning and not still at Pruitt's, or vice versa. Pruitt's neighbors keeping up their end of the unspoken bargain, making sure Molly wasn't "staying overnight" at his house. County Sheriff was a major public figure in a small county, and appearances had to be kept. It was such a relief not to have to think about any of that nonsense anymore.

His wife had just taken a sip of tea and was now looking him over, smiling. Actually, she was giving him what he thought of as her Molly leer. The one that came with one slyly-raised eyebrow. "What?"

"I feel like doin' it with you."

Pruitt laughed. "I always feel like doin' it with you, too."

"Right now, I mean."

Although he never pulled his watch on until walking out the door to his cruiser, Pruitt pointed to his wrist. "You've got to be to work in fifteen minutes, I've got maybe fifteen minutes more."

She rose and stood over him, bent so that he could see the tops of her breasts under the yoke of her top, the one he liked best on her. "I'll tell them I was having some morning sickness."

"Where?"

She got a curious look. "Here at the house, of course."

"No, no." He grinned up at her. "I mean where in this house do you want this doin' done?"

•••

At about ten, while he was in the midst of scanning paperwork and assigning it to various piles of completedness, thinking of Molly and smiling to himself, Pruitt got a call from Lewis County Sheriff Gary Bowman.

"I've got some discs with the data taken off the hard drive of that shot-up computer," he said. "I could mail them to you, or you could send somebody, but if you came over yourself we could powwow a little."

"Done deal, my friend. Arlis's? High noon?"

"High noon? Pretty dramatic. A couple of sheriffs meeting at high noon."

Pruitt laughed and rang off.

•••

Before he took off for Chehalis, Pruitt thought he'd drop in on Olivia and see how she was doing, see if Christopher was starting to embrace his impending fatherhood a little more keenly. But her diesel Rabbit was not in the parking slip. He'd forgotten she was at work. But since he was here anyway, he thought he'd duck in to the garage and check the pH level in his float tank, see how the salinity was holding up. And while the salinity was fine, it looked like it was time for a good cleaning. He hoped to get to that before his regular float on Sunday. Exiting, something caught his eye. In Bill Logan's back yard he saw Angela spread out on a chaise lounge holding up one of those silver-colored sun reflectors to her face. She was topless. Practically bottom-less, too, if you got right down to it.

"God-dangit, Angela!" he called out. "What are you doing? This isn't some nudist colony!"

Angela muttered, "Oops," and began fumbling with her swimsuit top. "I was just trying to keep from getting a tan-line!"

Surprisingly, she actually looked apologetic. When it came to public nudity, she rarely was.

"There wasn't anybody around," she said. "Not until you showed up, anyway."

"Can't you use one of those booths?"

"Unnatural light, man. Causes cancer."

Facing away from him, she clipped the bra. Low on her back was a tattoo of a leaping tiger, exquisitely rendered in vivid oranges and blacks. He wondered how he'd missed it, or if it was something new.

She then stood and walked over the low fence that separated the two properties. "I was being careful, Gav. Really I was. You're standing in the only place someone can see into our backyard."

He was angry, but also embarrassed at the flush of arousal he'd experienced. How could he have not? She was a beautiful woman. An ex-lover. One of his first. Voluptuous. *Why, why, why*, he thought, had she decided to stay in Elkhorn? To be with Bill? Really? He had noted her use of the word "our."

He took a breath and moved toward the fence. A friendly chat between neighbors in a classic Rockwell moment. Although Pruitt doubted very much that ol' Norm had ever painted anyone quite so unclad. What a scandal if he had.

Angela said, "Christopher's in Tacoma, those summer classes of his. Olivia's at her shift. Not that your daughter gives a rip about my boobs."

"Isn't it a little on the cool side for sun-bathing today?" He looked up at the sky. "There's clouds moving in."

"Around here," Angela said, "you grab what you can. Why are *you* here?"

He shrugged. "Just checking in."

Angela read right through that. "Yeah, she's going through a rough time."

"She said you've been helping her out. Thanks for that."

"Just someone to talk to, that's all."

Pruitt toed the ground. "Well, I appreciate it."

"Anything new on Wilma's murder?"

Ah, the rub. "Police business, Angela. C'mon."

"You find that laptop?"

Pruitt gave her a look. "Why are you interested in the laptop?"

"That romance novel I told you about. I was thinking I could edit it, get it in publishable shape, then pitch it to some editors I know."

"Why? Wilma's gone."

She gave him a look that cut right through him. His words unnecessarily harsh.

"A remembrance?" she said. "A memorial? Something nice to give to her family?"

Pruitt held up his hand. "I'm sorry."

She softened. A truce. "Just please tell me that if you do find the laptop and the novel is on it that you'll make a copy of it for me. You don't need it, do you? A romance novel? It's not part of the investigation, is it?"

"No, you're right. A manuscript you call it?"

She nodded.

"If we find the laptop and the novel's on it—" He raised a finger. "And if we deem it has no probative value, I'll make a copy of it for you."

•••

Then the clouds were upon the county, rolling in from the ocean. Pruitt's trip from Elkhorn to Centralia along Highway 6 took him through a thick, misty rain and a smart wind that blew the thin layer of water across the blacktop into patterns that reminded him of how breezes sometimes fashioned the surface of a otherwise calm bay.

Drifting and dreaming, he thought, *on a misty swirling sea.* He'd never thought of himself as that lost sailor in the Dead song, although the investigation into Wilma's murder had certainly gotten lost—or at least muted as the weeks had passed by.

Although not forgotten—certainly not. Maybe he was hearing her anew on the wind, a siren song calling from Lewis County. As the road snaked east through verdant farm land and hillsides that varied from rolling gently to steeply pitched, he hoped so. He passed through Menlo and Lebam, Pluvious and Pe Ell. Log trucks, clear-cuts, green hills still being logged. And milestones. The storybook-looking stone house near Walville, the World War II-era tank that served as a veteran's monument in Pe Ell, and Rainbow Falls State Park outside Dryad, with its old-timey hanging bridge. When he'd been a teenager, Pruitt and his friends would defy the rules and jump off the midpoint into the icy-cold water of the Chehalis River. Eventually a park employee would shoo them away, but not until they'd gotten a half-dozen exhilarating leaps in.

Once past Adna he sped across the Chehalis River floodplain towards Interstate 5, slowed down as he reached the overpass that led into town, then turned onto West Main. Arlis's was a mom-and-pop operation on NW Market, a couple of blocks away from the Centralia Police Department. There were places to eat closer to Sheriff Bowman's office in neighboring Chehalis, but both favored this little diner. Besides, Bowman, like Pruitt, represented all the people of his county. Being seen in as many places as possible was both good policy and good politics.

Under the eave of the restaurant's entrance Pruitt shook the mist off his hat, then entered to the tinkle of bells. Bowman had already found a booth and ordered coffee. He stood when he saw Pruitt. He was probably fifteen years younger, although unlike Pruitt was well into male pattern baldness. Yet he remained, as Pruitt had, trim and athletic. Both still played basketball, including an annual fund-raising game between their two departments: (Willapa County Pig) Skins versus (Lewis County Fuzz-y) Shirts. And while there were indeed some years between them, they were both newly elected first-termers, not to mention both U-Dub grads—a couple of Dawgs—and found a lot to talk about. Beyond all that, they liked each other. Helped each other out as much as possible.

They shook hands, then sat. Pruitt placed his hat next to him on the bench seat. Unlike some of his older counterparts, who would love nothing more than a return to cracking skulls first and considering civil rights later—not to mention keeping it a boy's club—Bowman shared Pruitt's affinity for contemporary law enforcement trends: proactive community networking, restorative policing, becoming more technically savvy—an issue Pruitt recognized as his personal shortcoming.

"It's Christmas early," Bowman said, and handed Pruitt a bundle of blue, square, three-inch plastic discs.

"What are these?"

"Floppies."

He fiddled with them. "They don't seem floppy to me."

"Yeah, I dunno. It's what they're called. Data storage. Our techs downloaded the information on the hard drive of that computer to these. Copy for you, copy for me. I haven't had a chance to assign this to anybody yet, but I will when I get back to the office."

"I will, too," he said, thinking of Raphe Jones.

"Great. Let's compare notes when we've got notes to compare."

Pruitt said, "Done deal," and placed the bundle of discs inside of his upturned hat.

When the waitress returned—a younger woman whose T-shirt sleeve covered only half of the bright tattoo on her upper arm—Bowman ordered a cheeseburger and fries. Pruitt ordered a coffee, a grilled-cheese sandwich, and a side of sweet pickles.

"You still on that meatless diet?"

"More like a lifestyle, once you get into it."

"No salmon, for crissakes?"

"Salmon, yes. Clams, oysters, crab. Seafood, man. I can't live where I do and not eat what comes natural."

"Deer are natural around here. All over the place. Nature's bounty, in some people's eyes."

Pruitt shrugged. "I'll admit I'm not consistent."

Bowman chuckled. "I remember a quote from a lit class, about consistency."

"Hobgoblin of little minds?"

He nodded. "There's that, too. But what I remember was 'with consistency a great soul has simply nothing to do.'"

Pruitt laughed. "I don't know if that makes me a great soul or just damn busy." Then he added, "I forgot to ask. Any prints?"

"Yeah, and they're off to the FBI. Just shipped them the whole thing. Maybe there's some other evidence on it, too. But you know how that works. All those cards they gotta look through? It'll be a while."

"Did you see that article in *Officer's Notebook* about computer-based fingerprinting?"

"I did. My computer guy told me they're building a database. Something called AFIS. Automated Fingerprint Identification System. Gonna be a while, though, before it's operational."

After the waitress with the tattoo cleaned their plates and refilled their coffee cups, Bowman said, "Speaking of the lack of consistency, you notice how there's no organized crime around this meth business?" He rapped his knuckles on the table. "Yet."

Pruitt scoffed. "Can you imagine trying to organize home cookers into some kind of syndicate? Be easier to herd cats."

"Outlaws," Bowman said, making quotes with his fingers. "Everything a frickin' conspiracy. I can tell you one thing, it's still about demand. And I haven't got a clue what to do about that."

When the waitress returned to drop off the check, Bowmen swept it up. "You want to see the latest act of in-your-face boldness?"

"That would be you picking up the tab?"

"Har-har." Bowman stood. "We won't even have to drive."

The rain had abated and the clouds were breaking up as they walked down NW Market to a video store. Inside, near the back, next to a row of shelving stuffed with tapes, was a very well-stocked display of Sudafed and generically-packaged cold tablets, their main ingredient being pseudoephedrine, crucial for cooking meth.

Bowman said, "My guess is they make their real money right here. I wouldn't say the videos are a front, necessarily, 'cause they've got a pretty good selection, really, and a decent location, but there's no way they're making the kind of profit off movies they are off this stuff."

"You can bust them for this." Pruitt looked around. "You probably already have."

"There's a forensic accountant going over their books with a fine-tooth comb as we speak. As soon as she's got it nailed down, all this will be confiscated. Centralia city cops got a little ahead of themselves. Did the bust in front of the paperwork. Can't officially take custody of the stock, or even close the store, for a couple more days." Bowman looked directly at the clerk, who offered a small wave of his hand.

He turned back to Pruitt with an un-amused smile. "Can you believe that?"

Chapter Eleven

WHEN THEIR FRIEND, Dr. Marion, had informed Pruitt and Molly of their pregnancy, they had stood and hugged her.

"That's a first," Marion laughed. "Usually folks hug each other."

Which they then did.

Then Molly wiped her eyes. "I've wanted this so much." She took Pruitt's hand and said, "Thanks, honey."

Marion, smiling, said, "If you say 'You're welcome,' Gavin, I'll have heard it all."

And although Dr. Marion delivered her fair share of babies, she had encouraged Gavin and Molly to use a proper OB/GYN, the closest one being in nearby Riverton, a city of some 35,000. "The Women's Clinic," she'd told them. "It's just what they do. Mommies and babies. You've got coverage. Why not?"

Why not, indeed. It was a great place. And here they were again, keeping on their appointment schedule in the clinic's well-lit and spacious waiting room, where the chairs were comfortable and the reading material close at hand. Pruitt held a *Field & Stream*, but was actually recalling their pregnancy celebration, their little gift to themselves, a nice bottle of red wine, most of which Pruitt ended up drinking.

"Half a glass," Molly had said. "I'm taking no chances."

"More for me," he'd joked, which got him reminiscing. "I remember my mother pregnant with my younger sisters and brothers, smoking, drinking. A few cigarettes a day, a few beers a week. It wasn't much, but she wasn't teetotalling. In the fifties, nobody gave it a second thought. We all seemed to come out okay."

"Moderation," she said, "probably is okay. But, you know, I'm not going to miss wine for nine months."

Their pregnancy also got him thinking about his family in ways he didn't recall thinking about when his first wife, Claudia, had been pregnant with Olivia. He was the oldest of five: a brother, two sisters, another brother. All had fled Elkhorn for other parts of the state, other parts of the country. He had fled, too, for that matter—although he was the only one of them to return. His parents had divorced in the late seventies. His father eventually remarried and moved to Ilwaco, the other end of the county. His mother remained single and moved near his youngest brother in Portland.

Pruitt considered them a medium-close family. Their father, especially, everyone kept at arm's length. Dr. John "Jack" Pruitt was what AA called a functioning alcoholic. He had an indefatigable routine: sober all day, then three martinis in the Torchlight bar before heading home to his liquor cabinet. All their lives he'd loved his children as ferociously as he'd aggravated them.

Acknowledging they were bound by genuine love, Pruitt also recognized their closeness as one survivors sometimes feel—a closeness where love was a component but not the full story. The psychological cocktail that defined their shared experience was such that being together a couple of times a year was enough.

And while he wasn't unhappy with his own family's dynamics, he wondered how much better things could be in a family. He felt very close to Olivia. He'd love to see her every day. He sometimes had to will himself not to drop in on her, especially on weekends when Christopher was home. But how close, he mused, would he be with the new baby? What kind of possibilities were out there for them—Molly, the baby, and him?

Of course, with their pregnancy had come all the logistics. First things first, he had to borrow the beach house at Tokeland again. So he could propose to Molly in a place that was meaningful to them, the place they'd first made love. That night, taking a knee on the plank floor of the rustic cabin, he'd kept it simple. "Molly, will you marry me?"

She'd laughed. "I'd rather keep living in sin, if you want to know the truth." Tousling his hair, she'd added, "Just to set Elkhorn's collective teeth on edge."

"Oh, you're a wicked one. Letting poor Elkhorn and their old-fashioned morals twist in the wind. But I want to stay gainfully employed, so I'm not getting up 'til you say yes."

Neither of them, however, wanted anything to do with a big, formal wedding. Instead, on the following Monday they applied for a marriage license. Then, after the mandatory three-day waiting period, took a long lunch and got hitched by Superior Court Judge Doug Sullivan in his chambers right there in the County Court House.

Pruitt had worn his short-waisted, full-dress jacket. Below his badge were his service pins: Medal of Honor (for his confrontation with a murderer the previous fall), Distinguished Volunteer Service Cross (for his community activism, including his free percussion lessons), and a Ten-Year Good Conduct Bar (in spite of the public beer drinking on his river floats). He also had the obligatory American Flag pin and, nestled in with the rest of his official decorations, his treasured Skull & Roses pin.

Molly had worn a green, knee-length frock whose soft hue offset Pruitt's dark greens beautifully. She had her dark hair up, the nape of her neck exposed. It had taken all of Pruitt's willpower to keep himself from kissing her there.

Their witnesses were practically everyone in the Court House who could get away from their desks for twenty minutes. Ing Yen served as best man, Jeannie Taylor as bridesmaid. Yen also wore his dress uniform; Jeannie wore a beige dress that complemented Molly's green one.

But it was Wilma who had really pulled the whole thing together—at least as far as color coordination. When she walked into the judge's chambers in a green wraparound dress of her own, she'd caught Molly's eye and tugged at the yoke. "Can you believe this?" she'd said. "And I didn't even get the memo." She'd laughed, then approached Molly in a cautious yet endearing way, and touched her forearm. Molly touched her back and smiled. Wilma had looked happy.

"A classic," Judge Sullivan had commented—though they weren't sure if he was referring to Molly's dress, Pruitt's uniform, or all the Court House employees stuffed into his office. Maybe the moment itself. Maybe all of it.

After the ceremony, Pruitt kissed the bride, then amidst a hail of rice thrown by staffers hanging out of the Court House windows, whisked her away in his cruiser. He remembered vividly that the last two rice throwers were Wilma and Dan. They'd been standing out in the parking lot next to Dan's Lincoln, apart from the rest off the wedding assemblage. He also recalled that somewhere between the judge's chambers and the parking lot, Wilma's demeanor had changed. She'd become downcast. At the time, he'd thought returning to work was bumming her out. Now he knew it must have been something else entirely. And he wished he knew what the hell it had been.

"Molly Pruitt?" A nurse's gentle call broke Pruitt's reverie.

Molly set down the *Parent & Child* she'd been reading, then leaned over to touch his arm. "Where have you been? I know you weren't reading that *Field & Stream*."

"Some place interesting, apparently," Pruitt said. He let her lift him up from his chair. "Molly Pruitt, eh? That's you, is it? Mrs. Pruitt?"

"Stop it," she told him, smiling.

CHAPTER TWELVE

ANGUS WAS SUDDENLY barking his fool head off, his muzzle right up to the windowed door, his slobber left on the glass something they had to clean weekly. This was an Omega dog's job, patrolling the perimeter of the pack's territory, alerting the Alphas—Molly and Pruitt—to trouble. That he was doing his duty was just fine, but that bark of his! So deep and menacing, as if coming from a dog three times his size. It never failed to stop Pruitt's heart for a second. "Angus!" he yelled. "Leave it!"

The little black cocker spaniel lowered his head and looked up with those sorrowful brown eyes at one of his masters for approval.

Pruitt bent over to pat his head. "Yes, yes, you're the dog. The best dog in the house." Then he opened the door to Raphe Jones.

"Hey, boss, hate to bother you. But I found something from that computer hard drive that can't wait."

He noticed that she had a folder in her fist. "Well, then. Come in. You want some coffee?"

Jones said "Sure," then raised her eyebrows as she looked passed Pruitt's shoulder. "Hey, Molly. Sorry for barging in like this."

"Coffee?" Molly asked. "Or some lemonade? I was just going to make some."

"Lemonade, actually. Thanks."

Pruitt made an expressive sweep of his arm. "Why don't we sit at the table in the dining room."

She nodded to a framed photograph on the sideboard. "Molly's parents?"

"Yes."

"And her husband who died?"

"Yep. That's Steve."

She pointed to a tiny sculpture in metal and porcelain of a wren perched on a branch. "I like that little bird." Then she gave Pruitt a sly glance. "And that would be?"

"Me at graduation. U-Dub, winter of '73. With the various sidetracks I got into, it took me a little extra time to get through."

"1973, eh?"

"Yes, the hair is long."

"And thick."

"And more than a little ridiculous. But you know what they say: if we don't remember the past we're doomed to repeat it."

Jones laughed, then seated herself at Pruitt's right hand, Pruitt himself taking his usual place at the head of the table. As if they were sitting down for a meal.

"So what have you got that couldn't wait until Monday?"

"First of all, it was indeed Wilma's computer."

Pruitt said, "Whoa." Thought about it a moment. "Great. We've got something new to go on."

She opened the folder like a book, then turned it to face him. "This is the crux."

What lay in front of Pruitt looked like entries in a ledger. "Accounting?"

"A spreadsheet. Electronic accounting, if you will." She paused. "I think this has to do with Dan."

"Louderback?"

She straightened her back and set her jaw, a practiced move many cops adopt when delivering bad news. "I think he was skimming."

"From the city?" Pruitt leaned back in his chair and drew his hand across his face. After letting this news sink in, he sat back up. "How was he doing it?"

"A variety of ways." She pointed to an entry. "For instance, I think here they're referring to parking tickets. See: PT? And also traffic tickets. See the TT entries? Other things, too. Anything where someone came in and paid cash."

"Somebody pays cash, there has to be a receipt."

Jones nodded. "Sure. But it doesn't have to come from an official receipt book. My guess is there were two."

"But the ticket number itself has to be reconciled."

"Yeah. I thought of that. Only one way it's going to work."

Pruitt finally caught up with her. "Wilma. She doubled as Elkhorn's court clerk. This doesn't work without her."

"Yep."

Pruitt sighed and ran his hand across his face again. "Crap."

"I know."

"Here we go." It was Molly, delivering the lemonade. "Enjoy," she said, then left them.

After a sip, Pruitt said, "He would have killed her over some money?"

Jones, too, sighed. "The gut says no. The evidence says we gotta look at him for it."

"Why was the computer at the meth house?"

"I've got no idea about that."

"Nothing in those floppies that could explain it?"

"Nothing I can find. Just this skimming operation."

"Do we need to get a forensics accountant down from Olympia to look at this, or do you think it's solid for a warrant?"

"If it gets to trial, we'll want the accountant. For turning the Elkhorn PD offices upside down, we've got plenty."

CHAPTER THIRTEEN

EIGHT O'CLOCK ON Sunday morning the July sun was still low in the horizon, casting a soft light over the Elkhorn Civic Building, causing its unattractive stucco siding to glow. The irony was not lost on Pruitt that the building would probably never look better than at this unfortunate moment, having to carry out this disappointing task.

He stood next to his cruiser in a small knot with Raphe Jones and Ing Yen, waiting but not talking. They already knew their roles, what each would do when Dan Louderback arrived, which he just now was, rounding the corner onto Commercial Street in his metallic-blue Lincoln Mark VII, a fairly ostentatious car for a public employee—a fact Pruitt really hadn't given much thought to until today.

Louderback parked behind the cruisers. He looked a bit shaky getting out of his car. "What's with the cloak and dagger?"

Pruitt pulled the warrant from his back pocket and stepped forward to hand it to his colleague. "It's quieter, Dan. Won't be so alarming to people."

Louderback took the proffered paperwork and appeared to read it, although it didn't look as if his eyes were capable of focusing on the words. Instead, he scanned the streets, down Third, up Commercial. Nothing extraordinary. A quiet Sunday morning in a small town. "Shit," was all he said.

"Dan?" Raphe Jones said, "can I have the keys?"

The police chief said, "Yeah, yeah," and fumbled through his pants pocket until he found them.

Jones plucked them from his hand, then she and Yen moved smartly to the Elkhorn Police Department's entrance, unlocked the door, and disappeared inside.

Louderback stood so that the rising sun caught his left profile full on. His skin looked worn. Beaten up and slack. He wasn't that old a man, probably mid-forties, but at that moment he could have passed for sixty—and a hard sixty at that.

"Dan?" Pruitt held out his hand as a directional.

"Yeah, yeah. Let's go in."

Once in the waiting room, Pruitt said, "You want to make this easy and tell me what was going on?"

Louderback gazed intently at the door to his office. "Can I get something from my desk?"

"Of course not . . . Oh. You want the whiskey?"

"Yeah." He held up his hand. "I got the shakes a bit this morning. It's a little earlier than I've been getting up."

Pruitt called out to Raphe Jones, who retrieved the bottle. Pruitt found a glass in the kitchenette. He then sat with his colleague on the uncomfortable chairs in the waiting room.

"When's your next shift coming on?"

"Came on about twenty minutes ago. But Arlie just starts from his house. There's nothing here he needs to come in for."

After a two-finger shot, which he knocked back without so much as a grimace, Louderback laid it out. "We had this scam going." And he explained it pretty much as described the day before in Pruitt's dining room by Deputy Jones. Any time cash came in, the receipt was written from a separate book. Wilma reconciled both receipts and ticket numbers.

"I'm having a hard time imagining Wilma going along with this," Pruitt said.

"She didn't want to go along with it. It was my idea. I told her I needed the money. Needed it bad."

Pruitt caught himself scowling. Had to quickly get his face back in order. This was not the time for judging. "Did you, Dan? Need it bad?"

Louderback gave a slight shrug. "Not really."

"Then why?"

"I dunno. I just wanted it."

"Okay." *Money*, Pruitt thought. Nothing led to sin more resolutely. "Did Wilma need the money?"

"No. Neither of us did. But it was exciting. You know? The whole idea of getting away with it? That adrenaline rush?"

His colleague poured himself another two fingers of whiskey. "Plus we were in love."

Ah, Pruitt thought. So all the rumors were true. And here it is, boiling down to money and love, the two sides of the sin-triggering coin. Dupree shoots a jeweler for a diamond ring to keep his baby satisfied, just because of that sweet jelly roll.

Yet the thought of Wilma involved in crime would still not take hold. Or maybe, because he'd liked her so much, he just wasn't allowing it to. "You were pretty discreet."

"That was a big part of what made if fun. Hiding the affair."

"And the scam?"

"That came later. At first it was only about finding time to make love."

"You do that here?"

"Sometimes." Louderback stared at the whiskey. "We had a couple of places we'd meet. Motels. One over in Lewis County, one up in Riverton. Olympia later. Portland once or twice." He smiled. "What do they call it? Al fresco? We had a couple of those, too. The whole clandestine aspect, I'm telling you, it turned her on. Turned *me* on. With Mark everything was so prescribed. One of those guys that has to have the towels folded over the rack just how he wants them. You know?"

"You don't think he knew?"

"Baseball junkie," Louderback said. "He used to go down to Arizona for spring training. All those games during the season? Then other sports, Sonics and Seahawks."

"So it wasn't just about the Mariners?"

"Baseball mostly, but he'd get his sports fix wherever he could."

The shot poised at his lips, Louderback said, "Once we got started, I let Wilma lead. Do all the scheduling, the arrangements. She loved it."

He knocked it back. Licked his lips. "Incredible."

Pruitt assumed he meant Wilma. Or maybe it was the whiskey. Either way, it was an uncomfortable moment. He sat silent, letting the booze kick Louderback in the head. He wished there had been something that would have kicked some sense into his colleague long before this.

"Why did the entries dry up a couple of months before Wilma was killed?"

"She wanted out," he said. "She wanted it to stop."

"Is that why you killed her?"

Louderback turned glazed eyes on him. "I didn't kill Wilma. Are you *crazy*? I *loved* her." He clutched his chest, the booze apparently loosening up his sense of drama. "With my whole heart. My whole soul! I can't believe you'd think I would do something like that!"

Pruitt let the histrionics die down before saying, "Motive, Dan."

The eyes were still on him, too glazed for only two pops to account for it, regardless of how early in the morning it was. "I would never. I wanted her to run off with me. Take the money and go."

"Why didn't you?"

He dropped his hand from his chest. "I already said. She wanted it to stop." He turned away, gazed out the small window high on the kitchenette wall. "She wanted to get the money back in the loop. Clean the whole mess up."

"Back in? What're you saying?"

"The money. It's . . . you know. Over there."

•••

Louderback had literally waved his hand in the direction of the kitchenette. "A box," he said. "You'll find it."

In the cabinet underneath the sink, behind a small garbage can and an array of cleaning items, Yen discovered a blue plastic container with a tightly sealed lid. Tupperware, it looked like. Full of cash. Few denominations higher than a twenty.

Stunned, Pruitt pulled Louderback into his office for some follow-up questions, then had Yen escort the police chief to his cruiser and place him in the back seat.

When he returned, Yen gave a Pruitt a look. "Dan said he forgot his whiskey."

Pruitt snorted. "He's going to have to wait."

The three of them stood silently in the kitchenette.

Jones finally said, "What were they thinking? This was all just a game?"

Pruitt said, "He told me their plan was to get a hundred thousand, then take off. 'Blow this pop stand,' were his exact words. Then Wilma had a change of heart. Wanted it to stop."

Hefting the tub, Jones said, "I'll bet there's thirty- or forty-thousand dollars in here."

"You'd think they'd be worried about somebody stumbling across it."

Ing Yen said, "Bet nobody cleaned up around here but Wilma."

"Night shift?" Pruitt said. "They spill something? Looking for cleaning products?"

"Probably just use paper towels. Hanging right there. Besides, shift officers in Elkhorn work out of their cruisers. They've got no holding cell here. Any arrests, they bring them to us."

"They've got keys to the place."

"Come in to do paperwork." Yen nodded towards the waiting room couch. "Get some sleep."

"Nonetheless," Pruitt said, "It sure as hell takes hiding a crime in plain sight to a new level."

"What are we going to do with the chief?" Jones asked.

Pruitt shrugged. "Book him. What else can we do?"

"Jail's crowded right now," Jones said. "We don't want to keep him in there, even overnight. He could get hurt."

"Well, let's book him, then release him on his own recognizance. I don't think he's going anywhere. And even if he does, I'm not going to lose any sleep over it. We got the money back."

His deputies went quiet on him. He looked at them. "You two are thinking he might have killed Wilma."

Yen said, "He's been acting weird. Wracked with guilt, I think you say."

Pruitt said, "Yeah, but guilt over what?"

Jones said, "Well, killing her."

Pruitt said, "Except we don't have any direct evidence he did that. He's involved in fraud, which we could obviously hold him on. But that's white collar crime. You set bail, if they can pay it, they walk."

Yen said, "He's got motive."

"Does he?" Pruitt glanced at the Tupperware tub. "Money's still here."

Jones shifted her weight. "We don't know how much money's been skimmed. Maybe someone else found out about it, started skimming the skim."

Turning to her, Yen said, "That person may be killer."

Pruitt said, "What are there, ten Elkhorn PD officers?"

"One his brother." Yen noted. "Heard him called screw up."

"A little lazy at times," Pruitt said, "but he does his job."

"The guy skimming the skim," Jones said, "maybe he wanted in on it. They freeze him out, he gets mad . . . "

Pruitt thought about it a moment. "It could be any one of them."

"Getting back to Dan," Jones said. "What'll we do with him?"

Yen said, "Work out deal with Sheriff Bowman? They got empty cell over in Lewis County?"

Pruitt said, "I might be able to make that happen. Let's keep him at the office for the immediate time being."

"Another problem," Yen said, "Who takes over for Dan?"

Jones looked at Pruitt. "That's up to the mayor, right?"

"It is. I'd better call her."

"Are you going to tell her she might be putting Wilma's killer in charge?"

Pruitt said, "At this point, I don't see how telling her that is going to help anything. All we've got is speculation. Mayor can't make a decision based on that."

"Another thing to do," Yen said, "is drop in on Mark Gillespie, see if he knew about this affair."

Jones said, "He's alibied, Ing."

Yen gave her a smile. "Lee Wilson say to me: 'You never argue with an alibi. You just work to prove it worthless.'"

•••

Pruitt called Elkhorn Mayor Vicki Stephens and brought her up to speed.

"Dan's been bilking us? Are you kidding me?"

"For a number of years, apparently."

"And Wilma was in on it?"

"Had to be." He explained why, the ticket reconciliations, the double books.

"I served on Elks Club committees with her. For charities. I counted her as one of my good friends. How can—" But she had nothing more to add. "And Dan. Goddamnit. How could he—"

Pruitt paused before saying, "We're all feeling betrayed."

"Everyone's still talking about her murder. And now this. It's so—" After another moment, she said, "You think this is related to her death?"

"We don't know, Vicki. We just don't."

"And there's nothing new on the investigation into that?"

Pruitt said, "Well, there's this, that just came up."

The mayor sighed. "Sorry, Gavin. I'm not thinking right."

"You'll need to appoint a chief, Vicki. Today."

"Yes, of course. Arlie Petit's sergeant, and next in command. As far as I'm concerned, it's that simple."

"Arlie's a good man," Pruitt replied, hoping it was actually true.

•••

After the call, Pruitt assigned Ing Yen to drive Dan Louderback to the department. He wanted Jones to come with him to Mark Gillespie's house because she'd been there before, might catch something she'd missed the first time.

When they arrived at the corner of Jackson and Gravel Pit it was still pretty early for a Sunday, so it wasn't surprising that Wilma's widower answered the doorbell in a bathrobe. Seattle Mariners logo on the pocket. His plaid cotton pajama bottoms were Mariners navy blue; his fuzzy slippers had a Mariners logo on each toe. Pruitt was thinking that being a devoted fan was one thing, but that Gillespie's interest in the team bordered on the obsessive.

Seeing two cops took him back a moment, but only for a moment. He invited them in.

"Coffee?" He turned, implying they should follow him, which they did, across the short hallway then right toward the kitchen.

Pruitt again noted the odd, but practical arrangement. The kitchen area was open to a television room—maybe they called it the den—full of quality but very comfortable furniture and high-end electronics. Next to this was a fireplace with dual hearths, the second facing a formal living room with no media and less comfortable-looking furniture, a place where one might sit rigidly and sip tea and discuss books. Wilma had been a reader—always with a novel at her desk—and, apparently, a writer. Pruitt seemed to recall she'd asked Molly once to join a book club. When Wilma and Mark had built the house, had this been the sole accommodation to her needs?

Gillespie held the coffee maker carafe up to them. The light from the window made it appear more brown than black. The same light emphasized Gillespie's pale skin—made it appear like parchment—and the delicacy of his fine blondish-red hair, which even this early had been combed into place.

"Had plenty already, Mark," Pruitt said. "But thanks."

Refreshing his cup—which was black ceramic with, of course, a Mariners logo—he said, "Did something come up, finally? About Wilma?"

"Did you know she was having an affair?"

Methodically, he took a sip. "Well, we were separated. It really wasn't any of my business."

"I mean before your separation. Like for the last two or three years."

Gillespie couldn't bring his gaze up off the floor.

"So you did."

"I didn't, in the sense you're talking about. There was something going on, but what . . . " He finally looked up, made a combination tight face and shrug. "I suspected but never had anything to go on. And I sure as hell didn't know who."

"You never once thought Dan?"

"Sure, of course. Only logical, I guess. She was there all day. He got that divorce. Good looking guy."

"You ever get a little upset with him?"

He made a tsking sound and looked out the window at the slope of lawn in front of his house, beyond which lay the home-strewn Riverview hillside and flats, then the sloughs and estuaries of the South Fork of the Willapa. "I was upset with everything. Anybody would have been. You're trying to do something to stop it, but you can't? Nothing's working?"

He finally turned to address Pruitt and Jones. "But you're talking to me again like you think I had something to do with her getting killed. And I didn't. I loved her. Besides, you know I was at the game."

CHAPTER FOURTEEN

CHIEF DAN LOUDERBACK spent the night in the Lewis County Jail, then was brought back to Willapa County for a bail hearing—expedited at Pruitt's request. Clearing out an entire cell to house one inmate was impractical. Sheriff Bowman had pulled it off for one night, but that was as much accommodation as he could provide. Back at Willapa County, they could take a chance and place the police chief in with the general population, but if an incident were to occur in that circumstance a lawsuit would surely follow. A law enforcement officer left unprotected and then shanked because of fraud? Fraud was bad, of course, but nobody wanted Louderback hurt because of it.

That he may have been Wilma's killer was moot in these circumstances. Even if it was him, there was no evidence of it. From an investigative stand-point, Pruitt thought it more likely they could move the case along with Louderback a free man. Let him loose but keep track of him, follow him—maybe something useful would emerge.

Carl Pulkkinen, the Prosecutor, however, didn't like the idea of simply allowing Dan Louderback an open pass—didn't think it would look good to voters in the next election—so arranged to have an electronic monitoring device strapped on him, an ankle bracelet.

"What if I need to go to the liquor store?"

"Call us," the tech told the police chief, handing him a card. "Let the operator know where you're going and how long you'll be. We'll call the office here and let them know."

Pruitt said, "We're paying for this privilege, right?"

It might have been a question aimed at the techie, but it was not. It was meant for Pulkkinen; Pruitt as angry with him. The bracelet situation was not going to allow Louderback the kind of freedom of movement Pruitt was convinced would help the investigation. Privately, he'd been clear with Pulkkinen about that, but the Prosecutor overruled him. Indeed, since about a year ago, their relationship seemed to move from one tense moment to another.

When he'd first been elected Sheriff, Pruitt had respect for the man, his intellect, and his ethics. He still admired his intellect, but no longer his ethics, which he saw now as driven entirely by politics. Events in last fall's murder investigation had changed his thinking. When Pruitt had needed support the most, all he'd gotten from Pulkkinen was threats. A turncoat covering his ass. More concerned about making sure the Governor and her minions blamed anybody but himself for the lack of arrests.

"It's not that bad, Gavin."

Pruitt wasn't sure who or what Pulkkinen was looking at—a fly? the wall? the air?—but it sure as hell wasn't at him.

"I thought the budget was tight. No cost-of-living for our officers, but we've got money for this bullshit?"

Before Pulkkinen could respond, Louderback said, "I don't care about it one way or the other. As long as I can get to the liquor store when I want to, I don't give a rat's ass."

After a moment of uncomfortable silence, Pulkkinen said, "Jeez, Dan. What's happened to you?"

Louderback raised his head, which looked a little loose on his neck, lubricated with alcohol already. Yet somehow he got himself together and stared directly at the prosecutor. "Go bite yourself, Carl. As if you could with that gut."

The police chief was a tragic figure, for sure, and Pulkkinen, a short, large man whose midriff had been expanding relentlessly in the years Pruitt had known him, was probably giving voice to a legitimate concern about his well being. But Pruitt had to turn and bite his lip.

•••

About a half-hour later, Pruitt took a call from his friend Sheriff Bowman, who usually had some pleasantries to share, but not this time. "You remember that video store we visited a while back? The one selling the Sudafed?"

"Yeah, sure."

"Well, our investigation turned up something interesting. They were bankrolled by Tom Conley, a guy who also happens to own one of the more extensive farm supply stores in the area."

Pruitt took a sip of coffee from his Steal Your Face mug. "I'll bet he's got a few tankards of anhydrous ammonia parked at his warehouse."

"You betcha."

"That's a lot of coincidence."

"Trouble is, he had a good story to tell. We didn't get anywhere with him. I know it's a little out of the ordinary, but—"

"—maybe it wouldn't hurt to shake him down a little more, keep some pressure on."

"Well, there's that, too. But really, I'd just appreciate your take on him."

•••

Tri-County Farm Supply had a Centralia address, and was located where Harrison Avenue and Sandra Avenue met and formed an arrowhead-shaped parcel of land. There were numerous buildings, all far more functional than attractive, essentially aluminum-sided warehouses accommodating the various branches of the business—farm supplies, tack, garden, tools—plus a peppering of open lots for display equipment, tractors mostly, and an array of tractor attachments like harrows and bushhogs. There was even a covered outdoor patio with all the latest gas barbecues, some of them more sophisticated than Molly's stove. *Oops,* Pruitt said to himself as if Molly was listening in on his thoughts. *Our* stove.

Also on site were trailer-mounted anhydrous ammonia tanks—fertilizer to farmers, but a crucial ingredient to meth cookers. Before meth it had been a common practice to leave the tanks in the fields. But when the tweakers started stealing the gas, siphoning off gallons of it at night, law enforcement had begun pleading that the tanks get stowed away when not in use—under lock and key, if possible.

At Tri-County the tanks weren't exactly hidden from view, but were kept well out of the public walkways, locked behind a steel chain-link fence near the back-end of the tool shop. They knew what they had and didn't seem to be playing games with it, taking appropriate precautions.

The owner of this empire was Tom Conley, who worked out of the garden complex. Located in the largest of the buildings, a steep set of stairs climbed up the back, leading to a catwalk, a string of windows, and a door simply marked Office. Inside that door, in keeping with the theme of function over fancy, the décor was reminiscent of what Pruitt had seen in both government offices and single-wide trailers: the walls paneled in thin, fake cherry wood-colored veneer, the reception desk manufactured from thin, fake cherry wood-colored steel. A small cactus plant with a magenta-colored bloom sat on a shelf behind the desk, offering the barest shred of personality. A Christmas cactus, he thought it was called. The receptionist, however, was exceptionally friendly, and led him to a corridor lined with offices.

As Pruitt walked down the hallway, a man looked out from his cubicle and took Pruitt's full measure in a glance. A hard, professional assessment. Pruitt nodded to him. The man did not acknowledge, but rather pulled his head back in his office. When Pruitt passed by, the door had been left ajar only slightly, so that nobody could see in.

Tom Conley's office was just past the curious man's, larger than a cubicle, but not by much, and filled with sunlight. He stood when Pruitt entered. Conley looked to be about five nine or ten. Trim. Dark hair and eyes. A nice looking man with a wary, but not unfriendly, countenance. Not exactly glad to see a cop, but not pitching daggers, either.

They shook hands and Pruitt sat when offered a chair. He noted a tidy office, no photographs of kids or family. All about function. Just like everything else he had seen so far in this operation. "You're out here on the flats. Did you flood in '90?"

"Just saw the tip of it. We're on a bit of a rise." He nodded towards his window. "You see that pasture out beyond our fence? There was water up to about twenty yards of us. But now the Army Corps of Engineers assures us everything is under control. Safe as milk, they tell us."

"I've seen you before? We've met somewhere?"

Conley gazed at Pruitt a moment. "I don't think so. I know Bowman, of course. He was out here asking what I imagine will be the same questions you're about to ask."

"About the video store. Seems outside your business model."

A pencil played through Conley's fingers. "Actually, it seemed like a good investment at the time. An old friend had an acquaintance who needed some start-up funds. Why not? The lease on that place was pretty cheap. Everybody's renting videos these days. It seemed like a money maker."

"You can see why I'm here. All this easy access to important meth chemicals. His, yours."

Conley raised his hands, a what-can-you-do gesture. "I was down there once, at the grand opening. Wished them well. I did not see any Sudafed for sale at that time. If I'd seen then what I've been told recently they were selling, what Bowman told me about two days ago, I'd have been as curious as you. At a video store? C'mon. But the fact of the matter is they started sending me checks thirty days after the store opened and kept sending checks like clockwork, so what did I care? I personally don't rent videos, and as long as they were turning the nut I had no reason to stick my nose in their business."

Pruitt, however, suddenly didn't care about this interview. He realized it was premature. He now thought he knew where he'd seen Conley. But before questions came out of his mouth that might or might not come with a lie for an answer, he wanted to be sure he knew the difference. "Well, that's good enough for me." He stood and stretched out his hand. "Thanks for your time."

Surprised, but trying not to show it, Conley rose, shook hands. "Glad to clear things up."

•••

Back in his cruiser, driving back to Elkhorn, Pruitt pondered the fact that he was sure he'd seen Conley before. And if it was when and where he thought it might have been, then Conley had just moved up to the top of his persons of interest list for Wilma's murder. The item he needed to confirm his suspicion rested with Raphe Jones, and he didn't want to wait until tomorrow to find out. He radioed ahead to the office. She was out on a call, due back in an hour. Pruitt asked that she wait for him.

•••

She was hunched over paperwork when he stuck his head in her door. "Raphe, didn't you shoot some video of Wilma's funeral?"

"Sure did. Sometimes a killer comes back to gloat, see their handiwork, the havoc they've wreaked—that sort of thing. Taking a second pleasure in it."

"I'm sure you reviewed it. Anything jump out at you?"

GARY McKINNEY • 135

"Well, the only thing I remember was seeing a lot of people I didn't know. But then I'm not a real 'local,' either. And I sure couldn't just walk up to them and ask what their relationship with her was. As much as I would have liked to."

"Let's take a look at it."

They adjourned to the break/conference room, where Washington State and Willapa County maps were hung, and a bulletin board with some wanted posters—and, of course, the obligatory framed photograph of William Jefferson Clinton, 42nd President of the United States. At the back of the room was a kitchenette, the ubiquitous red light of the coffee pot aglow. Pruitt's empty Steal Your Face mug was hanging from the peg just a couple of feet away. Alluring. A visual equivalent of the Siren's call. Did he dare drink the office swill just this once?

No, he did not. Calling that stuff battery acid was far too kind. Just a sip of it was a devil dance with heartburn.

There was also a television and VCR in the break/conference room, located next to the kitchenette. Jones commandeered the remote. Although hand-held and a bit jumpy, the video was in focus and she hadn't panned wildly left or right, just calmly kept filming, getting a record of everyone there.

After a four or five minutes, Pruitt said, "Him," pointing. "Pause it there."

They'd gone past, and Jones reversed the tape, started again, then hit the pause button at the right place. "Who is he?"

Some jagged video lines cut across the image, but Pruitt could see him well enough. "Guy named Tom Conley. Owns Tri-County Farm Supply, a little north of Centralia. He bankrolled that video store I told you about that was selling Sudafed. Why the hell," he asked, "was he at Wilma's funeral?"

"He lie about it?"

"No, but he conveniently left out the fact. Me sitting there in front of him, a cop from Elkhorn. You don't think he saw me there?"

"Busy? Distracted?"

"No way." Pruitt pointed at the screen. "Is there some way to get a photo off this. Something I can take with me?"

Chapter Fifteen

AS MUCH AS Pruitt itched to confront Conley again, Tuesday's staff meeting wouldn't allow it. His undersheriff, Ethan "E.L." Lamont, and one of the two deputies assigned to Long Beach had driven up, plus schedules had been jostled to assemble as many staff as possible.

Because officers needed to be doing police work 24/7, there would never be a meeting where all employees of the Sheriff's Department could be present, but Joyce had a system worked out that got nearly everyone there. And that was the first thing Pruitt said to his assembled multitude. "Let's give Joyce a hand."

After a heartfelt applause, Joyce said, "Thank god we only do this quarterly."

"The spread's good, too," Pruitt said, "but the homemade cinnamon rolls? C'mon, Joyce, you're going to spoil us rotten."

The applause for the cinnamon rolls was far more enthusiastic than for the meeting.

The agenda was of some length, then afterwards E.L. had some budget questions. Sitting in his office with his second in command, Pruitt said, "Before this thing with Dan, had you heard any scuttlebutt about any of the Elkhorn PD officers?"

E.L., at six-five, was an imposing figure, although a much trimmer one these days, thanks in some part to Pruitt's fitness programs. E.L. had been undersheriff for Pruitt's predecessor, Arthur Hujak, and most people had assumed he would run for the position when Hujak retired. But he just wasn't interested. "You go for it, Gavin," he'd said at the time. "I'd be proud to work for you." Yet in at least one way E.L. had, indeed, stepped in Hujak's shoes, serving as Pruitt's trusted elder statesman when Hujak had retired to the San Juan Islands in the northwest corner of the state.

"Not sure what you're getting at, Gavin."

"I'm trying to gauge some thoughts I'm having."

"Who to trust?"

"Or who not to."

E.L. put his hands up on top of his head. "Well, they always seemed like a good posse to me. Of course, nobody thought Dan would do anything like what he did. And Wilma, that's a real shocker. And now the whole force is looking bad. I mean, you and I know how it could work, how they could hide it, but to the constituency out there, they gotta be wondering why nobody figured it out."

"Town council got reamed in the *Elkhorn Echo* this week for not keeping track of the budget."

E.L. said, "I thought that was a little harsh. How can you keep track of something you never knew was going on in the first place? If Dan and Wilma started small, worked it over a number of years . . . ?" He brought his hands off the top of his head and placed them back in his lap.

"Keep your ears open for me, would you?"

"Absolutely."

"So," Pruitt said, "This budget question you've got. I hope this isn't about that damned cost-of-living raise. Or lack thereof."

•••

Lunch didn't happen until nearly two, so Pruitt wasn't able to drive back to Tri-County Farm Supply in Centralia until after three.

Again, Tom Conley rose when Pruitt entered his office. But this second visit had put the kibosh on yesterday's conciliatory countenance. This time he was patently annoyed. "You're back?"

Pruitt placed the screen shot—as Raphe Jones had told him it was called—onto Conley's desk. "Can you tell me why you were at Wilma Gillespie's funeral?"

Conley picked up the photograph, which was grainy but clear enough to identify him. He showed no emotion, just put it down after a moment and looked Pruitt in the eye. "I knew her. There to pay my respects."

"In what capacity did you know her."

The man gestured toward a chair. "Sit down, Sheriff. Please."

Pruitt did.

Conley, too, sat, then steepled his hands, his eyes still facing Pruitt but going slightly out of focus. "Wilma and I were having an affair."

A disarming admission, Pruitt had to admit. "Did you know Dan Louderback?"

"I didn't know him, but I knew Wilma worked for him. He was the Police Chief over there in Elkhorn."

"Did she mention he was dirty?"

Conley nodded. "Yes, actually."

Again with the disarming honesty. "She mention she was in on it?"

"That, too."

Was this real honesty, or selective? "You two talk about that?"

"Yes," he said. "When I found out I told her it was bad business. Which she didn't need to hear from me. She already wanted to come clean. Apparently the money was still intact. She was thinking they could get off with a slap on the wrist if they gave it back. Maybe some jail time, maybe not. She felt really bad about it."

"She say how much it was?"

He dropped the steeple and reached for a pencil. "She wasn't real specific. I ran some numbers in my head and figured it couldn't have come to more than sixty or seventy thousand. I mean, the way they were running it, it had to have built up slowly."

Pruitt took note of his numbers. They were different than what had actually been found in the Tupperware tub. "You ever meet Louderback?"

"Not directly."

Pruitt let a beat pass. "Can you expand on that a little?"

He made a gesture toward his business. "We've got a line of cleaning supplies we sell wholesale. We don't advertise it, it's not a big part of our overall business, but we make bids. Schools, cities—that kind of thing. City of Elkhorn is one of our customers. Toilet paper for the public restrooms and paper towels for the offices—you know, the usual stuff you gotta have. Really, no big deal, a little steady cash flow is all, but we've got some other customers over in Willapa County, so why not? Made a delivery once a week, maybe every ten days.

"Then one day our driver was out, the whole office sick with something going around, so I stepped up and did the delivery myself. That's when I met her."

"Kept it pretty quiet," Pruitt noted.

"That's the kind of lady she was."

"Did you know she and Dan were having an affair?"

Pencil down, steeple back. A forward/backward guy. "I thought she might be, yes. But I did not ask her one way or the other. It was none of my business."

"So it was just a sexual thing? Nothing deeper."

Steeple down, pencil back. A regular dance, props and everything. Drama. "Don't be an ass, sheriff. She was one of the most beautiful women I've ever known. And I'm not talking about just her physical beauty, I'm talking about how she radiated something you rarely see."

That admission was, of all the admissions he'd heard in the last few minutes, the one he believed. Nonetheless, Conley's hand dance was pissing him off. "You got an alibi for the time of her death?"

•••

The return trip to Lewis County pretty much shot his day. He was tired and he needed a float. During his second drive back from Tri-County Farm Supply, while he still had a strong signal available from the nearby I-5 corridor, he used the bag phone he'd brought with him to call Molly and tell her he was going to do just that, then drove straight to Riverdale and his former residence. He parked alongside the front of the garage, and when Olivia peeked out the kitchen window he took a step or two out onto the street to make sure she could see him and gestured to where he was going. She waved back, disappeared again.

He entered the garage through the side door and slipped into his float room, which looked from the outside like a sauna. In a way it was. A local contractor—Quint Ledford—had modified a kit to suit Pruitt's purposes. It had been the purchase of a lifetime, the equivalent of a fancy boat or a hot motorcycle.

Inside the cedar-walled room sat the tank and a baseboard heater, unnecessary this time of year. The room was cramped but efficient, with just enough space to change in, some hooks for his clothes. He unpinned his badge and set it on the bench, loosened his tie and stripped it through his collar, removed the shirt and hung it on one of the hooks. On another, he draped his gun belt. He stepped out of his pants, folded them neatly, set them on the bench over the badge, then stripped his shorts off. He gave his stomach a slap. He'd gained a few pounds over the last few months—the sympathy weight—but at 195, he was still only twenty pounds heavier than when he'd graduated high school.

Once completely undressed, he pushed open the revolving shelf, which blended so seamlessly into the wall of his tank room that even he had to look twice on occasion to find it.

He kept his supply of wax earplugs here. Many years ago, while still a deputy, he'd also kept a plastic film canister of marijuana there—but that was long gone. Once he'd become an elected official, he'd had to terminate that enjoyment. Too risky. Personally, Pruitt had nothing against smoking grass. Not for a moment did he buy the whole Just Say No jive—at best a glib, cynical response to a complicated problem. But he also loved his job and wasn't about to jeopardize it by appearing "soft" on drugs. On the other hand, he didn't really miss it either. Occasionally he'd have a memory of being high that tickled him, but yoga was good, the floating was good, a beer on a tubing trip was good, some red wine with dinner was good—with so many good things in the world to enjoy, it wasn't that hard to go without one of them.

He set the timer to seventy minutes, then ducked under the hatchback door and stepped into the foot-deep water. He reached to pull the door closed after him. The task required kneeling, and the buoyancy created by the nearly half-ton of Epson salts could make this maneuver clumsy. Once the door was shut, however, and he was stretched out, it was like being sprawled across a waterbed, a warm one. He felt liberated— as close to a free floating state as a person could get without the benefit of space flight.

The first thing he did once ensconced, always, was savor the effect of the salts on his body, which not only kept him buoyant but also leached the fatigue from his muscles like an invisible masseuse. Languidly, he twisted and flexed. He felt like Cleo, his cat, lolling on the concrete walkway on a hot day. He arched his back and rolled his neck from side-to-side. Aches heightened, then dissolved.

His routine was to take ten or fifteen minutes to get his body relaxed before tackling the hard part: relaxing his mind. Even with his body at rest, his brain remained in high gear, cogitating, planning, analyzing—anything but shut up. To gain control over it, Pruitt regulated, then followed his every breath. He thought of still water, his mind becoming one with it. The gentle opening chords of "Help on the Way" began playing in his mind, the song that had begun the May concert. Jazzy, reflective, hopeful. Yes, help is on the way. Jerry's voice ragged, ravaged really, but nonetheless soothing. Count on it was the unspoken message: we'll be there, in some form or other, if only in a recollected melody.

With the Dead inspiring him, Pruitt found that untroubled spot where he just let himself be. Not sheriff, lover, or father—not even father-to-be. He did not allow himself to feel responsible or duty-bound, but to feel instead his body secretly carrying on—life's steward, seldom referenced but always present, overseeing the miracle of his heart pumping oxygen and nutrients through his veins steadily and without emotion.

•••

By the time he got back to the door of his cruiser again, the day had gone soft with the setting sun. He thought of checking in on Olivia, but decided to forego it. The last thing his daughter needed was her father constantly hovering around her life. It was probably already weird enough for her living in his old house—probably as hard for her to call the house hers as he was having difficulty thinking of Molly's house as his.

"Gavin."

He'd been probing his pockets for his keys and the voice startled him. He dropped the keys to the ground. "Jesus-H!" He turned to find Angela.

"Sorry," she said.

"You could've given a guy a heart attack."

She grinned at him. "I've been told that before."

Pruitt said, "Oh, brother," then stooped to pick up the keys. Once retrieved, he looked at her. *What?*

"Wondering about that manuscript."

Still a bit astral from his float, he just continued looking at her. He noticed, again, how normal she looked—at least with her clothes on. No wild get up, just a blouse and shorts . . . . Well, the sandals did run up to her knees, and had a vaguely gladiatorial look to them—a little on the outrageous side, but nothing by comparison to how she was capable of adorning herself. There were even some locals who might have worn sandals like that. Yet footwear notwithstanding, it appeared that she and Bill were moving slowly towards each other, towards the middle—at least in terms of wardrobe.

She gave him another grin. For a second, he thought she was flirting with him.

"Wilma's romance novel?"

"Oh, right. That manuscript. I'll ask about it."

Chapter Sixteen

PRUITT WAS BACK at the Riverton Women's Clinic. This time with his daughter. Apparently Christopher had gotten hung up at school, in the computer lab to be specific. "Said he had some code to write for a class and this one computer is faster than the others, everybody wants to use it, so you have to take it when you can. It seemed real important to him."

Olivia had called just as Pruitt was heading out the door for the office. "Well, I'm sure it is important. And I'll be glad to go with you."

"Are you sure? Don't you have to be to work?"

"Hey, I'm the boss. Who's going to tell me I can't?"

"Pop-cop, thanks. I just don't like making that drive by myself."

"No need to explain to me, honey. I'll be right over to pick you up."

Now here he was again with that same silly *Field & Stream* in his hand, his mind drifting again. Thinking about how different this whole baby thing had been for him and Olivia's mother, Claudia.

For one thing, rather than seeing a doctor, they had considered a home birth, all the rage among their circle of friends at the time—even among those that were not pregnant, nor even considering a family. Which should have raised a red flag. That their friends' interest in natural birth was motivated more by the general political notions of the day than by sound medical ones. Alternative child-birthing was simply another way of pissing off The Man, whoever The Man might be. Because don't forget, The Man was a big liar. Pot didn't make you crazy. The Domino Theory wasn't real. The list went on and on. Birth is natural, the new thinking went. Big medicine is just one more way the government insinuated itself into people's lives, another way it subjugated the masses. Etcetera, etcetera.

And for the first six months he and Claudia had steered clear of doctors and hospitals; instead, they read books on home birthing that they had checked out from the library. They searched for a midwife. But the only midwife they actually talked to was a woman with no credentials who told them, essentially, that anyone who opted for a hospital birth was a wuss, a sell out. So on they soldiered, reading their books, making plans for Pruitt to tie off the umbilical cord and for the two of them to boil and eat the placenta—some sort of primeval connection to cave women or some other critical obsession along those lines.

For god's sake, what had they been thinking? How could they have been so cavalier about something so momentous? Never for a moment had he felt comfortable with the idea of standing in the kitchen of their little alley apartment boiling water (for what, hygiene?) and getting sheets ready (for what, bodily fluids?) and the blood all over the place. As it turned out, when Claudia went into a false labor at about seven months both of them panicked. Screw the organic method. Pruitt drove Claudia to the emergency room of the nearest hospital.

"You haven't seen a doctor yet?" said the incredulous nurse.

Just barely out of college, no steady employment, Pruitt called his father and borrowed money to pay for a doctor and a hospital stay. It had been the biggest relief of his and Claudia's life together.

"Thanks, Gavin," she'd said. "This whole 'natural' thing was scaring the bejesus out of me. I love our doctor. She explains everything. I'm a lot less worried."

Only for about two seconds had Pruitt considered himself a traitor to the "movement." For one thing, he had not swallowed hook, line, and sinker everything the counter culture had espoused. Yes, he had strongly identified with it and wanted to do everything he could to remain a part of it, but the decision he and Claudia made about their pregnancy had probably been the tipping point as far as his anti-establishment days were concerned. He remained a Deadhead, obviously, and would never embrace the values of his father's generation completely, but from that decision on he began to think for himself—or at least as much as anyone could honestly say they did. By simplifying his life to just Claudia and the baby, his dearest daughter, he changed. He was a number of years distant from college and teachers, drifting apart from friends he'd lived with in communes—he began to think critically of all points of view, not just the ones he and his hippie friends had targeted in their early twenties.

And Olivia's birth had gone without a hitch. One good thing about having her when they did, in the mid-seventies, was that he was allowed in the operating room. Of course, now they didn't call it the operating room anymore, but rather the birthing room. But it was the OR then, sterile and formal, but who cared. They'd gowned and masked him and let him stand near Claudia. Well, relatively near, anyway. He'd been allowed to hold her hand. It was a situation twenty years later he was glad to see had changed. No gowns or masks. He could be right there next to Molly. He could touch her, kiss her. Not only was more physicality allowed, in the Lamaze classes they were giving him all kinds of chores he could do when the time came: supply ice chips, encourage proper breathing, help her to the restroom if she needed to go, and . . . well, just being close. That's what he was looking forward to.

He looked over at his daughter, who was apparently as adrift in thought as he was, working a cuticle with her teeth.

"Have you and Christopher started your Lamaze classes yet?"

She examined her finger, bitten to the quick. "Not yet."

"His school schedule messing things up?"

"Yeah. He's doing a nine-week class."

"That's cutting it. Babies are due in September."

"Yeah, tell me about it."

With young people a thin line existed between genuine anxiety and simple hormonal drama. It was especially harder to know one from the other if it was your own kid. Yet Pruitt's interpretation at this moment was his daughter was hurting. "Something you want to talk about?"

"I don't know." She finally stopped examining her cuticle. "I'm really mad he's not here today. Why couldn't he have scheduled that computer for some other time?"

"This is it for him, right? He's graduating this term?"

"I know, I know."

Then the receptionist called. "Olivia Pruitt?"

"Okay, Pop-cop," she said. "I'll be right back."

"Olivia, he'll have his degree. That part of his life will be behind him. He'll be ready to move on."

She gave him a brave smile. He wasn't sure he believed his words either.

•••

After dropping Olivia off at home, Pruitt stopped by Java Junction, a drive-through espresso stand built to look like a little house out on Highway 101 at Commercial, and picked up his usual jumbo cup of drip. As was his way, when he got to the office, he poured the still steaming coffee from the to go cup into his Steal Your Face mug, which was as pristine as the day he bought it. He washed it religiously, never let coffee or tea grow cold or stale in it. It remained unstained.

One time, and one time only, someone other than himself had used it. Fervidly, he'd hunted them down. "You seen my cup?" he'd asked the guilty party.

"Oh, this yours?" E.L. had said. "I didn't know." To be fair, E.L. spent most of his time in the Long Beach office and not the Court House. In one of his infrequent visits north, he had just assumed the cup was up for grabs.

"In spades," Pruitt had told him. The story of his avid vigilance regarding his mug had become something of a legend, but ever since he could always find it exactly where he'd left it, hanging from a peg on the board behind the table with the coffee machine on it.

He transferred the precious liquid from paper cup to porcelain mug, then strolled through the Swamp and poked his head in the office shared by Raphe Jones and Ing Yen. "Besides that spreadsheet you showed me, what else was on those floppies?"

Jones put her hands behind her head and wove her fingers together. "Nothing else of probative value. Some personal financial files, most of which just bear out what we already knew." She let go of her fingers and popped forward, lifted one of the disks up as if by doing so she could show him something on it. "Oh, and what looks like a novel. Some sort of romance thing."

"You read it?"

Shrugging, she said, "Just enough to figure out what it was."

"Did it look like some coded message?"

"You mean like a *Key to Rebecca*-type of cipher?"

"Yeah, exactly."

"Well, the only way something like that would work is if someone had also created a code book. And there was nothing like a code book, or file, anywhere else on those floppies."

"And nothing we found anywhere else in Wilma's things that might look like a code book?"

Jones shrugged. "Nothing like that at all. Not from her home, not in the office."

"They've got a computer at Elkhorn PD she worked on. Did we check it?"

"Sure did, boss. Nothing probative there either."

"That manuscript, I think they call them, did it look like something a publisher might be interested in?"

"I read the first chapter, and it just seemed like one of those bodice rippers." She smiled sheepishly. "I read a couple when I was in high school. But I have no idea, really, if it was publishable. I mean, it seemed okay, for that sort of thing."

Pruitt told her why he wanted to know. "Can we make a copy of it and hand it over to Wilma's friend with a clear conscience?"

"The wild one? You trust her?"

"No," Pruitt said. "Not for a second. But at this point I think the only way we're going to move this investigation along any further is shake things up. Angela seems to want this manuscript pretty badly. Maybe if we give her what she wants, she'll lead us to something we want."

•••

Pruitt rarely fully closed his office door, and visitors usually lightly rapped and entered in one fluid motion. Ing Yen, however, always knocked and waited for permission.

Because of this, Pruitt knew who it was without having to actually see him. "Ing. Come in. What's up?"

His deputy entered and stood at ease. "Crime lab got serial number of gun to come up."

"The gun used to kill Wilma? Really? That's great. Taking us anywhere?"

"Traced gun back to dealer in east Pierce County."

"You're kidding me?" Pruitt motioned for Yen to sit. "We should call Pierce County Sheriff's Department, have them check it out."

"Already called."

"Wow. Great." He studied his deputy. "Actually, you don't look like you're here with good news."

"Gun shop owner wrote out receipt to . . . " Yen pulled his pocket notebook out. "To Mr. James Hendricks."

Pruitt glanced at the ceiling. "Oh, brother. Jimi Hendricks. What an ass."

"Play on words, as you say?"

"On a spelling, anyway. You know Jimi Hendrix, the guitar player?"

"Heard of him."

Pruitt wrote the name out on a memo pad. "Spelled like this."

Yen bent over to have a look. "Got it."

"I don't suppose the receipt had an address on it, did it?"

He sat back and said, "No."

"I don't suppose the shop owner could come up with a description, could he?"

"Deputy ask him that. Said . . . " He checked his notes again. "Said he sold it at gun show. Too many people in one day to recall what everyone looked like."

"For all the good it's going to do us, let's get a photo of Mark to Pierce County, have someone take it out to him."

Yen stood. "Will do."

•••

A while after his chat with Deputy Yen, Madeline Box, the combination office assistant and dispatcher, stuck her head around Pruitt's doorjamb. "Just got a call from that electronic monitoring service again. Dan's off to the liquor store again."

"Good criminy. Is anybody checking in on him? Making sure he's okay?"

Madeline always seemed to be in motion, even when sitting at her desk, but now she struck a comfortable pose in his doorway. Hip-shot. Conversation time. "The first time that beeper went off, Charneski drove over to make sure that he was doing what he was doing. And he was."

"So nobody's been visiting him? At home, I mean?"

"Nothing formal. Nothing I know of."

"Let's set something up. Can you make a list of three or four people who might be kind of close to Dan, who could drop by and make sure he's not doing anything to hurt himself?"

Madeline nodded to him. "Can I put you on that list?"

"Yes. In fact, I'll go over there this afternoon."

Then she gave him a hint of a smile. "What about Carl Pulkkinen, should he go on the list?"

Pruitt couldn't help but smile back. "C'mon, now, Madeline, let's be nice to Carl. Poor fellow can't bite himself."

•••

Pruitt spent most of the day catching up on paperwork. Lunch at the Boondocks with Molly had been excellent. Clam fritters and fries—lots of tartar sauce. The fries, especially, made Pruitt pause. It was kind of obvious where those five pounds he'd added were coming from. Molly ordered cheesecake for dessert, and when she asked for help finishing it, Pruitt obliged. Afterwards he felt a little guilty. Here he'd been judging poor Bobby Charneski's weight gain; the pot calling the kettle black. Sympathy pounds, indeed. When you were in love with your wife, how could you not? Bobby had two kids already! And he was barely thirty. He told himself to lighten up on the kid.

Then about four Pruitt checked out for the day and drove over to Dan Louderback's home, which was nearby in the Sawlog Slough district, maybe three-quarters of a mile from the County Courthouse complex.

On the drive over, Pruitt thought about Louderback and his current set of circumstances. His once trusted colleague had morphed into troubled friend. Their friendship was still part of his feelings for the man, but now Pruitt was holding him at arm's length. Thinking of him as a burden, someone who had to be dealt with. He'd broken a trust that Pruitt was having a hard time forgiving him for. Which was tragic. Things had started off so well.

After a statewide search, the town council had felt blessed at snagging a man with his credentials, chief of a town at least three times larger than Elkhorn. Looking to downsize a little, he'd told them. Plus he loved deep sea salmon fishing, and what better place than Elkhorn and Willapa County for that. He came with glowing recommendations from his previous position.

Moreover, he was handsome and tall. Up until this embezzling scandal it had been a great partnership. Maybe his divorce two years ago had tarnished his glow somewhat, but only temporarily. For one thing, divorce wasn't so uncommon anymore. Of course, everyone suspected his wife had left him because of his affair with Wilma—his phantom affair as far as proof went at the time. It just seemed obvious to everyone. She was beautiful, he was charming, they worked together—a divorce, a separation . . . C'mon. Who needed hard evidence? Yet not even a Peyton Place backstory bothered anyone—not really. No one spoke ill of them. No nasty whispering at the Elks Club, or The Torchlight. Jeez, Dan and Wilma looked so good together! It was like having Jack and Jackie in the heart of Southwest Washington.

He drove up Quincy Street, where it both intersected with and terminated at Water Road. Across Water a crushed oyster-shell driveway led to a wood-framed house with a blue aluminum roof that sat on a quarter acre, a wooded hillside behind it. Louderback's dark blue Mark VII was parked in front of the free-standing garage on the concrete slip. Pruitt parked behind it. At this time of day the house was lit warmly from the summer sun. The hillside behind it was trapping some of the salty river smell blowing up from the south. At one point the site had been professionally landscaped, and for the most part still looked it, except that now the bushes needed trimming and the grass a good mowing. His last thought before getting out of his cruiser was how the obvious had been just that. What had looked like a duck and quacked like one turned out to be a pair of good-looking ducks named Wilma and Dan.

The front door was thrown open for the breeze. Apparently Bendick & Son's were still cooking oyster stew because there it was again, that familiar aromatic counterpoint of river and soup. Pruitt knocked on the frame of the screen door.

"It ain't locked."

The suspended Elkhorn Chief of Police sat on a brown leather couch, his head lolling a bit, a tumbler of whiskey and ice on the coffee table in front of him. He had been drinking, obviously, though Pruitt wasn't yet sure how much. He took the easy chair. Made some small talk. Decided Louderback's level of intoxication was significant.

Oh, well. He waded in anyway. Asked about Tom Conley. Did Dan know him?

"Saw the name on an invoice . . . Or something . . . Heard the name . . . Pretty sure."

"I'm assuming you knew Wilma was having an affair with him."

Apropos of finding this out, or simply because of alcohol, Dan began weeping. Serious wounded-animal angst. "I screwed up, man . . . It's on me . . . Wilma's on me."

He sobbed.

Pruitt thought to move next to him, put an arm around his shoulder, but hesitated. Physically, Dan had never been very approachable. A handshake guy, not a hug guy.

It hurt Pruitt to see someone hurt this much. Regardless of the fact that Dan had lied and cheated and scammed, he'd also been a decent friend. Although it occurred to him that Louderback had chosen soberly—he assumed—and willfully to break laws and act with some degree of immorality, it didn't lessen the fact that he was also a human being in torturous emotional pain. Nonetheless, as Louderback got his sobbing under control, Pruitt said, "Why do you say that?"

He wiped across his eyes with the back of his bare arm, blew his nose on a nearby tea towel. "Because I loved her . . . Then I made her a criminal."

"C'mon, Dan. Why would that get her killed?"

His bead bobbed back, snapped forward again. "I dunno," he slurred. "The money? . . . Somebody found out?"

"Who do you think found out?"

"Some guys? You know . . . guys? Criminals? . . . Want the money? . . . Pulkinnen, that ass . . . He thinks—"

"Did you tell anybody about the money, Dan?"

"Wilma knew . . . Me and Wilma . . . Pulkinnen, that son-a bitch . . . Him feelin' sorry for *me*? . . . I mean, what's the shit there, man?"

The conversation was going nowhere fast and reminded Pruitt of similar futile attempts at communicating with his father, also an alcoholic, although of a much different sort. Whereas Louderback had indeed kept a bottle in his desk drawer, he had done it more out of style than substance. Before Wilma's murder, no one had ever thought of him as a particularly big drinker. Knowing Wilma, she probably wouldn't have allowed it.

But since her death, Dan had gone off the deep end, drinking during the day—maybe even first thing in the morning. Pruitt's father, on the other hand, wouldn't have been caught dead with a bottle in his office, but once the work day had finished would begin throwing back vodka martini's. Rarely did Dr. Pruitt get as drunk as Dan was now. His father's MO was a weird fusion of eloquence and belligerence. He sounded rational, and appeared in control of himself, but was neither. You thought he was being nice to you, then the hammer fell.

To each his own, Pruitt thought, although Dan and his father shared one thing in common: after about 5:30 in the afternoon you couldn't talk to either one of them. "Dan," he said. "Focus, will you?"

Louderback slumped down into his couch. "Oh, shit, I took somethin' today, Gav . . . "

Pruitt rose. "You took pills? Then you started drinking?"

"Not pills, man. *A* pill . . . It's there." He waved towards his kitchen. "Take the stress off . . . "

The bottle was on the counter next to the sink. A mild sedative, it looked like. Pruitt emptied the contents onto a plate he pulled out of the cupboard. He noted that the prescription had been filled that day, and that all the pills but one were accounted for. He also noted that the freshly-opened bottle of Johnny Walker Black had only about three or four shots taken from it. Pruitt checked the garbage can under the sink and found no empties: beer, liquor, or wine. He found the receipt for Louderback's booze run. Two fifths of whiskey, the second unopened in the cupboard. So his colleague was not attempting suicide. Nonetheless, he called Dr. Marion and asked her if Dan was in danger.

"It's good to follow up, Gav," she told him, "but he'll be okay. That's not a very strong dose at all."

He thanked her and rang off, and by the time he got back to the living room, Louderback was snoring. It was only around six o'clock, but what the hey. It was warm in the house, but Pruitt covered his friend in an afghan anyway, loosely, and made sure there was a pillow under his head. Then he set the deadbolt on the front door and let himself out through the laundry room door. He pushed in the button of the entry lock's inside knob and checked that the outside knob was set. Apparently, if he was going to have a sensible conversation with Dan he would have to catch him much earlier in the day—just like he had to do with his father.

Chapter Seventeen

WITH THE HOT weather fully arrived in Southwest Washington, Pruitt and Molly were sleeping with sheets only and the bedroom window open. The window faced north by northwest and managed to draw in what little breeze had begun twenty miles away as the crow flew off the ocean. The room was too hot for spooning at night, but cool now in the morning air. Pruitt rolled over to his lover's back, snaked his arms around her and cupped her breasts, her ever burgeoning stomach a pivot point for his elbows.

"God, yes," she murmured.

•••

Running a little late for work, Pruitt called ahead and let dispatch know he was going to check in on Dan Louderback again. What he didn't say over the radio was he hoped a good sleep would help his troubled friend stay on task, maybe help this investigation along a little. What bothered Pruitt more than anything was the fact of Wilma's computer showing up at that meth lab. He had some thoughts on the matter, but really needed a sober chat with Elkhorn's now ex-Chief of Police to sort some of it out.

Like yesterday, he parked behind Dan's Mark VII on the tongue of the parking strip in front of the garage. The morning mist was drying off the foliage surrounding the house—azaleas, purple ground cover, a couple of decorative cherry trees—the smell of it crisp, almost sweet. Everything looked as it had the day before. Based on the condition Pruitt had left him in, he wasn't expecting Dan to be up yet, which was fine, because that meant he wouldn't have begun drinking yet, either. Maybe some coffee, eggs, and toast would get him in a cooperative frame of mind.

At the front door he knocked . . . waited. Knocked again and called out his presence. Waited some more. Finally, he tried the door, felt the solidity of the deadbolt, as firmly set as he had left it. Maybe Dan was up but indisposed, in the bathroom, or maybe even out back. Pruitt walked off the porch to have a look.

The back lawn, like the front, needed mowing—although the longer grass also gave it a cozy look, especially with the hammock strung between a couple of fruit trees. The apples and pears were forming well, looking ahead to a fall ripening. But no sign of Dan.

Pruitt tried the side door. As with the front, the lock was firmly set, just as he had left it. On the porch again, he knocked loudly and called: "Dan? You in there, buddy? It's Gavin!"

By this point, even if he was in the bathroom, Louderback would have figured out some way to let Pruitt know he was home. In normal conditions, it wasn't his way to pry, but this was not feeling normal. He sidled over the window and peered through the glass into the living room. Using his hands like blinders to filter the morning glare, he could see Dan lying on the couch, afghan around his shoulders, face turned in toward the fabric, away from the sun just now beginning to stripe the room with light.

Pruitt didn't like the looks of it. He tapped on the window pane and yelled louder. When no response came, he studied the door carefully. Decided it was too well built for what he had in mind.

He trotted to the side door, examined it, then stood a couple of feet away and kicked hard below the doorknob, crashing it open. He stepped inside and called Louderback's name again. It was so quiet he could hear the distant roll of a truck tacking along West Port Drive, probably three-quarters of a mile to the north. He stepped into the kitchen.

By instinct more than necessity, he crouched and pulled his service pistol. Taking cover behind the door jamb that led to the living room, he peeked in, pulled his head back, and muttered, "Crap." After a quick peek-and-duck search of the rest of the house, he re-holstered his gun and walked into the living room, prickles rising along his neck.

Pruitt reached to place his fingers to the side of Dan's throat. By the coldness of his skin he knew there would be no pulse.

•••

Ing Yen had a clipboard out, sketching the scene on off-white paper lightly gridded. Using the pencil, he pointed to the back of Louderback's head. "Entrance wound. Very close. Angle of impact, point and area coverage not hard to figure out. Powder tattooing here on wound. Low impact velocity spatter here on couch. Small caliber pistol. Bet coroner finds .22 bullet in his head. Second bullet here, at back. Heart shot. Just to make sure."

"How'd they get in?"

"Don't know yet. You smashed pantry door, right?"

"I did."

"Locked before you kicked it?"

"Yes."

"Somebody he knew? Let them in?"

"He was drunk. Plus he'd popped a pill. Somebody might have banged loud enough to wake him, but it doesn't seem likely."

"Front door has dead bolt. Still set."

"That's the way I left it."

"Let's go see if someone jimmied their way in."

At the pantry door Pruitt had smashed, Ing took a magnifying glass out of his fanny pack/investigation kit, then bent over to look for tooling marks around the keyhole and cylinder. When he straightened up, he said, "Nothing. But there's other ways in. Windows, maybe."

Pruitt ran a hand across his face. "The gun, the situation. This looks like an assassination to me," he said. "Similar to Wilma's."

"Assuming we find point of entry to house," Yen replied, "I wouldn't say no to your theory. But we can't rule out someone with key. Someone he knew."

"Who would have one? His wife moved to California."

"Under one of these rocks?" Yen said, pointing at the Frisbee-sized decorative rockery on either side of the pantry door.

Pruitt said, "Crap," and pulled one of the rocks up, then another. Nothing.

"Up here, maybe." With his latex-gloved hand, Yen reached up into the joists that held up the porch canopy. "Ah." He held the brass key out for Pruitt to see.

"Somebody would have to know."

"Could be. Or could be somebody never been here before, but smart like you and me."

Pruitt caught one of Yen's quick smiles. "All right, wise guy. Point taken."

"But makes your point, too. About professional. Trying to make it easy. Leave as little behind as possible. No clues, nothing but dead man."

Damn, Pruitt thought, Yen's getting good at this.

Yen placed the key in an evidence envelop.

"Prints, maybe?"

"Doubtful." He gave Pruitt a look. "You want to start asking around anyway? Neighbors and such?"

"Yeah, I'll do that." Pruitt gazed over the crime scene. "What were these two into?"

"You think more than skimming?"

Pruitt raised his hands. "It wasn't that much money. To kill over?"

Yen said, "Where I come from, saw worse for less. And really," he added, "not much different here."

CHAPTER EIGHTEEN

PRUITT WAS RAISED Catholic, but converted to agnosticism as soon as he left home for college. He sensed there was something big and cosmic out there, but didn't think human beings were evolved enough to figure out what it was—and probably never would be. He agreed whole-heartedly with John Lennon that whatever got you through the night was fine and dandy. Just don't make the mistake of assuming the answers to your personal needs were also infallible truths. So no more Sunday morning church for Pruitt. He'd swapped pews for tanks. Float tanks, that is. An hour in his did more for his ability to forgive—whether himself or others—than all his years intoning prayers at mass or confessing sins to a priest. He particularly looked forward to Sunday morning floats. He'd joke with Molly that "It's like the relief you get from Penance, but full body."

Losing Dan Louderback on Friday had given him a particular need to get into a forgiving mood, to try to gain back a wider, deeper appreciation of the human condition. However long you felt the darkest hour would last before the dawn—and losing two friends to murder made it feel like a long, long time, indeed—you had to remember, too, that all humanity was but a moment's sunlight fading on the grass. Nobody here gets out alive, Morrison had said. All things must pass, Harrison had said. Be here now, Ram Dass had said. So float, man, float. Let it go. Try to make today better for yourself, then someone else.

He pulled up to his usual parking spot near his old house, a little perplexed that Christopher's car was not parked behind Olivia's. It was perplexing, too, that the sound of his car hadn't drawn Olivia to the kitchen window for a peek. Maybe she and Christopher had gone out for breakfast. He thought he'd better check in. At the back door, he knocked. Waited. Heard nothing. Tried the knob, which gave in his hand. He'd been expecting to find it locked, which Olivia always did, even if only going out for a few minutes.

"Honey," he called. "It's dad."

He heard a yelp-like sound from the living room and found her there with a wad of tissues in her hand, weeping.

"Oh, honey." He sat next to her on the hide-a-bed couch. "What's wrong?" He wondered if this was a reaction to hearing of Dan Louderback's murder.

"Christopher," she said. "I don't think he wants to do this."

"What? Have the baby?"

She rocked. "He won't talk to me."

"I noticed his car's not here. What's up?"

"He stayed in Tacoma."

Pruitt waited.

"That damn computer was available again, he said. If he stayed, he could have it for the whole weekend, he said."

Pruitt sighed.

Olivia held up the wad of tissues. "Why did he even have to go to summer school at all, knowing what I was going to be going through?"

"Well, for one thing maybe he didn't know what you were going to go through. Or maybe because he wants to get college behind him. The sooner he's done, the sooner he can get a job. It's his own way of getting ready. For you and the baby."

She wiped her eyes. "I know him. It doesn't feel like what you just said. It feels like he's trying to figure some way out of this."

"You're right, I don't know him like you do, but . . . "
And he really had nothing to add. Indeed he did not know
Christopher well enough to jump to conclusions—bad or good.
He seemed like a thoughtful kid. Gentle around Olivia. At
least that's what he had seen. He had to admit the dreadlocks
were a little strange. Kept your eyes off his face. He wondered
if they weren't there to help him hide. Hide from what, Pruitt
wasn't sure. The world? His responsibilities?

"When I first told him, he wanted to get an abortion."

Pruitt let that settle over him. "Well, Olivia, it probably
freaked him out at first. He's young, too."

Olivia stuffed the wad of tissues into a paper sack she had
nearby. "Maybe we should have," she said.

"Was that your first thought, when you found out?" He
patted her shoulder. "That you wanted to have an abortion?"

"No. I didn't think of that at *all*. Not until Christopher
brought it up. Did you and mom think about it?"

"No . . . well, that's not true. Yes, it came up. We were a
little older than you and Christopher. No much, but . . . "

"Poor?"

"Oh, yeah. Good and poor. But it didn't seem like such a
big deal then, being poor. In a strange way, it was almost cool.
An alternative way of life is how we thought of it."

She stared at a spot on the hardwood floor somewhere
between the coffee table and the kitchen door. "But it didn't
work out for you. You guys got divorced."

"It didn't work out between your mother and me, but we
had you. The best thing we ever did together."

She sighed. "Yeah, I always felt that. I had friends whose
parents were divorced, complaining all the time about them.
Really seemed bothered by it. But I wasn't . . . not really. I tried
to be mad, you know, to act more like my friends. All pissed off
at the world because of the divorce. But you guys wouldn't let
me. You guys were just mom and dad, living apart, but always
there for me." She patted his hand. "Thanks, Pop-cop."

The emotion was draining from her face. "I don't know
what he does up there in Tacoma without me. Not really."

"Classes, studying. He's doing well, isn't he?"

"He says so."

"You've seen his grade reports, right?"

She sighed. "Yeah, he's doing well."

"There you go, then."

After a moment, she said, "He could be seeing someone else."

"Really? You think so? He just doesn't seem like that sort of person to me."

She picked up the paper sack of tissues, which looked to be about half full.

Pruitt said, "Maybe just hormones, honey?"

She looked up toward the kitchen. "I think some tea would be nice."

He gave her another hug, then stood. "Let me make it."

"Aren't you here for a float?"

He took her hand. "I'm here for you, Olivia. End of story. And, hey—" He helped her to her feet. "You're going to have a baby brother or sister, too. How cool is that?"

She smiled finally. "I'm going to be a big sister. That is cool. Weird, but cool."

CHAPTER NINETEEN

OVER THE WEEKEND, Pruitt made a few inquiries into who might have known where Dan's spare door key was kept. It turned out Jerry, his brother, knew of it, and Arlie Petit, now Elkhorn's acting Chief of Police. Which, as far as Pruitt was concerned, meant that the whole department knew about it. Not a very comforting thought. As far as the investigation into either Dan or Wilma's murder was concerned, none of the Elkhorn PD cops were off the hook.

Dan's nearest neighbors, Marty and Evelyn Smithson, knew of the key as well. When Marty had finished answering Pruitt's questions, he had a few of his own.

"He was murdered practically right next to us, Sheriff. We've started locking our doors during the day. Do you think we should get an alarm system?"

"Well, Marty, that's up to you. But, really, it had nothing to do with you or Evelyn. It was targeted, not random."

Marty worked swing shift at Saginaw, pulling the green chain. Hard work that had kept him fit. "Everybody's upset, Sheriff. First Wilma, now Dan? I gotta tell ya, it would sure make everybody feel better if you could figure out who did it."

"It'd make me feel better, too, Marty. It really would."

Ultimately, Pruitt had to agree with Ing Yen that the hiding place wasn't hard to figure out, even for someone who'd never been there before. Yen's point that a pro looks for the easiest way in and the quickest way out was well taken. Lock-picking leaves marks. Why do so if you don't have to? Pruitt hadn't even asked about tire tracks. Dan's driveway was crushed oyster shells.

So the list of suspects was long: besides any one of the Elkhorn PD officers, it could have been an unknown assassin from a pool whose numbers were impossible to guess at.

•••

Monday, it was time to call Angela. Which he did from his office. "I've got a copy of that novel here for you," he told her. "I'm swamped. You want to come up and get it?"

"Sure. Would now be okay? Or later?"

"Now's good. Tell you what, meet me by the pond. It's nice out, and I'm going to take some of my correspondence out there and work and enjoy the day all at once."

He rang off, gathered the aforementioned paperwork. "Going to the pond," Pruitt told Joyce. She looked up from the department's new computer. He raised the clipboard he was holding up for her to see. "Taking this stack of memos and letters with me."

The pond was part of a Japanese-styled garden that served as a quiet picnicking and relaxation spot to the east side of the Willapa County Courthouse complex. In 1977, the main Courthouse Building had been entered into the National Register of Historic Places, which brought, if not exactly a flood of tourists, at least enough to justify the addition of this modest northwestern-styled oasis.

The pond itself was a wide and deep oval of water, murkily green and filled with impressive-sized trout, 10 to 15-inches, that cruised just under the surface searching between their regular feedings for insects and food crumbs. A burbling waterfall took up one end, an overflow drain the other. The whole thing was surrounded by a low, ivy-covered cement coping. Behind the coping wall, on the street side, a service pump encased in a small wood-frame box hummed quietly. The waterfall and the pump between them created a pleasant white noise. Native flora had been planted: rhododendron and azalea, vine maple and hemlock. These were in addition to a small copse of Western red cedar, which had probably begun life on this spot over a hundred years ago. It was going to be hot today, in the mid-eighties, but it would be shady and cool sitting at one of the picnic tables. In the summer, Pruitt did as much work out here as he could. An unconventional routine to be sure, but he was unconventional guy; besides, being the boss allowed him to get away with it.

While he waited for Angela, he gazed out at the calm surface of the pool, the trout creating small ripples as their fins or mouths broke the surface. He sighed as a moment from the concert came to mind. One of those contemplative moments during the "Drums" section of the show; that day, Kreutzmann and Hart had attempted to channel the softer side of the galaxy's energy.

The afternoon had been waning into dusk and the crowd had settled down. Nobody was yelling out song titles, or "Jerry, we love you, man!" Pruitt thought of these moments as the "Time of Magic." They could happen at any point in any song—though not at every show, and never at the same time as the time before. Last May the Group Mind had synched when the two drummers became engrossed in a simple conversation between doumbek and rain stick. Like a couple of gulls tugging at a colorful length of seaweed on a beach, at first they were careful, becoming more intense as it became clear that this bit of seaweed was actually connected to something much larger, maybe something important. They began pulling at their prize with more energy, moving, in their corporeal selves, toward louder instruments, more complex rhythms, the thing they'd uncovered becoming more diffuse and illuminated simultaneously.

"Yo, Sheriff Pruitt! What're you on there, man?"

Pruitt looked up to see classic Angela, done up in full biker-punk regalia: high-top Doc Marten boots, black hose, black leather jacket over a red camisole and black leather skirt. Goth make-up, including black lips and black-and-red eye shadow. Her ever-present AIDS ribbon loop pinned to her lapel. She was grinning at him. What he thought of as her piss-and-vinegar smile, this one with a hint of sugar underneath. As complex a woman as he'd ever known. Back in full force, apparently.

"Angie, baby," he said, a joke between them from the old days. After they'd broken up as a couple but before they'd lost track of each other. Early seventies, it must have been. He hadn't thought of it until just now.

"Yeah, yeah." She'd walked around the building from the parking lot and now sashayed over to the picnic table. "You can't say we didn't try. Gawd, I never thought I'd hear that one again."

"It was appropriate at the time, don't you think?"

She sat opposite him. "Yep. Very."

From his breast pocket he took out a floppy disc, orange-colored. "Raphe copied that novel for you."

"Thanks, Gav." Angela squirreled it away in one of her leather jacket's many pockets. "Really. This is going to mean a lot to her family."

"Glad to."

She turned away from him so she, too, could look out over the serenity of the murky pool. "Nice out here," she said.

He rose and crossed over to Angela's side of the picnic table. Sat next to her. Splayed his elbows behind him.

"This is a weird place to exist in Elkhorn," she noted. "It's like the Dalai Lama got together with Paul Bunyon and reached some compromise. Buddhist meets Methodist, creates the Zen Redneck Garden."

Pruitt chuckled. "So how did you hook up with Wilma on this book?"

"She called. Must've heard I had publishing connections. Came to talk to me one day."

"Is that how business is done in publishing, it's who you know?"

"Yeah, mostly. In Chicago, John and I were publishing a newsletter, but I was also doing freelance editing. Somewhere along the line I hooked up with a managing editor at a medium-sized house and worked on a couple of novels for her. When they got ate up by a bigger house and protocol changed, we kept in touch. So I knew her, and she knows people who know people. But the deal is, if the manuscript isn't good, none of that makes any difference."

"But you can open a door for her. Even posthumously."

"Exactly."

Pruitt watched a couple of swallows in a mid-air squabble above the pond, diving bombing at each other. Once they veered away, he said, "Were you having an affair with her?"

Angela pinched her eyes shut for a second, then turned to him. "What? An affair? No. What kind of—"

"You've never slept with another woman?"

She kept her gaze on him, more bewildered than angry. "Of course I have. But not Wilma."

Pruitt turned so that he could level his gaze back at her. "She was beautiful. You're not against such a thing on moral principals . . . " He shrugged. "Just asking."

"Jesus-k-rist, Gav, that's the last thing I would have expected to hear from you."

The swallows made another pass over the pond, darting, soaring, falling back again. "Well," he said, "the more I learn about Wilma, the more I realize how little I knew her. Yet I also think I knew her pretty well. Do you know what I mean?"

"Out here in the Land of the Zen Redneck, yeah, I guess I do."

•••

He let Angela catch sight of him back at his paperwork as she drove down the sweeping one-way curve leading out of the courthouse parking lot to Memorial Drive. She waved, he waved. He waited a moment more, gathered up the papers, then walked back into the Swamp. He caught up to Ing Yen microwaving a cup of tea in the kitchenette.

"You got that bird dog on that truck she's driving? Bill Logan's?" Pruitt was referring to the radio frequency-enabled tracking device they'd gotten from the FBI office in Olympia.

He nodded.

"How long can we keep it?"

"Said it's ours. FBI moving to GPS. Even by RF standards, this one old as hills. But don't worry. This'll work." The microwave dinged and he pulled his tea out, discarded the bag. "So what you tell Pulkkinen to get warrant?"

"Wilma was seen with that laptop computer of hers entering a person of interest's domicile twice."

"Who saw that?"

"My daughter, actually. And Christopher."

"They sign affidavits?"

"Absolutely."

"Thought it was about some novel or something."

Pruitt shrugged. "We don't know that. Same computer had incriminating evidence on it. The fact is, we don't know what they were doing together. For all we know, Angela might have been a part of the fraud. For all we know, she might have had something to do with Wilma's death."

Yen looked at him. "You think she killed Wilma?"

"No. But it's within reason to think that whatever the two of them were doing, it may have lead to Wilma's death. That's why we need to track her for a few days. Maybe we'll find out."

"When did you get chummy with Carl again?"

"He'd like to get Wilma's killer as much as we do. We may not like each other much, but we both liked Wilma. Not to mention the town's getting antsy for this to get solved.

Especially since Dan got killed, Madeline's getting a lot of calls about it. Not all of them civil, either. Anyway," he said, "I'm planning on taking a shift. You better show me how it works."

•••

Yen led Pruitt out to the back parking lot and over to a mid-eighties Volkswagen Golf, a faded sea-green color, tinted windows, and one mismatched hubcap. Scratched up. Not exactly a heap, but in the process of becoming one. A "work car" for a family with a modest income.

"Where'd we get this?"

"Police auction. Just cost the price of tabs. Perfect for this job. Even if she sees it, she won't think twice."

"But she's not going to see it, right? Isn't that the whole point?"

Yen nodded. "Shouldn't, no. But stuff happens."

"And it runs well?"

"Perfect."

Pruitt studied it for a moment. "Two antenna? I suppose that's not too obvious. One looks like it's for the radio, the other for a CB?"

"That's what I tried to make it look like."

Pruitt ran his hand along the passenger side quarter panel. "You bored a hole on this side, so you wouldn't have to just set it on there with a magnet. Nice job, Ing. Really. Very innocuous." On very close inspection, neither antennas looked like the kind used for radios, but it would take a close inspection indeed to draw suspicion. At a police conference a few years back, Pruitt had seen a presentation where antenna with magnetic feet were used, the same kind used for slap-on cherry tops. A person would have had to have been blind not to notice something odd about the setup.

"So what do I do?"

Yen indicated that Pruitt should get in on the driver's side; his deputy took the passenger seat. There was a rectangular-shaped metal box mounted on the floor between the bucket seats, angled so that the driver could see what looked like a VU meter, only one whose needle rested directly in the middle of its face—like a very skinny nose. On either side of the face were red lights the size a small animal's beady eyes.

"This is old technology," Yen said. "Nobody use anymore, only poor people like us. But works damn good. Only need one car. Plus . . . what do you call it? . . . common sense. If needle point left, you turn left. Then needle should move back to middle. If needle point left and you turn left and needle go more left, then target got behind you somehow. Radio waves," he continued, "bounce all over. Hills, buildings, whatever. Can't tell back from front. That's where you got to use your head."

"Got it. What's in this fanny pack?"

"Accessories. Putty knife I used to scrape dirt and grease where I put transmitter on suspect's truck. Penlight for seeing under chasis. Towelettes for cleaning hands after attaching transmitter. All greasy under there, get uniform grubby."

Pruitt smiled at that. Ing Yen and Lee Wilson, more than any officers he knew, hated things grubby. He wondered if such fastidiousness was a biological predilection for a forensics nerd. "That transmitter won't fall off, will it?"

"No way. Got good magnet, plus I taped it. Black duct tape on frame rail. Flexible antenna I bent so it doesn't touch anything, get scraped. We're ready to roll, boss."

"Did you have a siren mounted in our follow car here?"

"Switch there."

Pruitt nodded. "Who's got the first shift?"

"Jones."

"I wish we could've afforded something fancier. Unfortunately, the budget the way it is . . . "

"We got it free and it works good." Yen turned a palm up. "How long do you think before she shows us something?"

"She's anxious. I'll bet she moves in a couple of days."

CHAPTER TWENTY

IT LOOKED LIKE Pruitt would have to work late, so he called Molly to let her know. But then he got tired, said screw it, it'll wait until tomorrow, and left for home only twenty minutes later than he normally would have. His and Molly's rambler (*his*, he noted to himself proudly) was north of Jackson, seven homes total along May Street, a dead end. Five others were ramblers relatively similar to theirs, and one was a wild two-story that looked like a beach house, driftwood and ocean flotsom nailed to the natural-colored siding. The Wengers lived there, bohemian types with whom Pruitt got along famously. Rusty Wenger—now in his late seventies, short, thin, and feisty—made his own wine. Drinkable stuff he shared generously. Parking at the door to the attached garage, Pruitt was thinking a glass of it wouldn't be all that bad about now. But he would probably settle for some herbal tea, or maybe a beer.

Immediately upon entering he noted the house was unusually quiet. No Angus on patrol, barking his fool head off.

No one in the living room. He walked to the back of the house and found Molly in their bedroom, lying down, faced away from him. Angus, snuggled to her back, glanced at, then refused to look at Pruitt. Normally not allowed on the bed, he appeared to be willing himself invisible, not wanting to give up this coveted spot of comfort.

"Molly?"

She sniffled. "You're home sooner than I thought you'd be."

"You all right?"

Sniffing again, she said, "Sort of."

Pruitt crossed over to her side of the bed. Any other time, he might have shooed Angus away, but the dog looked so happy to have been allowed this cozy refuge, he didn't have the heart to. He hadn't lived with a dog since he was a kid. Cats just need food, love, and water. Dogs need all that and more. Discipline, praise. More like a child.

"You've been crying."

She sat up to make space for him. "Raging hormones."

"Is that all?"

"I'm worried." She reached for a tissue.

He put his arm around her. "Worried?"

"About the baby."

He hugged her. "Everything's going fine. We're ready. Wait—" he said. "Did Marion call? Or the clinic? Is something up?"

"No, no. Nothing like that. Not the physical part. I'm—" She took a deep breath.

"C'mon. I'm here. What's up?"

She looked at the throw rug. "I'm worried I'm not going to be any good at this."

"Good at what? Dealing with the birth?"

"No, not that. The mom thing."

Pruitt's thinking had to catch up to what she was saying. "You're worried you're not going to be a good mom?"

She dabbed her eyes. "Yeah."

Hugging her again, he said, "You're going to be a great mom. The best."

She gave him a weak smile. "The best in the house?"

He chuckled.

"Like Angus?" she chided him. "Best dog in the house?"

At the mention of his name, the dog poked his head up.

"Yep, the best mom in the house. Then in the universe." She laughed.

"Why would you think otherwise?"

"Never been here?" She shrugged. "Never done that?"

"Never been a grandpa, either. Never done that."

"Not quite the same. You're not getting huge."

Pruitt tsked. "You're not huge. You're pregnant. You haven't gained any more or less weight than you're supposed to."

She sighed. "Do we want to know before? Boy or girl? I had them send the ultrasound results to Marion, in case we changed our minds."

"I don't want to know."

"I don't either. It doesn't matter."

"Boy or girl, it'll be a child of countless trees and seas."

"Yeah." They sat for a moment in comfortable silence, during which Pruitt was sure they were both thinking about the concert. "Did they do that song?" she asked.

"No, but we were playing it on the way down."

"Well, we've got plenty of trees and seas around here." She patted his leg. "Let's go make some dinner. I'm all of a sudden starving. I want some barbecued ribs so bad."

Molly never spoke of herself as a vegetarian, although for the most part she adhered to Pruitt's diet with an easy good will. She did, however, get her meat cravings, and Pruitt just stepped aside and let her enjoy. "Do we have any?"

"We do. But what'll you have?"

"We'll have beans and slaw with 'em, right? And I'll make myself a three-cheese omelet."

Chapter Twenty-one

TODAY WAS ULTRASOUND day. Not for Molly and Pruitt, but for Olivia. Again, no Christopher around, Pruitt stepping in.

"That computer come available again?" he'd asked when she called. "The good one?"

"A test, apparently. Midterm."

"Well, let's not worry about that. I'll be right over."

The paperwork had already been faxed from the Women's Clinic to Riverton General. The hospital was perched about halfway between the working-class flatlands and the bluff that overlooked them, the so-called "Miracle Mile," where the beautiful homes of Riverton's elite perched.

Before these ultrasounds, the last time he'd driven Elm Street—more commonly known as "The Grapevine"—had been last fall. He had been in hot pursuit of a killer. Snaking along these selfsame switchbacks, Pruitt flashed back to that horrible day he'd gotten shot. He caught himself reaching to feel the scar up on his right shoulder, then pulled his hand away, worried that touching it would make Olivia uncomfortable. He glanced at her, but she was lost in her own thoughts.

For a moment, he swore he could feel that sickening hotness again. That he was alive today was Angela's doing.

She'd been dogging the investigation, had followed Pruitt up to the remote clearing at the top of the hill behind the "Miracle Mile," Bill Logan's 30-30 beside her. Just as the killer was raising his own rifle to fire on Pruitt, Angela had shot the man in the head, skewing his aim and saving Pruitt's life. Typical of her, not once had she brought it up. When he had thanked her, she'd said, "For what?" "Saving me up there." "Oh? I wasn't aware of anyone else but the son-of-a-bitch that needed killing." She'd been smiling eerily, outwardly joking with him, though with Angela there was always something deeper going on. Always.

He turned into the hospital parking lot. Olivia was just starting to need a hand with things like rising out of a car, just starting to waddle. Since Pruitt had been there recently with Molly, he remembered the maze of hallways that led to the right suite.

They didn't have to wait long. As Olivia was getting prepped with the goo, the technician gave Pruitt a look. "Weren't you in here last week?"

"Yep. With my wife. This is my daughter."

"This your first grandchild?" she asked.

"It is."

"Obviously not your first child."

"No, but my only."

"So far," she said.

Pruitt smiled. "Right."

"Looks like you're going to be a daddy and a granddaddy about the same time."

"Yeah, I've heard that rumor."

"More common than you'd think."

"'Round these heah parts?"

The technician smiled. "I didn't mean it that way. Just that I've seen it a bit lately. Older moms and dads."

Pruitt smiled back. "Young grandpas, too."

"Oh, yeah. Young as we feel."

Olivia said, "That stuff's cold."

"You're doing great, Olivia. It'll warm up pretty quick. You know how this works?"

"I think so."

"I'm going to run this wand-looking thing over your belly and the image will pop up on this screen. Old fashioned black-and-white."

Pruitt said, "That's a computer there, right?"

"Yep." She pointed at the various parts. "That's the CPU. That's the display. This is actually called a transducer and by using the computer I can control the pulse frequency, duration, and scan mode."

"Amazing," Pruitt said.

Olivia said, "I can't see very well."

"Well, how much do you want to see?"

"Everything, I guess."

"I mean do you want to know the gender?"

Pruitt said, "No."

Olivia said, "Yes."

Pruitt said, "Oops. Sorry, honey. Molly and I didn't want to know."

"I want to know."

"Really? Molly and I are thinking of it as the coolest Christmas present ever."

"I want to know if it's a boy."

He said, "Why?" and then wished he hadn't opened his dang mouth.

Olivia stared intently at the screen. "Maybe if Christopher knows it's a boy, he'll get into it."

Pruitt could have slapped himself silly. Olivia needed what she needed, not what he and Molly needed. That damn Christopher. The kid needed a good talking to . . . .

Or did he? And even if he did, was it Pruitt's place to do so? What about Olivia and him working it out on their own? Lately, he didn't seem to know what he should do.

The technician had gone quiet. "It's a girl," she said.

Olivia said, "Are you sure?"

"Yes, honey. See?"

After a moment of scrutiny, Olivia began weeping.

•••

It was a very quiet trip back to Elkhorn.

Eventually, he found himself sitting at his desk admonishing himself for his inability to ease his daughter's anxiety, rather than adding to it. He wondered if parenting ever finally got easy. Answered his own question: Of course it didn't.

Then Ing Yen knocked in his familiar way. Pruitt bade him enter.

Yen closed the door behind him. "Heard back from Pierce County, about gun dealer."

Pruitt said, "He recognize him?"

"Photo array had Mark in it, but dealer not recognize."

"You think we could ask Pierce County to lean on him a little harder."

"Sure, but what to use for leverage?"

"I don't know. That dealer must have figured out by now that gun was used in a homicide. Probably not the first gun he's sold that was used for a homicide, either. He's going to circle the wagons."

Yen stood quietly for a moment. "Well. Maybe something will come along."

CHAPTER TWENTY-TWO

SURVEILLANCE ON ANGELA Caracitto was add-on duty, and Pruitt didn't want to blow his budget on overtime. But maybe more importantly, he wanted to keep the thing as quiet as possible, so he gathered a small crew, just two deputies—Ing Yen and Raphe Jones—plus himself. He was third up, all day Thursday.

With limited manpower and outmoded technology, the only way this game plan would work was to use a combination of old fashioned covert vehicle tracking—keeping the suspect within visual range—augmented with the Radio Frequency Tracking device. The key was the starting point. From where Angela was based, at Pruitt's ex-next-door neighbor's, Bill Logan's house in Riverdale, there were only two ways for her to turn. She could take a right and head in a westerly direction toward Tokeland and the north beaches, or she could turn left toward the Highway 101 intersection, where she could go north or south. If heading north, she could also turn left on Larch and catch Highway 101 a few blocks up the hill. With each shift, the officer on duty took up his or her stakeout on the south side of Cedar Street, in Bert and Cynthia Williams' dining room.

Bert was a volunteer fireman, and Pruitt had called him to explain the circumstances. Eager to help, Bert moved one of his cars to his brother's so the Golf could be parked on his garage apron and appear as if it was his. Their dining room window looked out over Park, Bill Logan's house only a block away. Pruitt swore the Williamses to secrecy. He understood that the secret wouldn't hold long, regardless of whether their hosts talked to anyone or not. A neighbor would figure it out soon enough. See the Golf and wonder about it. See him or Yen or Jones entering by the back door. In a small town, it was inevitable. Yet if they could get just a few days, it might be enough.

"We might have to be here late, Bert," he'd said.

Bert had promised to keep a pot of coffee on.

And that was where Pruitt was ensconced at the beginning of his shift, in his civvies: jeans, Hawaiian shirt, running shoes and a baseball cap that read: "I'm Irish, but I'm taking pills for it." The dining room had a bow window, with lacey curtains and blinds. With the curtains drawn in, though not quite closed, and the blinds turned to slits, it was a perfect vantage point to keep track of Angela's movements, which had been practically nil since Pruitt had handed over the floppy discs. She and Bill had driven to Riverton for pizza last night, Ing Yen in careful pursuit. He had informed Pruitt earlier that their low-tech system had worked just fine. He'd had no trouble both keeping track of the couple and staying out of sight. But they'd done nothing out of the ordinary. Pizza and home.

Cynthia, arms glistening from having just returned from her morning jog, was setting a cup of coffee in front of him—her smell an enticing combination of spicy perfume and sweat—when Pruitt noticed the nose of Bill's green, two-toned F-150 at the corner of Park. He raised his binoculars. It was Angela, by herself, signaling she was about to turn left.

"Gotta go, Cynthia," Pruitt said, ignoring the coffee. "Sorry."

"I hope this works for you," she called after him.

As soon as Angela passed the Williams' home, Pruitt hurried out to the Golf. The tracker took its power off the cigarette lighter, and its beady red eyes came to life with the engine. The needle swung right. She was heading south.

He pulled out onto Park and was quickly at the Highway 101 intersection. When he turned right, the tracker's needle swung back toward center. But then he had to slow down. He could actually still see her. At this point the highway slid off the hills, swept across the bridge, then settled down on the flats, and there was little to hinder his view. The key, as Yen had said more than once, was to trust the tracker, making it good sense to stay hidden as much as possible. So Pruitt tried to lay back without slowing too far under the speed limit.

Yet she remained in view as she turned left onto Highway 6. The transmitter needle yanked left, too, and Pruitt was glad that by the time he got to the intersection the light had turned red. He needed to heed Yen's instruction and not stay within the sight of Angela's rearview mirror.

The light changed and when Pruitt made the turn the needle came back to center. So far, so good. He hung back, wondering where she might be heading. Logic dictated I-5 and a swing south to Portland. If her destination had been Tacoma or Seattle, she would have turned left back at Highway 101. On the other hand, relying on logic to figure out Angela didn't always work so well, so he kept an open mind. For all he knew she might be heading to the swimming hole at Trap Creek, or one of the many hiking trails in the county.

He noted the tracker's needle sometimes jittered, which Deputy Yen had said was caused by multipathing, the signal bouncing off hills and structures. But it was only a slight distraction. The hills of Willapa County, Yen had noted, didn't cause near the kinds of problems the skyscrapers in downtown Seattle would.

The route along Highway 6 was one he'd taken often the last number of weeks: the trips to see Sheriff Bowman, the interviews with Tom Conley. It was a warm day, and without AC, Pruitt had rolled the windows of the Golf down an inch or two. Yen had said it would be better not to use a police radio in conjunction with the RF transmitter, but there was a bag phone at hand. Pruitt checked its signal every once and a while. No service yet, but there would be as they got closer to I-5.

As he neared Pe Ell, the needle went from slightly right to hard left. She'd come to the intersection at 4th and Main, Highway 6's name as it passed through the little town. It would revert back to Highway 6 two miles on. By now—save for Rainbow Falls—they'd passed all the turnoffs that might have led to swimming or hiking in either Willapa or Lewis County. Maybe she was heading for the state park, but Pruitt didn't think so. He felt sure she was going straight for I-5 then heading south.

Sure enough, they blew right past the park and onto the flats and farmlands of the Chehalis River Valley. Pruitt picked up speed a little. He wanted to get a visual of her as she neared the freeway ramps. She'd hardly be looking out her rearview any more. Not with fifty miles under her belt and nothing suspicious behind her. A few minutes later he could just make out Bill's truck, getting into the left turn lane, ready to head north.

North? Okay. Not what Pruitt had expected. But then Angela's behavior was often not what he expected. He lost sight of her as she crossed to the east side of the overpass, but the RF tracker needle swayed left, confirming her direction. He followed suit. Pruitt was surprised again when the needle veered right. As he neared Exit 82, Harrison Avenue, he caught a fleeting glimpse of her again, this time turning left at the mouth of the intersection, heading north by northwest.

This was getting weirder by the mile. Pruitt now thought he knew where she was heading, although he couldn't make sense of it. But sure enough, as he drove past Tri-County Farm Supply, there was Bill's F-150. And there was Angela's backside, heading towards Garden Supplies and—Pruitt assumed—Tom Conley.

He shot on past, found a turn-around, reconnoitered, and pulled into the parking lot of a mini-storage complex across the street from Conley's business. He found a place to park that afforded him a view of Bill's pick-up, obstructed only by passing traffic, which was steady but light.

He was thankful he hadn't had a chance to drink the cup of coffee that Cynthia Williams had offered him; he didn't yet have to pee. It was one thing to park unobtrusively in a business' parking lot; it was something else again to have to pee into a bottle or a cup in that same lot—especially in the full light of day. Not something one could do with much discretion.

•••

When about twenty minutes had passed, just as the peeing issue was beginning to assert itself to the forefront of Pruitt's concerns, he saw Angela again, walking quickly back to Bill's truck, taking furtive glances around. At first, Pruitt couldn't read her expression. He realized it was because he'd never seen her rattled before.

She recklessly backed out of her slot. Solidly crunched the bumper of a car in the second row behind her, ignoring it. Slid the automatic gearshift into drive and shot out of the lot and onto Harrison.

Pruitt fired up the Golf and was about to shift into drive himself when Bobby Charneski, of all people—his on-the-verge-of-being-overweight deputy, the dad of Ranger, Little League Baseball star—came tearing out of the Tri-County Farm Supply parking lot behind Angela. Charneski was supposed to be on vacation, but here he was in his personal vehicle apparently in some squabble with Angela. What the heck? This obviously wasn't police business. Happenstance? Pruitt didn't think so.

As he sped across the parking lot for the entrance to Harrison, he considered slapping his magnet-footed beacon on the roof of the Golf. Hit that and the siren and stop this nonsense in its tracks. But 1) Angela was freaked out; 2) Bobby was up to something bad; and 3) neither would give a rat's ass about a beacon and siren warning coming from an unmarked heap with some guy in a baseball cap and flowered shirt. Instead he used his bag phone to call 911. When Centralia dispatch answered, Pruitt told him who he was.

"There's two suspects in a high speed chase. A white woman in a late model Ford pick-up, two-tone green, dark on top, light in the middle, dark again at the bottom. And a Willapa County Sheriff's deputy, undercover, in an unmarked Mercury Cougar, coupe, black." He added the plate numbers.

"It looks like I've got somebody out in that area. I'll alert them. Are you in pursuit, too?"

"I am."

"Do you have any idea what's going on?"

"Not a frickin' clue," Pruitt told the man.

CHAPTER TWENTY-THREE

PRUITT WAS ALREADY going sixty-five in a forty-five zone. He figured the Golf to be gutless, but he was keeping up okay. Driving these speeds was dangerous, especially with one hand, but he had to contact the office. He again used his bag phone—the coverage great now—and when Madeline answered, Pruitt asked her if she knew what the heck Charneski was doing over in Centralia—chasing a suspect, for chrissakes—when he was supposed to be on vacation.

"He's not part of the stakeout?"

"No. It was just Jones, Yen, and me. I wanted to keep it low-key."

"Then your guess is as good as mine. He didn't say anything to anybody around here."

He rang off, slapped the beacon on the roof and hit both it and the siren. Doing so would not slow Angela's escape run, nor Charneski's pursuit of her, but during the week Old Highway 99 was a popular route and there was a lot of traffic. Maybe the siren and beacon would help alert the civilian drivers to the danger approaching them.

Angela, apparently, was equally interested in clearing a path—although for very different reasons. He could hear her riding the horn. When that didn't work on a Honda Civic, she got off the horn and pulled recklessly into the left lane. As

188 • D_{ARKNESS} B_{IDS} _{THE} D_{EAD} G_{OODBYE}

oncoming traffic kicked up shoulder dust trying to avoid her, she jerked the truck back into her own lane.

Then she was back on the horn, muffled from Pruitt's distance. Just in case, he turned the RF tracker back on. No sooner had he done so and the needle swerved left. Up ahead he could see her veering onto Old Highway 9, approaching traffic honking angrily.

Now she was heading west by northwest. Why the dangerous change of direction, he wasn't sure, because he had no idea where she might be heading. Maybe she was just trying to get away from all the traffic on 99.

And traffic was indeed lighter on Old Highway 9. Between Angela's horn and his lights and siren, cars were pulling over to the shoulder more readily, allowing him to gain a little ground.

He was just streaking past the Grand Mound Driving Range when the Lewis County Deputy Sheriff the 911 dispatcher had said was in the area appeared at the intersection of 9 and Grand Mound Way. Old Highway 9 and Grand Mound Way ran parallel for a few miles, one on either side of the train tracks, and the deputy was making the switch from one to the other. Unfortunately, if he'd been thinking of a cut 'em-off maneuver, he was too late. The best he could do was join the parade, jamming in quickly between Charneski's Cougar and Pruitt's Golf and going Code 3, his bar lights chasing madly, helping to announce more visually to the traffic ahead to get out of the way.

He spoke to Pruitt over the radio. "You know what's going on?"

"I don't."

"Looks like we're in for a ride."

They flew by Maple Lane High School, a maximum juvenile detention facility. A group of students in yellow work vests doing yard work paused and gawked. Moments later the procession passed through the shadows cast by Grand Mound itself, an oblong, 200-foot tall geologic anomaly rising like a wen from the valley floor.

More farms and fields hurtled by, and copses of trees. The traffic was mixed. When it was light, Angela pushed Bill's truck up past eighty.

Then the Lewis County deputy was back on the radio. Over the wail of his siren, he said, "You know who these people are?"

"Woman in the truck is a friend. Man in the Merc is one of my deputies."

"A deputy." Then a moment later, "This had better be important, for the danger he's putting everyone in."

Pruitt said, "You got anybody up ahead could lay down a spike strip?"

"Highway 12's coming up. She's going to have to slow down and take a hard left. Would've been a good place for it, but it's too late."

Sure enough, as Highway 9 petered out, everyone in the chase began breaking down for the 12/9 intersection.

The deputy said, "He could PIT her right now."

A Pursuit Immobilization Technique involved pulling alongside a fleeing vehicle then "gently" making contact with the target's side panel in order to instigate a skid—a maneuver adapted from race car driving. Pruitt was not a fan of PITs, but had to admit it might be appropriate. Recommended for use at thirty-five or less only, they were below that right now.

But Angela did not give Charneski the opening. Barely slowing down, she ignored the traffic coming both ways on Highway 12 and slid screeching out into the intersection. Horns sounded furiously as civilians desperately tried to avoid the two-tone green truck that had suddenly appeared in front of them. It was another reckless move on Angela's part; cars could have rammed her from front or back. But it worked. A white Cadillac coming up behind her swerved over the shoulder and skimmed out onto a field of waist-high corn. A red Mazda's brakes began smoking as the driver stood on them, pulling right, holding on for dear life to the shoulder that nudged up to a ditch. While the officers behind her waited for the chaos to simmer down, she gained on them.

Back in pursuit, the deputy told Pruitt something he already knew. "Your boy's putting everyone at risk."

"My sense is he's not thinking like a cop right now." Pruitt let a beat pass. "You want to let 'em go?"

There was a silence. They were near the village of Gates, passing over a set of railroad tracks. Farmland beyond the guardrails: double-wides, barns, out-buildings, and stables.

Finally, the deputy said, "We don't know what your deputy's going to do. Nobody's going to be safe if he keeps after her like this."

Pruitt wanted to say *duh*, but held his tongue. This was not, after all, the kind of circumstance small county cops dealt with very often. The deputy was simply voicing his thoughts. An experienced cop wouldn't have to, but as good as their training had been, real life always played out unexpectedly. If it were only Pruitt and the Lewis County deputy in pursuit, then, by all means, let'er go. It wasn't worth the risk. If she thought she had outrun them, she would slow down. But with Charneski playing the wild card, they really didn't have any choice in the matter. The risk assessment had been taken out of their hands. Pruitt had already thought all this through, but this was no time to be getting in a fellow officer's face about it. Not exactly an ideal "teaching moment."

They passed a nursery on the left, then another mobile home park. No landscaping but a ditch and scrub.

Heading due west, they approached Rochester, the largest small town out here in north Lewis County farm country— maybe 2,000 people. Up ahead was a wide intersection with a turn lane. A feed and seed was on the left, a used automobile and tractor business on the right, a red Mustang parked next to the red tractors with white roofs. Pruitt's stomach lurched when he saw the light. Angela careened into the turn lane to avoid the traffic that was slowing down for it. She shot through the intersection with an abandon based on a fear he had no understanding of. If she crashed, she crashed. If she died, she died. What could possibly evoke an emotion that powerful?

Miraculously, the maneuver worked. While Angela flew ahead, the three pursuit vehicles took advantage of the fact that the drivers at the light were now too stunned to move, and got through without incident. Then it was back up to speed, sometimes near eighty. They sped past Rochester High School, home of the Warriors. Then the newly opened Lucky Eagle Casino, on the left. Then a lumber mill with a yard full of logs, stacked like bundles of pick-up sticks.

Pruitt listened as the deputy contacted the Washington State Patrol and brought their officer nearest to the chase up to speed. "Suspect is heading for Elma. Is there time to set up a spike strip?" And he gave the vehicle description and an ETA, and a quick summary of the situation, including Pruitt's presence.

"Negative on that," the trooper responded. "It's just me."

The deputy said, "Any local LE available?"

"I'll try to raise 'em. Don't count on it."

"10-4 that. How about a box-and-stop on the freeway?" The deputy explained that one of the pursuers, although a cop, was not in radio contact.

"Sheriff Pruitt," said the trooper, "your man know the maneuver?"

Grabbing his microphone, Pruitt said. "He's had the training. But I don't know where his head's at."

"10-4 that. Let's give it a try. You're assuming she's going to go Olympic Highway?"

Pruitt said, "Roger that."

The trooper said, "I'll run up the entrance ramp and get in front of her."

The tiny villages of Oakville, Porter, and Malone flew by. Landmarks blurred: a small brick bank, an antique store ornately painted, a variety store housed in a World War II-era Quonset hut. Then they were approaching the 8/12 intersection. Highway 8 was as wide as a freeway, but with left turn lanes. Highway 12, also known as the Olympic Highway, had no turn lanes, at least not until past Montesano.

As she had done at the other intersections she'd already barreled through, Angela crowded the cars in front of her as she approached the freeway entrance, even bumping a compact hard on the backside.

By the time Pruitt had made the turn and blasted onto the freeway, he could see that the trooper had indeed put himself in front of Angela's pick-up. The Lewis County deputy was just pulling up alongside Charneski. Pruitt could make out Charneski holding something up to his window. Probably his badge. The deputy signaled "okay" back to him.

So maybe Charneski did have a legitimate reason to place everyone in this peril. Lord knew how many times Angela had pissed Pruitt off.

The Lewis County deputy now gunned ahead and took a position just to Angela's left, in the passing lane. Charneski, finally appearing like he was part of the team, dutifully pulled up behind her.

Pruitt positioned himself behind Charneski, although he hung back a good dozen car lengths.

The tactic now was for the three surrounding vehicles to slow down, which would force Angela to slow down, eventually to a stop. And it looked like it was working. Angela signaled to the deputy that she was backing down. Judging by hand language, it actually looked as if she was relieved. Maybe it was seeing cops in uniform. Unlike Charneski, whom she clearly saw as a threat, the Washington State trooper and Lewis County deputy had encountered her at random. She might be in some trouble with them, but they weren't out to hurt her. As wary as she was of the system, of The Man, not even Angela was so paranoid as to think these officers were part of a conspiracy.

They were down to nearly fifty miles an hour when Charneski suddenly gunned his Merc and rammed her, an expertly executed but completely perilous PIT maneuver.

CHAPTER TWENTY-FOUR

PRUITT FELT A sickening explosion in his stomach as the pickup truck lurched right from the impact, then slowly drifted back, Angela counter-steering, but too late. The vehicle rolled to the driver's side, a horrible skid of metal on asphalt while the officers ahead and to her side darted forward.

Undercarriage exposed, Charneski rammed her again.

Charneski's inexplicable set of directives caused Pruitt to take evasive action to avoid a collision with his deputy's coupe. Adrenaline exploded through him. The profundity of the feeling was one he'd experienced only once before, last fall, when through a cloud of dust he'd pitched over the side of a mountain, surviving only by the grace of a couple of miraculously-placed trees and the deepness of the scree.

The difference was he'd been blinded then, but was in full view of the disaster now. Muscle memory, not trees and scree, would be the only way to save himself. He braked hard, but felt for lock-up, easing back when it felt like the Golf's rear end might lose traction and swing out behind him. When Charneski's rapidly-slowing Merc got close enough that Pruitt knew he would hit it, he stepped off the brake and steered to avoid him. He did not question his arms or his instincts. When he went into a slight skid, he looked ahead at where he wanted to go, not to either side. At this point another car's presence wouldn't matter anyway. In the outside lane he gained control over the skid, got on the brake again. He pulled across both lanes to the inside shoulder, and came to a full stop. He took a couple of deep breaths, got on the radio, called in his location, and requested an aid car.

Calls made, he rolled his head over his right shoulder and backed up the fifty yards or so to the Ford and Angela. When he got out of the Golf he heard a sound he knew immediately would haunt him the rest of his life: painful, harrowing, weirdly sexual. I'm dying, I'm hurting, I know something now about life I never really wanted to know. It was utterly ghastly, and it was coming from Angela.

Then an eerie silence. Across the freeway he could see the twin cooling towers of the Satsop Nuclear Power Plant, a strange sight at any time, but a bizarre one now. Huge and useless. Not even a watt of electricity produced. He ran to the truck, which was lying driver's-side-down in the middle of the inside lane of the freeway.

Angela still moaned in anguish. Less loudly, but maybe more horrifically, the idea that her life was draining from her.

He got up on the short bed panel and pulled the door open, using his weight to crumple it forward and out of the way.

"Angela," he said. "Hang in there, honey. Everybody's on their way."

She was in her belt, her left arm pinned underneath her at an odd angle. Clearly broken. She'd suffered a gash across her forehead, although it didn't look like it was causing the pain.

"Oh, god, Gavin," she said, breathless. "Oh, my god."

"I don't dare do anything for you, Angie. Angie, baby. Okay? I'll make it worse. Talk to me, babe."

Her breath was labored. "Your man," she said. "Where is that pisswad?"

"Charneski?" Only then did he realize that his deputy had fled the scene.

"He's in on it."

"In on what?"

Her eyes started fluttering, consciousness dimming. "Look in the section breaks," she said, then passed out.

•••

A few minutes later an ambulance arrived and Pruitt got out of the way. Standing a few yards from the wreck, he was trembling. For all the hassles she had caused him over the years, especially last fall, he realized how much he loved Angela. She may not have been his soul mate, but she had taught him about physical love, helped a boy become a man. They had partnered well, then parted well. She was his friend. She had saved his life, but he could do nothing for her. He had betrayed her with his distrust; he had played her with this computer disk ruse. He may well have caused her death. He felt utterly useless, totally shamed.

Then: the pisswad. Charneski. Where had that son-of-a-bitch gone? Pruitt strode back to the Golf. Got on his police radio and called in an APB on the Cougar. For all the good it would do. Bobby was a local, born and raised, and knew the back roads and logging roads as well as anyone. If he was intending to stay hidden, to run, he could probably do so for weeks.

Pruitt got on his bag phone and called the office. When dispatch answered he brought Madeline up to speed.

"We'll bring that prick in cuffed and bleeding if we have to," he told her.

CHAPTER TWENTY-FIVE

PRUITT FOLLOWED THE ambulance to Providence St. Peter Hospital in Olympia, where Angela had been ushered directly into ICU, then surgery, then out of surgery and back to the trauma center.

While she was in surgery, Pruitt was able to call Bill, who gasped and went silent.

Pruitt said, "Bill, get a breath, man. Sit down if you can."

After a moment, Logan said, "Where is she?"

Pruitt gave him directions. "She's in the best of hands, here, Bill. I'm worried about you being able to drive right now."

"But I've got to—"

Pruitt said, "Bill, look out your window, over to my place. Is Christopher's car there?"

Logan said, "Yeah, it is."

"I'm going to call him and have him drive you up here. Just stay where you are, he'll be right over."

Then he called his daughter's house and explained to Christopher what he needed.

"I'll take care it, Gavin. Count on it."

When he hung up he realized those might have been the best words he'd ever heard out of the young man.

•••

Finally Pruitt was able to talk to the Trauma Center doctor. "We'll just have to see," the doctor told him in the waiting room. "This kind of injury, there could be internal issues going on that we aren't aware of because of the swelling."

When Bill and Christopher arrived, Pruitt helped explain to the front desk receptionist who Bill was and the nature of his relationship to Angela. She listened attentively, then spoke to Bill, assuring him that he could see her when that became possible. Pruitt noticed that the whole time she could hardly keep from staring at Christopher's dreadlocks. Having grown somewhat used to them, seeing the reaction of the receptionist reminded him that the kid could be a pretty strange sight.

Bill then announced to Pruitt that he wouldn't be going back to Elkhorn without Angela.

"If I can't sleep in a chair next to her, I saw a motel down the street. I'll stay there."

"Christopher," Pruitt said, "you want to come back with me or stay here with Bill?"

"I don't have class again until next Tuesday. Maybe I should stay here with Bill. Olivia can come up and get me. Tonight. Tomorrow. Bill can use one of our cars."

"I can get a rental," Bill said.

Christopher said, "We'll work it out, Bill. Don't worry."

•••

So Pruitt ended up driving back to Elkhorn alone. Got to the office just after six. Although past quitting time, Joyce and Madeline were still there. Looked like they were waiting for him.

He thanked them for their concern. "You have any idea where Bobby is?"

They looked at each other. Then Madeline said, "We don't know."

"Called his house?"

"Absolutely," Madeline said.

"Anybody answer?"

"Judy," she said, Charneski's wife. "She thought he was at work. Said he told her he was undercover."

Raphe Jones walked into the Swamp. "Hey, Chief."

"Raphe, you have any idea where Bobby might go if he's freaked out about something he's done? Because he's obviously up to his eyeballs in something bad."

"I don't, Chief."

Pruitt stood there in the middle of the Swamp thinking. He looked up at Jones. "Angela said something about section breaks. That we're supposed to look for something in the section breaks. You got any idea what she was talking about?"

"Section breaks? Jeez, not a clue. Do you think she's talking about something in the computer files?"

Pruitt shrugged. "Beats me."

"I'll look into it. I might have to make a few calls."

Pruitt turned back to Madeline. "We're going to need to have someone sit on Charneski's house."

"Weekend evening shift just started. So we've got two on: Goelz and Staricka."

Pruitt sighed. Here he was in a crisis and the thought of paying overtime flashed across his mind. It worried him that a bureaucratic thought process would rear its ugly head at such a moment. "Who's on call?"

"Deputy Goodin."

Geraldine Goodin was his rookie. Hired with the money the state was paying back to them to cover Lee Wilson's salary to teach at the Police Academy, which because of financial technicalities, Willapa County had to continue paying. Jeez, some people thought sports salary negotiations could get Byzantine.

"Get hold of her," Pruitt said, "and let her know she's on."

CHAPTER TWENTY-SIX

THE NEXT DAY around ten, Pruitt got a call from his colleague, Sheriff Gary Bowman. For a few moments they talked Husky football. Bowman had season tickets and offered a game to Pruitt.

Pruitt said, "We're due in September. Even into November, we're still going to be sleep deprived."

"Don't do what I did. I just got Eddie fed and dozing off. Got him all wrapped up in his blanket and resting in my arms, and I'm watching a Sonics game, got the volume down. Payton gets a steal and a breakaway, Kemp right on his tail. So Payton decides to go show time and throws a pass off the backboard for him. Of course the pass is too hard, Kemp misses the dunk, ball caroms practically back to half court. And I'm all, goddamnit! Just make a lay-in, you idiots! Yelling at the TV."

Pruitt chuckled. "How long did it take to get him settled back down?"

"Hours. I'm telling you, I scared the poor little guy half to death." Then Bowman said, "How's your friend doing? The one in that chase yesterday?"

"Moved from critical to serious. Still in ICU. They're hopeful. Whatever that means. Thanks for asking."

"You're welcome." Then he said, "We finally got the prints from that computer you found at that meth lab. Besides the owner's, they found prints from a woman named Carracitto—that's your friend's name, right?"

"Yes."

"Well, apparently she'd had some run-ins with the law back in the sixties, so she was in the data base."

Bowman had paused, the plum from the pudding. "They also found one more set: guy named Geoff Adams."

"Who is he?" Pruitt asked.

"Supposedly an employee of Tri-County Farm Supply. In reality, we suspect he's Tom Conley's muscle."

"Does he have an office there at Tri-County? Like right next to Conley's?"

"He give you the look when you visited his boss?"

"Oh, yeah."

"He's a vet. Army Special Forces. Trained to kill."

"He on meth?"

"Don't know about that, but he's got attitude. He had a fender bender with a guy last year, guy who'd been drinking. Thought it was Adams' fault. Got out of his car and came at him. Adams broke his nose and two ribs. Then called 911 on his cell phone. When the officers arrived Adams was standing there cool as a cucumber, drunk guy at his feet looking about dead. Officer says, 'You could have killed him.' Adams just shrugs and says, 'Didn't need to.'"

Pruitt gave that some thought. "So you're keeping up surveillance on Tri-County and Conley?"

"Absolutely. I don't know where all this business is going, but we should be ready to move and move quickly."

Pruitt made a tsking sound. "We just need something solid to move with."

•••

Around two o'clock, Pruitt got a call from Bobby Charneski's wife, Judy. "Bobby just showed up. Out of the blue, like nothin's wrong, like he hasn't been gone for nearly two days without callin' or anything, and says he's taking the boys swimming. He doesn't look good, Gavin, not at all. He hasn't slept, he hasn't showered. He wouldn't talk to me, just rounded up the boys and said he'd get them back later. I'm worried," she said, "really, really worried."

"Judy," he said, "has he ever hurt them?"

"The kids? No." He could practically hear her mind churning over the phone. "He disciplines them. No supper. No TV. He doesn't hurt them."

"Then it's very unlikely he's going to hurt them now. Do you know where he's taken them, the boys?"

"Yeah, I've a pretty good idea."

•••

Pruitt raised Raphe Jones on her radio. "Thought Bobby's house was being watched? I gotta hear from Judy he's been there and gone?"

"Ing got called out on a domestic. I'm overseeing an eviction. Goodin got called away on a traffic accident. We're always thin, can't be everywhere at once. That's the best I can say."

Pruitt immediately felt bad for snapping. That just wasn't his way. "Sorry, Raphe. The deal is Judy thought she knew where he went. Forget the eviction." He told her where to meet him.

On the way out, he hollered to dispatch to get hold of Ing Yen and send him out to East Elkhorn, too. Pronto. It sent a shiver up him that he had total confidence in only two of his deputies.

•••

He met them on Cole Street, the far edge of the Elkhorn city limits, technically out of Pruitt's jurisdiction. A technicality he didn't give a damn about. At this point he didn't trust any of them, not even Arlie Petit, the interim chief. Although not usually Pruitt's MO, right now he was in a "screw all of 'em" frame of mind. As Yen often noted, easier for forgiveness than permission.

Maybe fifty yards from where they'd parked was an oxbow bend in the Willapa, and an access path that led to a T-shaped sandbar that offered safe swimming—a rare commodity this far down river, where the current was strong and unforgiving. The sandbar was nearly a hundred yards long, equally spread out along each arm. The furrow between the back of the sandbar and the shore was sandy—another rare commodity. Swimmers didn't have to wear old sneakers like they did at many of the swimming holes in the county, with their rock or pebble beds. Not only was the current held at bay, the sandbar helped the water stay relatively warm. Parents could catch some sun and watch their kids enjoy the water and the day, which was beautiful, upper seventies.

Pruitt, Jones, and Yen parked their cars in a line on the narrow shoulder of Cole Street and walked the access path to the swimming area. Dense foliage covered the path, shadowed it nearly all the way to the isthmus that was the bar of the 'T' and the walkway out to the sandbar. But they held back where the foliage began to thin, knelt to remain hidden. They spied Bobby, sitting in a foldout camp chair out along the north-side arm, slumped and watching his young sons playing at the edge of the lagoon. He had a boom box next to him. Sounded to Pruitt, from this distance, like some sort of soft rock. The light was just a few degrees off of directly overhead, the swimmers splashing, the sun-worshippers basking.

Pruitt signaled his posse further back into the shadows of the grove of trees and foliage. They took up a makeshift command post alongside the path. Maybe a half dozen families spread out along the breadth of the sandbar. About twenty kids were there—including Bobby's—and half that many adults.

They stood there a few moments, observing, before Pruitt finally said, "Ing, would you go back to your cruiser and radio Goodin to go pick up Judy? When she gets here, bring her down."

Before Yen could obey the order, Pruitt said to Jones, "Raphe, go with him and retrieve the rifles, yours and Ing's."

The two of them hustled away.

Then Pruitt managed to catch the eye of one of the parents, a cousin of his office manager, Joyce, although he couldn't remember the guy's first name, not a Cody, but rather a Betrozoff. He signaled him over. Held a finger to his lips.

Wary, the man said, "Sheriff?"

"Could you get your kids and yourself out of here? And tell the other families, too?" He held the man's eye a moment. "But not Bobby Charneski down there, okay? Don't make a fuss. It's just time to go home is all. Your kids raise a stink, tell them you're taking them to Dairy Queen."

Dutifully, Joyce's young cousin went to take care of business. While he was doing so, Jones returned with the M-16s. She set Yen's down. Began preparing hers.

"Make sure those are hidden by the time Judy gets here."

Fifteen minutes later the only people on the sandbar were Bobby Charneski and his boys, Ranger the older of the two, and Jeremy, the younger.

If Charneski took note of anything strange going on, he didn't register it. He looked to have a thousand yard stare, his gaze fixed on his boys. Pruitt noted that their playing had brought them to about halfway between Bobby and where he and his deputies were standing in the shadows. With the other families now gone, it was quiet enough that Pruitt recognized "Dreams," from Fleetwood Mac's *Rumours* album, playing on Bobby's boom box.

Then Yen and Judy Charneski walked up, Yen with his hand gently at her elbow, a delivery. An odd looking one, Judy, a former all-star center for the Elkhorn Sea Eagles girl's basketball team, standing nearly six-three, towering over Yen.

Judy looked manic. Her dark eyes jittering, her breathing shallow.

"Thanks for coming." Pruitt spoke as if this were nothing more than a church bake sale.

204 • Darkness Bids the Dead Goodbye

"Where's Ranger and Jeremy?"

"Just paddling around in the lagoon. They're fine."

"There's Bobby."

"Yep." Pruitt let her drink him in. From the corner of his eye he noted Yen hefting the second M-16. He almost turned to tell him not to chamber a round, not with Judy standing there, scared out of her wits already, not needing to hear that sort of sound. But Yen already knew what not to do. Kept behind her, too, where she couldn't see. Unspoken communication was a priceless commodity in a team. To Judy, he said, "How's he look to you?"

After a moment, she said, "Does he even know we're here?"

Pruitt kept his voice low. "Here's what I want you to do: walk a little ways down the sandbar and wave to your boys and call to them. Time for ice cream, or whatever it is you know they'll drop everything for and come running."

"Do I say anything to Bobby?"

Pruitt acted as if he were giving this some thought. "No, no need. Not unless he says something to you. Even then, gather up the boys and walk back here."

She stood there before finally saying, "Now?"

"Yep. Just call them in like it's the most natural thing in the world."

Her gait looked a little shaky at first, her knees trembling, but then she looked to get hold of herself, her body.

"Deputies," Pruitt said quietly, "please train your weapons on our colleague, Deputy Charneski." With Judy far enough out of earshot, Yen and Jones brought their rifles to shooting position. "If he shows a weapon," Pruitt continued, "do not hesitate to take him. Let me know when you've got him in your sights."

When they indicated they had, Pruitt said, "Yes, he's a colleague, but he's crossed the line. He's potentially dangerous. He placed our law enforcement brothers in jeopardy. A civilian is in critical care because of his actions. He may have killed one of our own. You will shoot to kill if you must. You got that?"

Both acknowledged with finality that they would perform their duty.

Judy walked to within about ten yards of her sons and called gently to them. They turned and smiled, heard her say "Burgers at the Barge," and immediately dropped everything and skipped over to her.

Bobby didn't move. Fleetwood Mac played "Go Your Own Way"—Pruitt for a split second admiring Mick Fleetwood's phenomenal drum track.

Judy had her boys under wing. Pruitt caught her eye and signaled "take it easy" with his hands—like her coach surely must have many times from the sidelines. He could see that athletic poise of hers kick in, those years playing in front of rabid Elkhorn fans. Looking natural, she ushered her brood in Pruitt's direction.

Before he had to issue the order, Yen and Jones lowered their rifles and held them to their sides opposite Judy and her boys.

When at hand, Pruitt said, "Hi, Ranger. Hi, Jeremy."

Ranger, the baseball player, said, "Does dad have to go back to work?"

"Naw. He'll catch up to you at the Barge. I just gotta have a quick chat with him. He's good. No big deal."

And then they were gone and the sound of a breeze rustling the leaves mingled with Bobby's boom box.

Pruitt said, "Can either of you tell if he's armed?"

Rifles raised again, his deputies used their scopes to take an assessment.

Jones said, "Nothing in his hands."

Yen said, "Glock could be in waistband. Sitting back against it."

"Keep your beads on him. Shoot him, please, if he comes up with a gun. I wouldn't be happy with a suicide by law enforcement, but if he's determined to have it that way, we'll oblige."

Pruitt then left the thicket. He walked casually toward Charneski. Waved. Weakly, Bobby waved back. With his right hand, Pruitt noted, Bobby being a right-handed shooter. He hoped it was a good sign.

"Bobby," he hailed, "can you hold both your hands up where I can see them?"

He did as told.

Close enough now to use a normal voice, Pruitt said, "Can you stand up for me?"

Again, he did as told. Smiled. "Hey, boss. Sorry for all this crap. My bad, man."

His use of a phrase that Pruitt himself used all the time in pickup basketball games was unsettling. *My bad?* Pruitt wanted to say. Are you fucking kidding me?

But he shook it off. "What's this about, Bobby? You working for Tom Conley on the side?"

His deputy shrugged. "Wasn't sure who I was working for, actually, until just the other day. We never knew where Dan was getting the money, only that he had it and he was giving it to us to look the other way."

"So you shot Dan 'cause he wanted it to end?"

He held his hands up higher. "I didn't shoot Dan."

"You shoot Wilma?"

"I did not. No way."

"You were chasing Angela 'cause Tom asked you to?"

He lowered his hands, but not in a threatening way. Nonetheless. "Hands, Bobby. You gotta keep them up."

"He called me after Dan got arrested."

Pruitt couldn't tell if Charneski had just not heard him about keeping his hands up, or if he was being intentional. Was the Glock in his waistband at the small of his back?

"Conley said there were going to be new arrangements. Going to cut me into Dan's position. A lot more money. I was over at Tri-County yesterday, talking it over when she shows up, all pissed off, threatening she had him by the balls."

"Why'd you do this, Bobby? Just jump into this whole shebang? Huh?" Pruitt knew why but just wanted to keep him talking.

"Same ol', same ol'." He rubbed a thumb and fingers together.

"All about the money?"

He nodded. "A lot more money, Chief. And I really needed it. We got behind on our mortgage. I mean, Judy having to go back to work at Dairy Queen? That's crap, man."

"Bobby, I see your point. But now we gotta get you in. Can you turn around, cross your wrists at your back?"

Charneski was staring at him now, but wasn't really seeing him. His moment of decision.

"Those boys, Bobby, they love you. Ranger. Jeremy. They need their dad. You haven't done anything yet that's going to keep you in jail for long. If you cooperate, it may not be long at all. With good behavior, full cooperation, maybe only a few years. You'll see Ranger graduate from high school, Bobby. You'll see him play college ball, man. 'Cause he's that good."

From the boom box, Christine McVie was singing "Oh, Daddy." If this whole thing wasn't so damned serious, it would have almost been comical. Pruitt was hoping Bobby had, if not a sense of humor, then at least a latent sense of irony.

"They're going to be ashamed of me." Charneski held his arms up to chest level, like he was beseeching someone for an answer. His voice had begun to quaver. "When they find out what I've done."

"They won't, Bobby. Kids have a short memory for stuff like that. They don't care, really. All they care about is their dad. But if you do this the bad way, man, they'll never forget it. That's what'll make them ashamed of you, man. That you left them. They'll think you never loved them. They'll think you didn't care about them. They'll blame themselves. Don't scar those boys because of your pride, Bobby. I'm asking you, brother, turn around and cross your wrists at your back."

CHAPTER TWENTY-SEVEN

WHILE PRUITT WAS making a couple of notes before he interviewed Bobby Charneski, Bill Logan called. They'd moved Angela from serious to fair.

"She's breathing easier, Gavin. Squeezed my hand, even."

"Great news, Bill. Christopher still there?"

"Olivia came up for him earlier. But I sure appreciate him staying with me last night. He even offered me his car, but I got a rental that my insurance company's paying for. He's a good young man, Gavin. You tell him that."

Then Raphe Jones was at his door.

"Bill," he said, "gotta go. But you call me again tomorrow, okay?"

He rang off and turned to Jones, who said, "I got something you need to know, before you talk to Bobby."

"Hit me."

"It'll be easier to show you."

Pruitt followed her into the office she shared with Yen and E.L., when he was up from the Long Beach office. Since Yen and Jones were both neat freaks, the space was well squared away. The county itself owned only the recently-purchased computer that had arrived in the cow-colored box, which was being kept in pretty constant use. So when Wilma's laptop had been found and there was some computer investigation to do, Jones had brought her personal one in from home. It was off-white, with one of those small television screens. At least they looked like television screens to Pruitt. When he'd asked Olivia why they couldn't just hook a computer up to a television, he'd been told that it didn't work that way. Some sort of incompatibility issues that were explained to him but that he couldn't follow.

He took Yen's chair and rolled up next to his deputy.

"Okay, so I made some calls, including Emily over at the library. She said section breaks are those little design thingies you see in books when there's a change in theme, but not one big enough for a new chapter to start. So I figured this had to do with that manuscript of Wilma's. Here the title page."

Up on the screen, appearing in large letters, was *The Pirate and the Virgin*.

Pruitt couldn't help himself. "You gotta be kidding me."

"Probably sell like hotcakes." She pushed some keys and the screen changed. "Then you got, obviously, Chapter One, etc. But as you go through there's a couple of section breaks. Little black squares. See, here's one."

"Yeah, got it."

Then the screen flashed quickly a number of times. "Now look at the one on this page."

"Little black square."

"Right. Watch as I put the cursor on it."

"Blinks to the side."

"Right." She flashed through some more of the manuscript. "Now a few pages later there's this one."

"Another little black square."

"Watch when I put the cursor on this one."

Pruitt squinted. "It's kind of underneath it. Suppose to be that way?"

"No." She wiggled the mouse. "Now I'm going to highlight it."

"Weird. Now there's an asterisk-type thing under it."

"So this is where I called my college roommate, Neil. He's a computer guy. He's the one got me interested in them in the first place. We bat this back and forth. Then we come up with this: now watch, I'm going to go up here to 'format,' then 'picture.' You following this?"

"So far, so good."

"Now I'm going to go to 'size' and bring it up to regular paper size."

Suddenly something entirely different popped up on the screen. Pruitt said, "Whoa. What the heck?"

Jones sat back in her chair, more than a little proud of herself. "Somebody, Wilma or Ms. Caracitto, embedded this PDF file in this document and shrunk it to make it look like a section break marker. This one's a spreadsheet. But I think there might be a few more."

Pruitt let the implications wash over him a moment. He wasn't sure what embedding was, or a PDF file, but he was impressed. "What's the spreadsheet telling us?"

"That Dan was into a whole lot more than just skimming some cash on parking tickets."

"We know he was into something with Conley. Probably having to do with meth. Any details here we can use for a warrant?"

"Only that there was a considerable amount of money involved." She sat forward again, pointing, but not quite touching, areas of the screen. "Here's money coming in, here's payouts."

"Can we figure out who he was paying?"

"It's initialed, but . . . Look at these two in particular: RFC and JRL."

"RFC has got to be Bobby. Robert Fredric Charneski. How much has he been paid?"

"Rough estimate?" She made some quick calculations in her head. "Maybe $12,000 over the past eighteen months."

"JRL? Is that who I think it is?"

"Jerry Louderback? Dan's brother? Isn't his middle name Ronald?"

The idea that popped into Pruitt's mind made him feel a little sick to his stomach. "Same amount?"

Again, Jones did some fast calculations. "No. A lot more. Maybe twice as much."

"That's gotta be for abetting the tweakers."

"At the least. Maybe worse." She looked at Pruitt. "Maybe murder?"

Pruitt pointed at the screen. "Where's the money coming from? Can you tell that?"

Jones' lips were a tight line. "Doesn't say. Income entries are just dates and dollar amounts."

•••

Armed with a whole new set of facts, it took only twenty minutes for Charneski to finish his tale. By the end of it Pruitt knew a lot about how the methamphetamine operation his deputy had been protecting—the players involved, where they lived, etcetera—but not who had murdered Dan and Wilma.

Chapter Twenty-eight

IT WAS JUST after eleven, Saturday, when, at Prospect, Pruitt turned left and raised his hand to acknowledge Dan Louderback's younger brother, Jerry, situated strategically in the vacant Texaco parking lot. From this position, Jerry liked to train his speed gun on the exit ramp at the end of the Highway 101 bridge. Picking up speed across the bridge was almost impossible to avoid and, technically, the limit switched from thirty-five to twenty-five right at that point. A great place to catch tourists going forty or forty-five, a good fifteen to twenty miles-per-hour over. A sweet ticket, especially as out-of-town offenders were not allowed to simply drive away with a piece of paper they would in all likelihood ignore. Rather they were escorted by the issuing officer to headquarters to pay it immediately.

No checks, no credit cards—cash only. Don't worry, they were told, there's an ATM nearby. During the late spring, summer, and into fall, there were easily a dozen such occurrences every day, sometimes more. Ground zero of Dan Louderback's initial descent into crime.

As usual, Jerry was smoking, the long, ash-tipped cigarette sticking up through fingers resting on the steering wheel, the inside of the patrol car looking like bottled fog.

Jerry had followed his brother to Elkhorn just a few months after Dan had been named police chief, a move that had generated some consternation on the part of the City Council and local populace, although the controversy passed relatively quickly. Jerry was not quite everything his brother was—not quite as handsome, or tall, or charismatic—but people liked him, especially kids, who knew his pockets were always full of red-striped peppermint candies, which he sucked on between cigarettes and also shared generously.

When Pruitt parked next to him and Jerry rolled down his window, smoke roiled from the cab like a fire was lit inside. Pruitt said, "Gotta minue, Jer?"

"Sure. You want to go somewhere?"

"Naw, just take a second. But I'm afraid if I get in there with you I'd catch lung cancer easier than a cold."

Normally Jerry was a jovial kind of guy, always up for some good-natured ribbing. Pruitt's little joke, however, barely drew a smile. Jerry just crushed his smoke, then joined Pruitt, getting comfortable in the passenger seat.

"What's up, Gavin?"

Jerry was pale, his skin blotchy. He'd come to Elkhorn with eczema, although initially it had been noticeable only when his sleeves were rolled up. Now it looked to be crawling up from under his collar toward his ears. Pruitt thought he had read somewhere that the disease fed on stress. Yes, his brother had just died, but Pruitt had noticed it before that. Back on the day they discovered Wilma's body. Since then, too, he'd lost more weight.

"It's your brother's case. We've got some new evidence."

"Oh, good."

Pruitt watched him carefully, where he was holding his hands, which were still on his lap. "So, Jer, we want to do this casual. Not make a scene. That's Officer Jones pulling up behind us now, and Officer Yen coming up in front."

Jerry's eyes skittered. He didn't turn around, but did glance in the passenger side rearview mirror, ducking his head for an angle, then looked up to note Yen's arrival. Both of Pruitt's deputies were quickly out of their cars, pulling their batons.

"Jerry, go ahead and put your hands on the glovebox door, would you?" After he did so, Pruitt used his left hand to reach across him and remove his service revolver, which he then placed at his own side, out of reach.

"All right, buddy, sit back, relax."

Pruitt let him get a couple of breaths. Find his center.

"First, let's clear up the easiest part. You were in on this money scamming deal with Dan and Wilma, right?"

When Jerry didn't answer, Pruitt said, "Believe me, Jer, you might as well come clean on that one. It's the least of your worries."

"Yeah. Right. I worked it with Dan. I never talked to Wilma about it, but . . . "

"This whole ticket thing."

"Yeah."

"Okay. Let's move on. What we're trying to figure out here is who killed your brother. Was it you, or Bobby?"

When Jerry tried to speak, Pruitt raised a hand. "Not yet."

Pruitt sighed. "We found the .22 about an hour ago. Served the warrant at your house."

"But—"

Again, Pruitt stopped him. "Ginny was home. It was a good search."

"I wasn't gonna say anything about that."

"The thing is, you know as well as I do that the ballistics will match."

"But—"

"Wait. Just hold on. I understand that just because the gun was at your house, it doesn't mean you killed Dan."

"I would never. No. He's my brother."

"But you've been doing some bad shit, Jer. Don't even tell me you haven't." Pruitt kept his eyes on the side of Jerry's face. "We've got evidence now."

Dan's brother wrapped his hands around his face. He began weeping. "I'm a son-of-a-bitch," he moaned through his tears.

Pruitt let him cry for a few minutes. He even patted his shoulder, waiting for the emotion to pass. "What were you and Bobby doing for the money, Jer?"

Jerry wiped his nose on his sleeve. "Help out the cookers. Look the other way. Let them know if anything was coming down. Get them safe passage if they thought they needed it."

"The cookers. So this was about meth?"

"Yeah. Crank, man. Jesus."

"You using it?"

Jerry thought a moment. As if trying to remember. "A little."

"A little?" Pruitt said. "Didn't think that was possible."

Another pause. Then, "Yeah, maybe more than a little."

Weight loss? Encroaching eczema? Yeah, more than a little. "So Bobby shot Dan because he was giving you guys up?"

Jerry immediately shook his head. "No. Dan would never have done that."

"Then why did he shoot him?"

"I don't know who shot him. I would'a never thought Bobby would do something like that."

"Well, why would anybody have shot Dan? Did Arlie have anything to do with it? Kyle? Did those guys know what was going on?"

Jerry said, "I don't think so. I mean . . . Well, I don't know. But the thing was, Dan was going to stop. He told them no more."

"Told who?"

"Whoever he was working with."

"You don't know who it was?" Pruitt, of course, already had a pretty good hunch who it was, but was in search of confirmation. One more source and his requests for warrants and extra resources would get granted expeditiously.

"I just knew the cookers. And the main guy's muscle. A vet, or a biker, or something. Crazy eyes, Gavin. Nasty-ass son-of-a-bitch. There was him and some other guys like him. Scary, man. Scary as hell."

"Got any names, Jer?"

"One of 'em was Geoff. Don't know the others."

"So this muscle, these scary guys, they're the ones told Bobby to shoot Dan?"

"I dunno. Maybe they shot Dan. Makes more sense than Bobby shooting him. I just don't think he would. They knew I sure as hell wouldn't do it." He looked up at Pruitt. "It ain't ever over with guys like that. We should've never got started."

"Was it you killed Wilma, Jer?"

His expression was as if Pruitt had slapped him hard across the face. "Jesus Christ, no! Wilma? God, no. I'da never hurt her." He dropped his head back in hands. Started sniffling. "When that happened, I felt like I'd been condemned to hell."

"But she was part of the drug thing you and Dan had going, right?" Again, Pruitt felt he already had a pretty good idea of Wilma's role in this sordid mess.

Jerry sat still a moment. "I'm not sure. She had to have known, because she was with Dan. But maybe not. She never talked to me about it. I just assumed she was part of it. 'Cause she was in the skimming deal. With these tickets," he said, nodding to the exit ramp. "You know?"

"So you covered the town issues? Charneski covered the county?"

"Yeah. Bobby was working the county. He was assigned to East Willapa. A no-brainer. We'd work together sometimes. Like the lab you found near the South Fork. I'm telling you, man, you don't know how close you were to busting that in full swing."

Pruitt now sat silent a moment. "Okay, Jer. Go ahead and step from the cruiser. Jones and Yen will take you in. We've shuffled some people around at the jail, moved a couple over to Lewis County. We can't keep you separate from the general population, but we'll put you in with the cupcakes."

Jerry said, "Thanks," and reached to shake Pruitt's hand. "For making this clean. Thanks a lot."

Though it sent a cold shiver up his spine to do so, Pruitt took his hand. "No problem, Jer."

CHAPTER TWENTY-NINE

BACK AT THE Sheriff's Department, Pruitt gathered Raphe Jones and Ing Yen into his office. "This absolutely sucks."

"Which part?" Jones asked him.

He looked at them. "That you're the only two deputies I've got that I have complete confidence in."

They stood quiet a moment before Yen said, "What now, boss?"

"We're paying a visit to Centralia."

"When?" Jones asked.

"Right now. We've got everything we need for a warrant, and Conley's got every reason to cut and run. I'm going to have Sheriff Bowman get the warrant."

"We going in hot?" Ing asked. "Do they have SWAT?"

"Hot as fire. With SWAT and whoever else may be on the Meth Task Force. Let's stay off the radios. Just in case Conley's listening to police band. I'll set things up with Bowman. Once we get around Pe Ell we'll have signals for our bag phones. We're taking no chances, here. Vest up."

•••

Sheriff Gary Bowman, after hearing everything Pruitt had, said, "Not an hour ago that Geoff Adams I told you about put a box in the trunk of Conley's BMW. Then they high-tailed it out of Tri-County Farm Supply."

"Where'd they go?"

"Home, I guess you'd say. Conley's place out near the old Elks Club Golf Course."

"We need to intercept him," Pruitt said. "He may be destroying evidence already."

"Trouble is," Bowman said, "this isn't a matter of just walking up to his door and arresting him. We gotta figure he's armed. Ready to resist. Maybe not Conley himself, but Adams for sure. Maybe some of the others involved, too."

"You guys have SWAT, right?"

"We've got regular officers who volunteered for SWAT training. It's a combined team: Lewis County, Centralia and Chehalis PD. But with a guy like Adams, we gotta go with State Patrol SWAT. They've got more training, more experience."

"So we wait?"

"No, we've got to contain the situation. Immediately. We'll set up tactically. Set up our L. Make sure nobody up there can escape."

"Your what? Ell?"

Bowman said, "SWAT always starts with three points where they place their teams. Got an L-shape."

"Gotcha. How long will it take to deploy your SWAT?"

•••

Going Code 3, it had only taken Pruitt, Yen, and Jones about forty minutes to get to the rendezvous—what Bowman told him SWAT called a chalk talk—in the parking lot of the Amtrak Station on North Railroad. The day was beginning to fade, the sun half-lidded at the brow of the hills to the west.

The SWAT leader laid out a map on the hood of Pruitt's cruiser and circled the team around it. Tom Conley lived east of downtown Centralia on the sloping shoulder of Seminary Hill. It was isolated and the occupants had good sight lines—at least on three sides.

He pointed out that four stems branched off from Roswell Road and led to four properties. Conley's perched highest, just shy of the crown. A sparsely populated enclave, it looked like country living only minutes from the tight, urban streets of the city.

"There's only one road in," the SWAT leader said. "Which is good, because that also means only one road out."

The "Mansion on the Hill," as the SWAT leader called it, lay northwest by southeast. Northwest was the garage entrance, three cars wide but only two doors. Southeast were windows to the bedrooms, no doors. Northeast was ostensibly the "front" of the house, although it was obscured by the trees along the steep hillside, under which the road leading to the property ran. Southwest was the back of the house: patio, hot tub, and gazebo. Running in parallel to the layout of the house was a wide field, mowed but not watered, brown and brittle this time of the summer. Beyond the field was the abandoned Elks Club Golf Course, where clumps of trees delineated the former fairways.

A small house sat at the northwest edge of the property—a rental, maybe, or guest house—that abutted the thick hedge that ran for a good fifty feet before ending abruptly at the property line.

The SWAT leader looked at Pruitt. "This your first time working with SWAT?"

"Yes, sir."

"We start by setting up our L. If you're standing in front of it, looking in, so to speak, the team to the left is Bravo Team. For this op, they're our sniper/observer. Observer is a K-9 unit, officer Parker and K-9 Rowdy. We're placing them at the edge of this hedgerow."

"Never worked with K-9," Pruitt said. "Will Rowdy stay quiet?"

"Absolutely. Parker's his buddy. He obeys him completely. He's a great dog, Rowdy. One of the state's best."

Sheriff Bowman said, "That hedgerow thick enough for cover?"

"Kind of inbetween cover and concealment. About eight feet tall, thick. A shot probably couldn't get through with any accuracy, but that doesn't rule out blind luck. But the sun is setting and the shadows are long from the trees on the old fairway. So we'll have shadows over our sniper, and he'll be camouflaged and positioned on the ground at the end of the hedgerow. K-9 will be covered, too, low behind the sniper, watching for anyone who might try to escape from the house by running across the old fairways.

"We call the team to the right our Delta Team," he continued. "They'll be positioned at the other end of the hedgerow. They'll intercept if the occupants of the guest house try to escape by heading east.

"Sheriff Pruitt," he said, "tonight our Alpha Team, which is our front team, will be non-SWAT. You, Sheriff Bowman, and your two deputies. You'll set up a road block. It's the only road out, so it should work pretty effectively.

"Plus we're using a fourth team. Usually Charlie Team is positioned at the rear, but for this op we've got them down here in the old club house."

Pruitt nodded. He appreciated the debriefing. "We've got Alpha in front, Bravo to the left, and Delta to the right. Plus Charlie."

"Yep. Charlie Team will have a panoramic view of the fairways. If anybody manages to get past the K-9 or the sniper, they'll have to contend with Charlie."

The SWAT team leader was hatless and ran his hand over the stubble of his military cut. "Our main duty is simple: we're going to make sure no one leaves. We're just holding things together until the WSP SWAT gets here."

Pruitt said, "When's that going to be?"

Sheriff Bowman: "I made the call. Maybe two hours?"

"If they know we're here holding down the fort, they're probably not going to hurry," said the SWAT leader. "It's an overnighter."

Pruitt said, "Why's that?"

"The last thing we want to do is engage the occupants of the house in a fire fight. State SWAT is going to want to make their move just before dawn. It's the safest time. That's what this is about: taking no chances, getting everybody home safe . . . even the bad guys, if possible."

One of the other SWAT officers pointed to the map. "What about the people living here? Behind the hedgerow to the north? Won't they be in danger?"

Bowman said, "The Starks. Retired couple. I went to high school with one of their kids. I called them when all this started to come together. They've got a daughter that lives in Winlock. They went to stay with her. I'll call them when it's over."

"I've got an idea," the SWAT officer continued. "That guest house abuts the hedgerow. Gotta be a window on that side. What about taking some pruning shears and a saw and hacking our way through? The occupant sure wouldn't be expecting that."

The SWAT leader said, "But can it be done quietly? We don't want that hedge shaking, giving you away."

"We can make it stealthy."

"Okay. Let's assign Delta Team to that. If we move Alpha Team up a few more yards, they should be able to spot anyone trying to escape on foot going east. Can we get pruning shears and a saw? Not exactly standard issue."

Bowman said "I'll bet the Starks have both. Probably in their garage. Let me call Dave right now." He turned away to use his cellular phone.

The SWAT leader looked at Pruitt. "We have a motto. 'No plan survives first contact.'"

"Which means?"

"It's our contingency if, for whatever reason, we get detected. Adams is the enforcer. Based on the intel we got from your office we know he stays in the guest house. We know he's got a small arsenal. We know he knows how to use it. He's smart, trained, and dangerous. If things go awry, we need an alternate plan. Which starts with Alpha Team heading up the road, all three vehicles. In that scenario, here's what I want you to do."

A few minutes later, Sheriff Bowman returned. "We can use whatever we need from the Stark home. Dave said that we'd find everything in the garage."

•••

Pruitt was comfortable with Plan A, wary of Plan B—even as he saw the logic in it—and impressed with Gary Bowman's SWAT team. Within ten minutes everyone was in place. A half-hour passed, on the verge of dusk. Everything was quiet. The teams were equipped with two-way radio communications, each officer with a speaker-mic on his lapel, but they were trying not to use them. Then over Bowman's speaker came a harshly whispered, "This is Bravo. Adams is taking his dog out."

Sheriff Bowman said, "Shit. We didn't know he had a dog."

"Can we do anything?" Pruitt asked him.

"Just hope it's old and lost its sense of smell."

"Is this what SWAT was talking about, our plan not surviving first contact?"

"We better get ready to move."

Tense moments passed before a dog began barking. Then shots rang out—mere pops, really, from Alpha Team's location. Then the SWAT leader, who had decided to oversee Delta Team, the one sawing through the hedge, gave the order for Alpha Team to move out. Plan B was in effect. All three vehicles hit lights and sirens and sped up the road.

As designed, the lead vehicle, Sheriff Bowman's, swung wide right parallel to the small house and jounced to a stop. Pruitt, following him closely, did a turn not quite as wide, keeping Bowman's cruiser on his right, then swung left and ended up with his passenger side parallel to the big house. Raphe Jones and Ing Yen pulled in between the two, forming an arrow. The maneuver allowed both Bowman and Pruitt

224 • Darkness Bids the Dead Goodbye

to tumble out their driver's sides and stay covered, the cars between them and potential fire. The cars also protected Jones and Yen. All four took their positions quickly. Jones and Yen each shouldered their M-16s, aiming respectively at the large and small houses. Bowman and Pruitt had their service revolvers drawn. Pruitt, in addition, had his megaphone in hand. The tactic was smooth and brisk. Mere seconds had passed.

There was no sign of life whatsoever in the big house.

Over their speaker-mics, they heard the SWAT leader whispering. "Adams fled back in the guest house. His dog picked up Rowdy's scent, started barking. Adams didn't even investigate, he just started shooting toward Bravo Team."

The SWAT leader was at his mic again. "Status check. Everyone good to go?"

There were affirmatives from each team.

"Anybody return fire?"

"One shot," replied the sniper. "To back him away. High and to the right."

"Stand at ready, then. Let's see if Alpha Team can get him to come out."

Bowman nodded to Pruitt, who lifted his megaphone toward the guest house. "Geoff Adams! Police! Come out now with your hands up."

When nothing happened, he lowered the megaphone and said to Bowman, "How close is the team cutting through the hedge to having something for us?"

Bowman relayed the question.

Whispering, the SWAT team leader said, "We're there."

"Do you have a visual?"

"No yet. We're at the bathroom window. Door's ajar, but not enough to see anything."

It was eerily quiet. Pruitt again demanded that Adams come out. Still no response. He waited for a minute, then tried again.

He was still speaking when an unearthly barrage of gunfire blew out the guest house's east window—roaring and continuous. Pruitt and the others in the driveway team ducked behind their cruisers and waited for it to end. Adams must have been using an assault shotgun with a drum magazine. The rounds were coming so fast it was impossible to count them, but there were well more than the eight a box magazine held.

Although it felt like forever, the salvo was over in moments. Windows had been blown out of Yen and Jones' cruiser, the one parked in the arrow shaft position. Pruitt could only imagine the extent of pellet markings that must be strewn along the body of Bowman's cruiser, parked broadside to the guest house. Pruitt knew an Atchisson could fire 350 rounds per minute. A mere twenty or thirty wouldn't take long to unload. The only positive in their favor was the Atchisson was notorious for jamming.

As soon as the volley stopped, Jones returned to keeping an eye on the big house while everyone else raised up and returned fire on Adams. Bowman had exchanged his sidearm for an M-16, and he and Yen pock-marked the siding, and exploded the remaining windows.

Then, from what was probably the kitchen window, a second barrage of shotgun fire erupted. Again, the driveway team had to duck and cover.

This time the salvo ended abruptly. Pruitt assumed that the Atchisson had indeed jammed. But before the driveway team began firing back, Bowman held up his hand, signalling "No fire." Somehow he'd heard something over his radio.

Then there was a mixed sound of MP-5 submachine gun cracks and tinkling glass. Then silence.

Bowman said, "Delta Team? What've you got?"

Another burst of muffled cracks sounded. Then, finally, from Delta Team, "Suspect down. Give us a minute to secure the scene."

The SWAT leader and two officers appeared shortly at the east end of the hedge. Pruitt figured the bathroom window had probably been too small for any of them to squeeze through.

Using well-rehearsed tactical maneuvers, they advanced to the front door and kicked it open, their MP-5 submachine guns raised. They entered the house. A couple of minutes later, they came out again. Thumbs up.

Joining Alpha Team, the SWAT leader said, "The bathroom door just all of sudden swung open, maybe because of the percussion of that freakin' Atchisson. Soon as we had a clear shot, we took it. Suspect went down, but we must have got him a little high and to the left 'cause he rolled over, a handgun clearly visible. Second burst settled him. One was a throat shot. He was dead when we got in there."

Bowman said, "Conley next."

Adrenaline coursing, Pruitt took a breath, then turned his megaphone toward the big house. "Conley! Come out hands raised! You hear me? Adams is down already. Let's not do this the hard way."

Utter stillness from the big house.

To the SWAT leader, Pruitt said, "Can you get some tear gas in there?"

"Looks like we'll have to."

"Probably safest," Pruitt said, "from the front of the house." The front looked over the northeast hillside, which was densely wooded, providing good cover. The windows, on the other hand, were typical for a house face: large, easy targets.

"Good call."

The SWAT leader sent Delta team. A few minutes later pops were heard, followed by the sound of breaking glass. Smoke began rising from the smashed window.

Into his mic, the SWAT leader said, "Bravo be ready. You got your night scope on, right?"

"Roger."

"Use K-9 if possible. I want someone left to interrogate."

"This is Bravo. Gotta runner on the south side of the house."

"He armed?"

"Hand gun."

"We need one of these guys alive. Send the K-9."

Pruitt said, "Jesus, he might get shot."

Bowman said, "Dogs are expendable."

Before he could add another protest, Pruitt caught sight of Officer Rowdy streaking toward the armed man. A mostly black German Shepherd, he was a furious blur. For a big dog, he was incredibly fast. Then the slope of hill took him out of sight. A shot fired, sounding like a handgun. Then Rowdy was growling and a man was screaming.

Bowman said, "It's dark enough, I didn't think the suspect could get a clear shot." He looked at Pruitt. "I hate putting a dog at risk, but better a dog than one of my officers."

"Sorry. We've never had a K-9 unit. It makes sense."

"But it also makes you feel bad."

Then over their speaker-mics came another report: "Got another runner."

By now Pruitt recognized the sniper's voice.

"Shall I take him?"

The SWAT leader said, "Is he armed?"

"Not in his right hand. That's all of him I can see."

"Red light that."

The SWAT leader spoke to Charlie Team, situated in the old club house. "Can you get a warning shot at the second runner?"

"Yes."

"Take it."

They heard the retorts of the M-16. Two. Evenly placed. Then, from Charlie Team, "He's standing there now. Hands up. Looks unarmed."

Bowman said, "Good. Now we've got to clear the house."

The suspect engaged by Officer Rowdy was still screaming at the top of his lungs.

"Have Rowdy stand guard."

Pruitt heard the dog's master yell something that sounded like "Piss-te." He turned to Bowman. "What'd he say?"

"Guard," Bowman said. "In French." He shrugged. "I don't know why. Parker likes French for all his commands.

Says that way the bad guys don't know what the dog will do. I think he just wanted to be different."

The screaming stopped, replaced by pained moaning.

Bowman winked. "That guy won't be going anywhere."

The SWAT leader said, "We don't know if anybody else is in there. We don't know who the guys are on the slope, for that matter. One could be Conley, for all we know."

Bowman said, "Gavin, let's see if we can talk anybody who might be left in there out. If there is anyone, their eyes have got to be watering practically shut."

Pruitt raised the bullhorn to his lips, but lowered it to the ground again before saying a word. He aimed his sidearm at the garage door, which had begun opening smoothly, a powerful but quiet electric motor hum. Two bays but only one car, a BMW sedan. Engine running. Then revving. Conley hunched down low behind the wheel.

Bowman said, "Shit."

Just as the garage door opened enough for the BMW to clear, it shot out, veering left away from the police cruiser roadblock.

In spring or fall, purchase would have been light on the grass, but the sun had dried everything up and the tires found enough traction to get some speed built up relatively quickly.

The SWAT team leader was at his speaker-mic. "Bravo, got a silver BMW making a break. Get Rowdy out of harm's way."

Pruitt heard Officer Parker yelling, "Ici! Ici!"

"Jesus H!" said the sniper. "He's going to hit that guy."

Because of the slope, Alpha Team couldn't see what had happened, but they did hear the thump.

The sniper said, "Knocked him on his ass. He may not be coming up again, either."

The SWAT Team leader said, "Charlie Team, if you can, stop the car. If you can't, let him run."

Bowman was already calling for back-up, indicating to the nearest patrol officers which direction the BMW was heading and where the most likely spot would be to intercept the fleeing Conley.

Some M-16 shots rang out. Then, a few moments later, a loud crashing sound.

The sniper said, "Holy shit! He just smashed into that tree!"

The SWAT team leader told Bowman, Pruitt, Yen, and Jones to attend to the mess on the slope of the old golf course. "We'll mask up and take care of clearing the big house."

Over the ridge there was just enough light left that Pruitt could make out one suspect hunched in a ball and moaning, another to his left quiet and motionless. Up ahead of the two prone men, vapors rose from the engine of the silver BMW, front end smashed into the trunk of a big leaf maple.

Pruitt told Yen to take the moaning suspect, Jones the quiet one. He and Bowman ran ahead to the smoldering BMW.

Service pistols raised, they pulled up a few yards short of the car. "Hands where we can see them!" Pruitt yelled. "Conley! Hands up!"

The window of the sedan rolled down. The engine had stopped running, but the electrical system was still working.

"I gotta get out of here," Conley said. His voice was both adrenaline and pain fueled.

With no further negotiations, he did just that, opened his door and spilled out onto the brittle fairway grass.

"Spread eagle!" Pruitt shouted.

Conley was in obvious discomfort, but did as told.

"Jesus, man. Don't shoot."

Pruitt said, "Just stay down."

Crouched, both Pruitt and Bowman approached. Pruitt kept his aim on Conley, while Bowman cuffed him.

Once the suspect was cuffed, Pruitt looked back up the hill, where the beams from the cruisers raked off in different directions, one up over the houses and the other into the darkening sky. Residual tear gas smoke rose from the house. The dust stirred from Conley's attempted getaway was just

230 • Darkness Bids the Dead Goodbye

settling back down. The sniper stood in a dual shaft of light, rifle lowered, posing like an actor on stage. Nearby, Officer Rowdy looked disappointed that he'd been called off the chase and now had to sit—or "assis," as Officer Parker had ordered him. SWAT officers were standing by the gazebo in gas masks. It looked like the set of some twisted movie.

Cuffing Conley, Bowman said, "Maybe we'll get you for vehicular homicide, too. Your own guy, for chrissakes."

"I didn't see him, man. It was dark."

"Ambulance time," Bowman said, and made the call.

Pruitt turned to his colleague. "Can I have this?"

Bowman said, "Please do."

"Tom Conley, you are under arrest for methamphetamine trafficking." From memory, he recited him his Miranda rights. "And soon enough, I'm sure, we'll have some murder charges to add as well. Wilma's for sure, and maybe your buddy over there, too."

PART THREE:
AUGUST, 1995

CHAPTER THIRTY

THE LAST TIME Pruitt had visited Angela she was still in intensive care. Tubes running into and away from her, IV bags, infusion pumps, heart monitors—the works. Technologically impressive and scary as hell. At that point, just over thirty-six hours after the accident, the best she could do was open her eyes and give him a pained smile. When he took her hand she could barely squeeze it back.

But it had been over three days since then, and she had been moved out of intensive care and into a recovery room, a double occupancy whose other half was currently unoccupied. She still had the IV, but the rest of the machines were gone. Bill Logan was sitting in a chair next to her side when Pruitt arrived. Angela's eyes were closed, but when the two men made their greetings she opened them. Pruitt wasn't sure if she'd been asleep or just resting.

"Angela, jeez, how are you feeling?"

She tried to smile but could manage only a grimace. "Like twisty dancin' in the front of the Wall of Sound, Gav. How about you?"

Pruitt chuckled at first, but then found himself unable to control his anger with her. "What were you thinking," he said, "going over there and confronting Conley like that?"

Bill Logan said, "Easy, there, Gavin. We don't want to get her excited."

"Oh, yeah, you would." Angela gave him as sultry a look as possible, given the circumstances. "Pretty soon, anyway."

Bill stroked her hand. "Okay, I'm going to take a walk around that park next door. Get some air. Sounds like you and Gavin need to talk some police business."

Once Bill had left, Pruitt said, "Sorry, I wasn't trying to criticize."

"Yeah, right, Pruitt. You've never had any issues with me, have you?"

Pruitt raised his hands. "I was . . . I am . . . that accident." He groped to find the words. "I'm telling you. It scared me to think I might not have you around any more . . . you know? To drive me crazy?"

Both had teared up. "Sometimes thinking's not my strong point," she confessed.

Wiping his eyes, Pruitt said, "You were just going to waltz in and take him down?"

"Yeah. Kick his ass."

"Because you thought he killed Wilma?"

"I didn't think *he* killed Wilma. I thought he might have ordered her killed. I was seeing red angry, Gav. I don't know . . . " She sighed.

Then like a cloud passed over, her demeanor changed. "What were you doing following me?"

Pissed at him now. The old familiar. "I had a hunch."

"You just can't do that, can you? Just follow anybody around? Jesus. I'm a private citizen. Don't you have to have a warrant to do something like that? Can I sue you fuckers for that?"

"We got the warrant based on your relationship with Wilma," he told her. "You had access to her computer. There was incriminating evidence on it. It was reasonable to think you may have known what was going on with the fraud." He gave her a look. "C'mon, Angela. We were right. There was something going on with you and Wilma and this whole meth business. We could have had you arrested."

"Instead you use me for bait."

He raised his hands. "Well, you could have trusted me. Just told me what was going on."

Pouting now. "I just felt so . . . I don't know. Violated."

"It could have been worse."

"Worse than this?" She looked at him. "What're you, working on a stand-up routine?"

Pruitt pointed to the water jug on the table next to her bed. "I'm going to help myself if that's all right. You want some?"

A faint shake of her head. "No, I'm good."

He poured himself a cup and took a sip. "As far as Wilma is concerned, Conley's got an alibi. Besides, I don't think he killed her or had her killed. I think he loved her, actually."

Still pouting.

"C'mon, Angela. Talk to me."

"Yeah, I don't know. I didn't get that far with him before he sicced the pisswad on me."

"Charneski."

"Yeah, your boy there."

"So how did Wilma find out about this meth business? Did Conley confide in her?"

Angela contemplated the plastic water pitcher on the tray. "I'm changing my mind about that drink."

Pruitt poured, then held the glass for her as she sipped through a flexible straw.

She settled back, the blankets, so expertly turned down, gave the impression of a white cummerbund. "No, Conley never said a thing to her about his business doings. At first, it was a series of coincidences that didn't make sense to her. Then she found a set of books in Dan's desk. Under his bottle of whiskey. Copied everything down into that laptop of hers."

"When he was out of the office? That type of thing?"

She nodded.

"Wilma came up with that—what was it?—PDF trick?"

"Yeah. She was damn clever that way."

"So was it a love triangle? Her, Dan, Conley?"

"God, no. Wilma and Dan were through. He didn't want it to be through, but it was. Wilma wasn't some player. She fell for Dan, and felt guilty about it, but couldn't help herself. She was a romantic that way. That heavy falling in love thing. But then Dan got her involved in that skimming deal."

"She didn't have to do that."

"No, but she loved him. And at first the skimming was exciting, too. But then it wasn't. All it was doing was making her feel bad. You knew she was working to get that behind her?"

"Yeah. Even Dan said so, that they were trying to get the money back."

Angela raised her eyebrows. "That's only part of the story. Louderback wanted to get it back in without anybody knowing. Reverse skim it. She just wanted to come clean, take their medicine. There was a lot of arguing about that."

"Did Mark know anything about any of this? Did he know about her affair with Dan?"

Angela thought about that a moment. "She didn't think so. The thing about Mark was he just didn't get her. You know what he's like: brooding sort of guy? More into that baseball team than their marriage. Met him once." She gave Pruitt an impish look. "He didn't take to me."

Pruitt smiled. "Gee, really?"

She chuckled, then grimaced. "Stop it. Laughing hurts."

"Angela, why did Wilma get *you* involved in all this?"

"It was your boy, the pisswad. When she found out that he was part of the meth dealing, she didn't know who to trust."

Pruitt sat down in the chair Bill Logan had been using. "Jeez Louise, she could have trusted me."

"I thought so. I actually told her that, but she couldn't bring herself to. Christ, Gav, her ex-boyfriend was the freakin' chief of police. And one of your guys is dirty, too?"

"Still, why not go to law enforcement out of the county? Gary Bowman would have been a good guy to go to."

"She didn't know any of that. If there's dirty cops here, why not dirty cops there, over where Conley's doing his meth business?" She gave a faint shrug. "But she knew she could trust me, an outsider with media contacts. The plan was to gather up as much evidence as we could, make it as air-tight as possible, then have me run with it. Take it to the FBI."

Pruitt laughed in spite of himself. "You, Angela, hooking up with the feds? Oh, man, that's a rich one."

She held a hand up. "Don't think I didn't get the irony."

"Was she doing all this thinking she might get off scot-free?"

Angela gave the idea some thought. "My gut feeling? The only thing she kept coming back to was making everything right, accepting her punishment, whatever that turned out to be. I never doubted her motives. I think she was ready to go to jail."

"But Conley," Pruitt said. "She falls for him?"

"She actually thought Conley was an ally. She couldn't believe it when she figured out what he was up to. Dealing meth, of all things."

"Struck me as a pretty compartmentalized sort of guy. Doing it strictly for profit, not because he was a user. Those kind of people can be hard to read."

Angela nodded to the water glass. "Gimme another hit there, Gav."

She took a healthy sip. "Wilma, I'm telling you, was complicated, too. I don't think she was looking for that affair with Dan—or with Conley, for that matter. But even so, if it had just been about love, I think she'd have just moved on. Divorced that schlub of a husband. You know?"

Pruitt nodded.

"But the scam. That's where it started to go bad for her. Then she finds out this new guy she loves is running meth with her ex-boyfriend. Setting things right, that was the only way she was going to get back to being the person she thought she was in the first place."

Pruitt was quiet a moment. "The odds against her increasing, but hoping to pull through."

She looked at him. "Dead song?"

"Yup. 'Saint of Circumstance.'"

"Well, if you're trying to sum it up, that's not bad."

Then they sat in silence, Pruitt thinking how utterly terrible this had turned out for poor Wilma, a good soul pulled into an unexpected and, to her, inexplicable set of circumstances. Perhaps fate had similarly bushwacked Dan and Jerry Louderback, and Bobby Charneski, too, for that matter, although he saw them as far more culpable than Wilma. They had embraced the corruption they became a part of. Wilma certainly had not.

"The thing is we've pretty much excluded Dan, his brother, and my deputy as the ones who killed her. We've taken Conley down. The guy we're investigating as Dan's killer—who then tried to pin it on Jerry—was killed in a police shootout. So the fact of the matter is we're no closer to figuring out who killed Wilma than we were in the spring."

"Gotta be her husband."

Pruitt gestured. "Yeah, but we've got nothing on him."

"Maybe just his guilt?"

Pruitt mulled that over a moment. "I don't know. Mark plays his emotions close to the vest."

"Maybe if I took a shot at him."

Pruitt looked at her. "I'm not real happy with your choice of words."

She raised a hand. "You don't think I meant . . . ?"

Here she was again, pushing his buttons. Which was fine, if pushing his buttons was all she was doing. The trouble with Angela was you never really knew what she meant.

"Don't even play with that kind of thinking. It's not going down that way again. C'mon, Angela, look at you."

"There's time, man." She settled back against her perfectly fluffed hospital pillows, a slight smirk on her face. "Time is on my side, as they say."

"Don't. I mean it. Look . . . I love you, Angela. We go back too far for us not to feel good things for each other. But you stay out of this. Leave Mark Gillespie alone."

Angela's role in his life was certainly a mercurial one. But, whether his friend or nemesis, scrubbed clean of makeup with an IV leading into her pale skin, she didn't look like someone to fear. Yet that smirk on her face spoke to the other person he knew her as. She'd shot and killed a man once. The man had deserved it, and her actions had probably saved Pruitt's life, but the fact that she understood the dark and violent side of her nature—was not, in fact, at least that Pruitt had ever seen expressed, in any way tortured by the event—did not make him feel comfortable.

CHAPTER THIRTY-ONE

WHEN PRUITT ANSWERED his phone, Molly said, "You doing anything for lunch?"

He smiled. "Yes. I'm meeting you somewhere."

"Barge? In fifteen?"

Though its name didn't engender visions of vegetarian delights, Pruitt got along fine with The Burger Barge. The fact was he had long ago figured out how to make his diet proclivities work in a town where the idea of a meal without meat, while tolerated, was also considered weird. But so be it. He was Willapa County's weird sheriff, and there were but two choices left to him: embrace it or walk away. And so far so good. He had a reelection campaign coming up in eighteen months and, despite rumblings from the enclave of Republicans in the county, from all he could tell there was no one even planning to run against him. So while Molly would assuredly order a Rueben—the sauerkraut something she had been craving of late—he would thank the food gods again for where he lived and have a plate of fried oysters and fries. He knew for certain the Burger Barge owner got her oysters fresh; her husband, after all, was an oysterman.

The Barge, as everyone knew it, sat in the most unlikely of locales. Grandfathering had allowed it to remain literally half on the banks of and half over the Willapa River, just off

Highway 101 as it shot through from the north to south ends of Elkhorn. No business in the foreseeable future would ever be granted a building permit within a hundred yards of a river, much less be allowed to perch over one, not to mention exist within a stone's throw of two lagoons (Morriss and Cutoff), and a vast marsh. With a location so unique and beautiful, The Barge could have sold stale chips and sodas as their lunch fare and still done a roaring business, especially during the summer when tourists could sit out on the deck that surrounded three sides of the establishment and feel nature practically in their laps—particularly on a day such as this, mid-seventies with a light breeze ruffling the sedges and cattails that spread in a seemingly endless carpet from the opposite banks. The bouquet of hot oil, salty breeze, and fecund marsh mingled into something Pruitt had never smelled anywhere else. If not exactly transcendent, it was definitely memorable.

Of late, Molly's gusto for foods she craved had been waning a bit. The cravings were still there, but her need for quantity had slackened. After finishing half her Rueben and maybe a handful of fries, she pushed her plate away.

"Just no room anymore?"

"I'll eat the other half later. I just can't eat much at a sitting."

"I'd probably be better off leaving the rest of these fries alone myself." Then Pruitt, too, pushed back his plate.

Molly was drinking iced tea with lemon, Pruitt coffee with cream and sugar.

"Funny," he said, "how your basic American beverages seem almost decadent when you're drinking them out here on this deck."

Molly nodded. "It's an amazing location, that's for sure."

Why hadn't he noticed before that Molly looked sad?

"Something wrong?"

"Gavin," she said, "have you listened to the news today?"

"No."

"Nobody's said anything to you?"

"About what?"

"It's about Jerry Garcia, honey." She gave him a tender look and he realized that it wasn't for herself she was looking sad. "He died today."

When he didn't say anything back, she added, "I wanted to tell you here. Where, maybe, it might be easier to keep everything in perspective. The world and all. How it goes on with us or without us."

His cheeks were suddenly wet and he wiped his face with the napkin that had been resting on his lap. Molly leaned over her exquisite watermelon belly and put her arm across his shoulders. The breeze cooled his face with the aroma of marsh.

•••

He just didn't feel up to going back to work. Called the office and told Joyce that he was going home. Calling in sad.

"Sad?" she said.

"A friend died, and I need to call some other friends about it."

"Oh, right. That guitar player you like. I just heard. So sorry, Gavin."

At home there was a message from Biscuit. Through sobs he asked Pruitt to call him back. Which he did. They cried at first, but soon were on to favorite moments and stories. Afterwards Pruitt and Molly spooned on their bed, window open to the cooling breeze blowing overland from Long Beach. Fell asleep for an hour and woke up groggy.

"Coffee, honey?" Molly asked as she rose.

"You know, I think I'm going to uncork that bottle of red wine I got from the Wengers."

"Well, I don't blame you. And in spirit, I'm joining you."

Pruitt drank half a glass, but then lost his taste for it. He wasn't sure what he needed, but knew this wasn't it. He went to stand in the kitchen, thinking he might call Biscuit back. While he was still considering it, the phone rang. It was Ing Yen.

242 • Darkness Bids the Dead Goodbye

"Thought you might like to know. Some folks sitting in Logger's Park with candles."

"Disorderly? Do you need backup?"

"No, no. Nothing like that. Good people. Got pictures of that musician you like. You know, gray beard and hair? Little glasses?"

"Oh. Gotcha. Thanks, Ing."

He hung up the phone and thought about it. Went to stand in the door well between the kitchen and living room where Molly was sitting with her feet up on an ottoman. "Hon? I'm thinking I'll go down to Logger's Park for a little while. There's a little memorial going on down there."

"For Jerry?"

"Yeah."

"You want me to come?"

His wife looked exceptionally comfortable. "How're you feeling?" he asked her.

"Honestly, I'm tired."

"I'll just be an hour."

He took the light jacket he wore sometimes on summer evenings off the hook near the back door. Stood there a moment. Then went to the bedroom to find his Steal Your Face pin. Everybody's Store was on the way to the park, and they were open until eleven. He'd stop in there and pick up a candle. And a rose, too.

•••

Maybe a dozen people were down at the park. A clump of teenagers, a knot of gray-hairs, a cluster of indeterminate mid-agers.

"Gavin."

It was Dr. Marion. Smiling at him. Her gray-streaked raven hair and high cheekbones. A little teary for having encountered him here, unspoken, unbidden.

"Look at you," he said. "You took it out of the frame."

Dr. Marion was wearing the T-shirt. The one her boyfriend from high school had so painstakingly created for her. Because she'd worn it only once before, and taken such good care of it ever since—it had been in a frame, for god's sake, for nearly fifteen years—it looked practically brand new. And yet it had a patina of age—not of something grown dim, but of something imbued with depth, of meaning. LSD-influenced fonts, a bouquet of peyote buttons, mushroom caps on long, twisting stems—an amazing work of art. Must have taken him weeks to create. ("He got a little hung-up with it," Marion had told him once. "Maybe more than a little.")

"When I heard," she said, "I knew what I'd been saving it for."

He hugged her.

Someone had brought a boom box and tapes. Just at that moment "I Know You Rider" morphed out of a jam. The first verse out of Jerry's mouth said it all: "I know you rider, gonna miss me when I'm gone."

"Hey, brother."

He broke his embrace with Dr. Marion. Someone was handing him a lit joint. A fat one.

Oh, the temptation.

Pruitt said, "Can't, brother, but pass it on in peace."

Then he got the look. "Hey, wait a minute. Aren't you the sheriff?"

"Not tonight, brother. Not tonight."

CHAPTER THIRTY-TWO

WHEN HE COULD fit it in, Pruitt played in the TNBA, the Thursday Night Basketball Association, a regular gathering of aging, ex-high schoolers like himself and a few ex-college players at the Elkhorn Sea Eagles High School gym, the same floor most of them had played on as teenagers. During the winter, there was a townteam league, sponsors providing matching T-shirts and referees calling the games, but the Thursday Night "league" was just pickup, skins versus shirts, offense calls the fouls. It could get chippy, but generally the atmosphere was collegial. Knowing that an opponent could just as easily be your teammate in the next game kept things from getting overly competitive—for the most part. There were also times when any one of them could act out, the "grumpy old man" lurking somewhere in their psyches suddenly unleashed—like a werewolf at full moon. But apologies and forgiveness usually came quickly afterwards. It was an affliction they all suffered from and easily recognized.

During the summer, attendance could get a little sketchy, especially with nice weather and long days. Sometimes they had to play half-court three-on-three, or even just shooting games like Pressure or Horse. But a hard rain had started earlier in the day, chasing barbecuers, water-skiers, and other outdoors enthusiasts back inside. A good summer eve for basketball, five-on-five full court.

Pruitt was a shooter. Had been in high school, still was. He could post, and his mid-range game was adequate, and he could play strong defense. But his key asset was shooting behind the three-point line. There'd been no such line when he'd played for the Elkhorn varsity in the mid sixties. In those days, when two points were awarded whether a shot was from two feet or twenty, Pruitt's forte had been used sparingly, a strategy to stretch a defense that was clogging the middle. An indispensable skill in the modern game, even back in the day it was useful enough that over the course of a season he averaged around eight points a game on a team that averaged just over fifty overall.

Thankfully, the Thursday night game used contemporary rules: teams kept track of twos and threes, and it was a badge of pride when Pruitt received a pass on the wing and his opponents started yelling "Shooter! Shooter!" Of course sometimes his buddies would also rib him for the fact he was a cop by yelling things like, "Look out, he's got a gun!"

The attention defenders paid him was also a pain in the ass. His reputation required him to work harder than ever to get open. But he could be patient, cutting across the middle to take advantage of picks, or simply letting his defender get bored by spotting up and waiting for one of his teammates to cut into the paint and dish out.

With squalls battering the roof, the usual insularity of the games had been less pronounced than usual. Nature felt oddly close on this warm, humid evening, rain battering the roof. In Southwest Washington rain and warmth ordinarily manifested themselves separately, and at very different times of the year. Maybe he was letting the strange but interesting confluence of weather pull his mind from the game, but so far his night had been so-so.

It wasn't helping matters that Mick Stevens was guarding him. By day, Mick taught chemistry at the local community college over in Riverton, but on Thursdays he was both a clever point guard and a tenacious defender. Yet he was also one of those team-oriented guys always looking to help out.

Pruitt's best ploy with Mick was to spot up beyond the arc and wait for him to get bored. Eventually Mick would turn his head, just a little, to see if he could backpedal into the lane for a strip. When he did, Pruitt would sidle left or right away from him and wait for a pass. But it had taken half a game for Pruitt's passive-aggressive strategy to finally start working. Unfortunately, even then, his first two shots missed.

When he finally drained one, Mick said, "I can't turn my back on you for a second."

Pruitt smiled. "Love it when you do, man."

During a reset, Mick playfully grabbed his arm. "That's it, buddy. No more shots for you."

The games were played to twenty-one, and this one was at nineteen to eighteen, favor of Mick's skin team, when Troy, who ran a used bookstore by day and was a shirt tonight, cut through the paint. Mick took notice and lunged, Troy dished, Pruitt raised and shot: three-point swish . . . game over.

"Damnit!" Mick cried, throwing his hands up. "Who was supposed to be guarding that guy!"

Pruitt laughed. He and Mick slapped fives, as did everyone, that being the last game of the night. "Good Thursday." "Good games."

From his gym bag, Pruitt took a towel and began wiping sweat off his face and arms.

The last person he expected to see at this place and time was Christopher. Or at least a person who looked a lot like Christopher. It could have easily been his short-haired clone. Not just short, either, but corporate short. Pruitt realized that those long, thick dreadlocks had done more than just set him apart, they'd drawn attention from his face. Without them, it was his face you noticed. A good-looking, and now clean-cut, kid.

The father of his grandchild-to-be was standing by the double doors that led to the hallway and the exit. Christopher raised his head in acknowledgment. Pruitt did likewise, then changed into his street shoes, zipped up his gym bag, and threw the towel over his shoulder.

He reached out his hand. "Chris, man. I haven't seen much of you this summer."

Chris shook with appropriate firmness. "Busy, Gavin. School and all."

"Appreciate what you did for Bill, man. That was standup."

"Hey. Bill needed us."

Us, Pruitt thought. *Nice.*

"My god," he said, "you cut your dreads."

Christopher shrugged sheepishly. "You know . . . unlikely I was going to get a job looking like a white Rasta."

"Surprised to see you here. I thought you stayed in Tacoma until Friday."

"Usually, yeah, but I'd put in some late days the last few weeks, so I earned a few days off. Wanted to check in with you, see how you were doing."

Had Christopher just spoken his personal feelings, or had he read Pruitt's mind? Either way, an interesting choice of words.

"Well, let's catch up, then. You want to catch a bite? Torchlight?"

•••

Pruitt opted for a plate of clam fritters and a beer, something new called a micro-brew. He'd read about them somewhere, how it was the next big thing in beer. This was called Red Hook, an ale, and it was pretty darn good. More body than the Vitamin R he and Duane Wildhaber had taken with them on their ill-fated river float over a month ago.

Christopher ordered a shrimp salad. They ate in silence for a few minutes, Pruitt waiting him out. It was the young man's play.

Finally it came. "I know I haven't been holding up my end of the bargain with Olivia."

Pruitt wanted to jump right on it, but held back. "Well, like I've been telling her, you're trying to finish up that degree."

"I have. It's nearly over, actually. Those times I stayed late, I was getting my senior project done. For the code I'm writing, I needed something with a lot more speed."

"You mean, like, computer speed, right?"

"Yeah. But it's pretty much done now. I've gotta write up my report, but, ah . . . "

Pruitt speared a clam and dipped it in tartar sauce. "So that's a good thing."

Christopher looked away. "I didn't want to go through with this at first, but, ah . . . you know, the pregnancy and all."

"Yeah, I understand. It's a lot to think about. A lot of responsibility."

"Maybe I've been hiding from it a bit. I think I have been."

"You're still unsure."

"Yeah. That's putting it mildly. Unsure, that's for sure. But, ah . . . "

He looked back at his food, but couldn't seem to get up the nerve to look at Pruitt, who said, "You ready now?"

Christopher finally looked him in the eye. "You make me nervous to talk to."

Pruitt wiped his mouth with his napkin. "Am I doing that cop look thing? I'm sorry. I try to leave that at the office. But it's hard sometimes."

He closed his eyes and passed his flat, opened palm over his face as if it were a magician's silk scarf. Then he opened them again, smiled. "Did I lose it?"

Christopher chuckled. "Yeah, that helped. You see, I'm not trying to be that guy, that one that people think is an ass. The one who can't take it and bails out? I'm trying to get with this thing, you know? But it wasn't what I was thinking was going to happen to me."

"I know, man. I do." He gave Christopher a recap of his past with his ex, Claudia.

"Yeah, Olivia kind of gave me a background. The thing is, this doubt, it's . . . you know?"

"Yeah, I know that part. It stuck with me right up through finally seeing Olivia born."

Pruitt flashed on the fact that this young man could easily be part of his life for a long time to come: as a potential son-in-law, or whatever he would be called if he and Olivia were to remain unmarried. Common-law son-in-law?

"But it's cool, too," he said. "You know? Like, really great. I mean, I'm going to be a dad. Those sonograms. We're going to have a daughter."

"That's awesome, Chris, it really is."

"I'm trying to straighten my head out on this. Trying to do the right thing."

"I know you are. I can see that. I mean, nobody knows what the future holds. You can't beat yourself up trying to live up to someone else's expectations. How do your folks feel about becoming grandparents?"

"They're okay with it." He looked away again. "Naw. I lied. They're not exactly thrilled. They're not giving me a real hard time, or anything, but, ah . . . "

"Not exactly throwing down with the program, either."

"I've got an older sister. They thought she'd be the one bringing the first grandchild around. But she, you know, ended up managing this business. She's doing pretty well."

"Well, don't be too hard on them. Once they see the baby, it could change a lot of things."

"Yeah. That's what I've been thinking. We just hang in there and wait for the baby."

•••

When he got home, Pruitt replayed his conversation with Christopher for Molly.

"Jeez, I didn't mean to, but I put a lot of pressure on that poor baby of theirs. Like it's entering this life with a job: must save mommy and daddy's relationship."

Molly thought that one over. "Yeah. Poor kid."

"I wish I hadn't gone there now."

"C'mon, Gavin. He was talking to you. That's the important thing."

"Yeah, I suppose."

"But I agree with you. Not even born yet and your little granddaughter already responsible for something."

Pruitt let a beat pass. "Your granddaughter, too."

Molly looked at him. "Legally, yes." A slight smile creased her lips. "Youngest grandmother you ever slept with."

He grinned at her. "Hey, Grandma," he sang, "you're so young."

She gave him her famous raised eyebrow look. "What's that, a Dead lyric?"

"Moby Grape lyric."

"Moby Grape was a band?"

"You know what's purple and swims in the ocean?"

"They named themselves after a joke?" She looked at him. "A horrible joke?"

"In the sixties, we were laughing at the cosmic weirdness of it all."

"I'll tell you who's weird around here tonight."

Dancing around her, he held his hand over her belly and sang again. "Hey, Grandma . . . you're lookin' so good, you're lookin' so good, you're—"

She put her hand over his mouth. Pulled it away and kissed him. "All right, Mr. Moby Grape. Prove it."

CHAPTER THIRTY-THREE

LAST NIGHT, ANGELA came home.

For Pruitt, the first weird thing was thinking of Bill Logan's house as Angela's home. He wondered when the dream would finally end and things would get back to normal. But he was also beginning to suspect that Angela with Bill might just be the new normal.

The second thing he thought about wasn't so weird but rather scary: what Angela might be up to now that she was out of the hospital and feeling better. He hoped recuperation wasn't giving way to revenge scenarios. Gazing out his window, he contemplated the moment, the irony. The heat had returned, as they liked to say, with a vengeance. Upper eighties, a blue sky, not a cloud to be seen. Humid, of course. This close to the ocean, it was always humid. In the fall, plenty of days were similarly clear, especially in October, but they didn't look hot. Not like it looked hot out there right now. Thank god for the air conditioning. Since none of the windows in the Sheriff's Department opened, installing it had been a necessity. Humming at full throttle, trying to hold its own against the sun and humidity.

His phone rang. It was Lewis County Sheriff Gary Bowman. After a couple of quick pleasantries, Bowman said, "Conley wants to talk to you."

252 • D<small>ARKNESS</small> B<small>IDS THE</small> D<small>EAD</small> G<small>OODBYE</small>

"Yeah?"

"A chat, he said."

"A chat? Him and his lawyer?"

"No, just you. And he'd like you to bring him—and I quote—a decent cup of coffee."

Pruitt thought there might be more coming, but there was not. "What do you think this is about?"

"Not a clue, man."

"Well, then. Anytime?"

"Whenever you want. He's—"

"Don't say it."

Bowman chuckled. "Not going anywhere?"

•••

Tom Conley's bust had gone down in Lewis County, therefore he was being held in the Lewis County Jail, part of the county's complex of buildings in downtown Chehalis. After a quick introduction to Conley's lawyer, who rambled off some boilerplate lawyer-speak about his client's upcoming conversation being held against his advice, and that he thought Conley might be under duress, Pruitt entered the interview room. Windowless. Bare walls. A table and a couple of chairs. A video camera mounted up on the wall. And of course a suspect in inmate coveralls—in this case wine colored—waiting. The fluorescent tube lighting reflected off the pale green walls casting a sickly glow over the proceedings.

Pruitt pushed Conley the cup of coffee across the desk that separated them. An Americano, black, 16-ounce, purchased barely five minutes earlier at a drive-through Starbucks, still steaming.

"Okay, I'm here. You're here—against your lawyer's counsel I've noticed. What's this about?"

Carefully, as if it were a can of wasps, Conley pried the top off the cup of coffee. When a drop or two fell onto the upturned plastic lid, he sucked it up. He closed his eyes and inhaled the wisps of steam. "Oh, man."

As if he were a sous chef at a four-star restaurant, he used his hand to fan more of the aroma up his nose. Finally, he opened his eyes, lifted the cup to his lips and took a sip.

"Coffee in here not quite up to par?"

But nothing—especially not Pruitt's sarcasm—was going to get between Conley and his coffee.

The meth king closed his eyes again and sighed. "Man, this is what I've been missing."

Pruitt just waited him out.

Finally, Conley spoke. "There was an eyewitness. The night Wilma was murdered."

Pruitt sat up. "You've got my attention."

"It was me, actually. I saw the whole thing."

Disappointed, Pruitt settled back again. "No you didn't. Are you saying now your alibi people were all lying?"

"Every one of them. Wanted to keep their jobs. I told them what to say."

"Bull."

Conley took a deep breath and had another sip of coffee. "There was an eyewitness, I swear it."

Pruitt thought of the car that Millie Johnson had seen in the copse of alder and huckleberry across from Wilma's. "Maybe so. But it wasn't you."

"Her husband doesn't know that." Conley gave Pruitt a look. "Does he?"

Pruitt was irritated. "Make sense of this, or I'm bringing your lawyer back in here."

He had another sip. "The guy the SWAT team killed that day? The one in the little house? Geoff? He was there. He was the one who saw everything."

"How do you know that?"

"I sent him there. Afterwards he told me."

"What'd you send him there for?"

"I sent him to steal Wilma's computer."

"You sent him to do that? Creep the house of the woman you say you loved? The guy died in a shoot-out with cops. Why shouldn't we assume he killed Wilma, too?"

One of his hands Conley kept on his cup of coffee—as if someone might try to take it from him—the other he held up to stop Pruitt's train of thought. "He had strict orders. Creep the house, get the computer, get the hell out. Don't touch her."

"So you knew Wilma knew something?"

Conley shrugged. "I knew she knew *something*. Wasn't sure what. But I figured whatever she knew she was keeping on that computer. When I first met her, she was on that thing all the time. Then as things were breaking up, I never saw her with it. It was like she was trying to hide it from me."

Pruitt said, "That's a strange way to show somebody you love them."

"It was over between us," Conley said. "But I didn't want anything to happen to her. I didn't. I just wanted the computer, put an end to whatever nosing around she was doing."

"So your man creeps the house? What did he find?"

"He gets there, and there's a truck already parked next to Wilma's Volvo. A white pickup. Chevy S-10. He waits to see if the owner of the truck is going to leave."

"I don't suppose he got the license plate number?"

"No. Just the description. Late model Chevy."

"All right."

Conley took a sip of coffee. "So he waits. Hears a pop. A gunshot."

"He's sure it was a gunshot, not something else?"

"Geoff was ex-military. He would know. A soft pop, he told me. Probably a .22. A little ways off in the distance."

Pruitt thought about the veracity of what Conley was saying. The distance from the copse of alder across from Wilma's to the edge of the slough was maybe a hundred yards. And the location of the murder had been isolated, quiet. Given the description Conley had given him of the man he claimed had been there—his military background, the expected high level of acuity such a man would have had on such an assignment—it was entirely believable that he could have heard the sound and recognized it for what it was.

Pruitt said, "Then?"

"Some minutes pass, guy comes from around the house, gets in his truck and takes off."

When Wilma had been killed there was still some light left in the day, and there had been a three-quarter moon already risen. Enough light to support the theory that if it had been Conley's man hiding in the copse, he could have seen the truck, seen Mark, if that's who it had been, walking out from behind the house.

"Your guy describe him?"

"Naw. Wasn't important at the time. Just glad to see him gone."

"Then he creeps the house, gets the computer?"

Conley cherished another sip of his beloved coffee. "He waits for something to change. Lights to come on. A door to close. Something. But nothing happens. House just stays black. After an hour, he creeps the place. Finds the computer."

"Why did he give it to the cookers?"

"It was a busy night. That was just his next stop. Checking up on those guys. Left it there with them. Told them to get rid of it. Then, from what I understand, 'cause I heard about this later, the cooks started playing around with it. Had some games on it, you know? Solitaire? Minesweeper?"

"Just can't trust a tweaker, can you?"

"Anybody who actually uses that shit is a moron."

"A sucker born every minute, right?"

"It's a solid business model, actually."

Pruitt was thinking that Conley was equal parts ruthless and smart. Thank god they'd gotten him off the streets.

"Tom, we got two problems with this. Number one, your man didn't really know who he saw that night."

"It was him. It was his truck."

"Mariners bumper sticker?"

Conley shrugged. "He didn't mention that."

"How tall was he?"

"Average."

"Wearing anything distinctive?"

"Baseball cap. Maybe a Mariners hat. Can't recall that part."

Pruitt went quiet. Conley didn't know the kind of cap it was because it had never been mentioned to him. He was only trying to pick up on what Pruitt had implied by asking about the bumper sticker. He shouldn't have said anything about that damn bumper sticker, but this was such a surprising circumstance he muddled the interview protocol.

"C'mon, man. You know it's him. Everybody knows it."

After another moment of silence, Pruitt said, "And of course the number two issue—the big one—is the guy's dead."

Conley made a gesture of conciliation. It almost looked like he was blessing the whole deal. "I'll be him."

"What? The eyewitness?"

Conley shrugged. "Yeah. Just substitute me for Geoff."

"Don't be ridiculous."

"My alibi people can rescind their stories. They will. At the drop of a hat."

Pruitt shook his head. "Never going to fly, Tom. Too preposterous."

After a pensive moment, Conley said, "I should have had that cocksucker whacked. Soon as I heard about it."

"Well, I appreciate the candidness. Why didn't you?"

Conley gave him a caustic look. "I thought you guys would get him." Conley gripped the paper coffee cup with both hands. Still protecting it. That it was empty now seemed not to matter. "That son-of-a-bitch is going to walk. I can't have it. She deserves better than this."

CHAPTER THIRTY-FOUR

PRUITT KNEW RAPHE Jones and Ing Yen were beginning to feel uncomfortable, but he wasn't quite ready to speak his mind. Heck, he couldn't even find his topic. Instead, after calling them into his office, he just sat in his chair and stared out his window. Outside it looked like fall, the sky evenly drab, from one gray horizon to the next. Vanished were the heat and humidity, not to mention the blue sky, of earlier in the week. Although far from an unusual occurrence in coastal Southwest Washington, it was nonetheless disconcerting. Willapa County summers fled too quickly as it was and this sky worried him. Surely the summer of 1995 had a few sunny days tucked away in reserve. Contemplating the fleeting quality of the season brought images of Jerry to mind, and also of Wilma and Dan—three people with whom he'd felt some kind of closeness—and the equally fleeting quality of life in general.

All of this heaviness also brought him around to the moment.

He willed his gaze from the window and looked at his two most trusted officers. "I've been thinking about Wilma's case. Thinking about it a lot." Actually, it had been on his mind ever since Angela had returned home, but he wasn't going to share that with his deputies.

258 • DARKNESS BIDS THE DEAD GOODBYE

Jones and Yen remained quiet. Their body languages spoke of interest. Elbows comfortable on the armrests of their chairs. Eyes neither hooded nor widened.

"There was this poster that was popular in the late sixties," he said. "Pair of vultures sitting up on the branch of a bare tree looking out over an empty desert. Desolate. The one is saying to the other: 'Patience my ass. I'm gonna kill something.'"

Jones got a little smirk. Yen was probably thinking his boss had lost his marbles.

"It kind of sums up where I'm going with Wilma's case. Correct me if I'm wrong, but we got nothin'. Or at least next to nothin'. And that's not likely to change any time soon."

Although neither said anything, both looked to be in agreement with him.

"So I've got an idea."

He glanced out the window, then back. "Again, correct me if I'm wrong, but as long as we don't illegally threaten him or her, we can lie to a suspect."

Yen nodded. "Pretty much."

"Whoppers, right?"

A little less resolutely, Yen nodded again. "Well. Stuff we hope suspect will believe."

"Raphe, we've still got the Gillespie's financials, don't we?"

Jones sat forward. "Yeah. Filed away safe and sound."

"I need you to go through them again. What I'm hoping might be in there would have been easy to miss, even going over them a couple of times like we did. It might have seemed inconsequential at the time. It might be something in their credit card reports, or in their checkbook history. Do you remember how far back they went?"

"I think it was a year or so."

Pruitt pursed his lips. "Possibly, it might be something further back than that. We might have to get another warrant. But for now, let's just go through what we've already got. I'm looking for some purchases. Something in the range of twenty or thirty dollars."

"Can you give me a hint what purchases you think might be there?"

"A book, maybe? A video? A subscription to a magazine, like *Soldier of Fortune*?"

"Are we trying to figure out if Mark studied up before creating this murder scenario?"

"Exactly. It was carried out with a degree of expertise that doesn't track with Mark's history. But it might track with his obsessive nature. That spotless house, all that Mariner's stuff."

"Are you expecting to find a connection to the murder weapon? A receipt?"

"No, actually. That we won't find. Not in his financials, anyway. But I am thinking he did the research first, then bought the gun. Obviously he paid cash for it. Used that phony name."

Jones said, "So we probably won't find a check with 'Gun to kill Wilma with' written along the bottom?"

He looked at her. She was trying to keep it light. "Stick with me here, Raphe."

She held a hand up. "Sorry, boss."

"What he may very well have written a check for, or used his credit card for, would be a book or a video. *That* we might be able to trace. And Ing, remind me again what all we got on the gun?"

"Ballistics were a match. It was gun that killed Wilma. No prints, as we figured. Got the serial number, but no way to connect it to anyone. Got some trace chemical."

"Matched the baby wipes from Mark's house?"

"Well, yes. But too generic to mean much. Like Lee Wilson say, weak circumstantial at best."

"Damnit, I wish we'd swabbed him for gunshot residue."

Yen shrugged. "After that many days, probably not there. Besides, if you think he studied first, probably wore gloves, toss them somewhere between crime scene and home."

Pruitt thought a moment. "The chemical analysis is weak, but we've got a report, right? Like a printout of some sort?"

Yen nodded. "Put in it box with gun. Put box in your safe."

"What's it look like? Pretty official?"

"Sure. Got seal of state crime lab. Whole schmeer, like you say. But thin. Attorney tear to shreds."

"Plus, boss," Jones said. "He's got that alibi."

He turned to her. "Right. About that. Here's what I want you to do."

CHAPTER THIRTY-FIVE

WHILE RAPHE JONES read Mark Gillespie his rights, Pruitt waited in his office. He sipped herbal tea to try and calm his nerves. The subterfuge he was about to attempt might have been within his legal rights as a cop, but it was also risky. If it worked, then kudos all around. If it didn't, in all probability Wilma's killer would lawyer up and that would be that. No justice. A creep gets away with murder.

He could call it off. Just send Mark home with some cock-and-bull story. It was not too late to opt for the second option: patience. Wait for new evidence, for a slip-up on Gillespie's part. But once again his thinking brought him back to the same place, that if he didn't do something, nothing would happen. Or maybe something would happen all right, Angela would gun him down on the street in broad daylight. Elkhorn the new Tombstone. The alley behind the Torchlight the new OK Corral.

Jones appeared in his doorway. "He signed it."

Pruitt picked up the yellow legal pad resting in front of him. It was for show only. He didn't dare write anything down on it that had anything to do with his scheme. Mostly, he wanted something to have in his hands. Something to make things appear as official as possible.

•••

Pruitt entered the interrogation room and tossed his legal pad on the table. "Hey, Mark. Thanks for coming in."

"Well, you asked."

As usual, Gillespie wore a navy blue-and-teal Seattle Mariners baseball cap, and a light blue shirt under a dark blue track jacket with ribbed cuffs, a Mariners insignia that matched the one on the cap on the left breast panel.

Pruitt sat. "I like the gear, man. Noticed it before. You're a big fan. And this is the year, too, don't you think? Junior c'mon back from the wrist injury. Bone and Edgar starting to heat up? The Big Unit? I think they're going to get into the playoffs this year, don't you?"

Gillespie made a face. "Yeah, they're playing well."

"I see Boston's in town this week. You going up for a game?"

"My turn's coming up Friday. Baltimore's back."

The fluorescent lighting made Gillespie's pale skin appear practically translucent. The light also emphasized his rosacea, the fine veins around his nose and cheeks standing out like a roadmap printed with blood. He smelled slightly of a familiar after-shave, Old-Spice, maybe.

Pruitt sat back, brought his foot up and rested it on his knee. A couple of buds talking baseball. "Ol' Lou, man. What a guy. Old Lou is old school." He chuckled. "Kicking dirt on the umpires. Throwing bases around. I love Pinella. He was a helluva hitter in his day."

"Didn't know you were a baseball fan."

"Well, I'm fair-weather. Not exactly devoted. But when they're winning like this?" He smiled. "Love 'em."

"Why'd you make me wait for half-an-hour? You said you had some developments."

Pruitt placed his foot back on the ground. Disappointed to have to move on to business. Baseball's so much more interesting. He took out his pen. "We do. In fact, we've got an eyewitness."

"Eyewitness to what?"

"The murder."

"An eyewitness to the murder? I thought she'd been shot by the river?"

Although it had nothing to do with this interrogation, Pruitt pick up the legal pad and wrote *River*. Looked up. "The murderer is what I said. Eyewitness saw the murderer."

"No, you said the murder."

Pruitt shrugged. "Whatever. They saw him."

"Who?"

Pruitt sighed. So disappointed to be the bearer of bad news. "You, my friend. Somebody saw *you*."

Gillespie smirked. "No way. I was at a ball game. I even called Harold Strozyk on my cell. Crowd was going nuts when Griffey hit that double in the gap. Wanted him to hear it."

"Ah, yes. The alibi." Pruitt wrote *Over the top*. "Been looking forward to talking about that. We did a little research. Funny you went to that game alone."

"Harold bailed out."

"Harold told us you called him, said you had to go up there early. Couldn't give him a ride."

"I had some shopping I wanted to do. He could have driven up on his own."

"Not Harold. Hated driving in Seattle. But you knew that." Then before he could respond: "Funny you getting that cell phone just a month before you killed her."

"I did not kill her."

Pruitt ignored him. "The coroner established a 24-hour window around Wilma's death. Sometime between six in the morning Friday and six in the morning Saturday."

When Gillespie opened his mouth to speak, Pruitt held up his hand. "Let me lay it out, Mark. Then you tell me what you think."

He shut his mouth again.

"On that Friday, you worked from seven to eleven-thirty. Then you drove to Seattle, checked into the 5th Avenue Hotel about two-thirty. You checked out at eleven on Saturday. We had Seattle PD run your photo over there, and the desk clerk remembers you, because you're a regular. He said he saw you when you checked in, but nobody remembers seeing you again until you checked out. Which he remembers you did at the desk. Struck him as funny, 'cause you usually just leave your key in the room.

"So then we checked the box score for the game that night against Baltimore. First pitch came at 7:10, and the game ran three-and-a-half hours. That's about three innings every hour and ten minutes. That big rally happened in the bottom of the fifth. So we figure you held your cell phone up for Harold around eight-thirty or nine. The thing is, there's no way you can establish what time you entered the Kingdome."

He looked at Gillespie. "You could have passed through that ticket gate five minutes before Griffey hit that double in the gap."

"I was there."

"Of course you were. Alone. You go in on a deuce, then you go to the game alone."

"I told you, I called Harold on my—"

"Yes. You called Harold on your cell phone. Why? Because you felt bad for not giving him a ride? Or that you knew he'd be home?"

But before Gillespie could respond, Pruitt said, "Lemme get back to that."

He glanced at his note pad. "So we got you with a gap of about six hours where you can't really explain where you were. It takes about two hours or so to drive from Seattle to Nalpe. You could have left Seattle immediately after checking in. We made a call to the Washington State Department of Transportation. Traffic going south that day at that time was light to medium. You could have easily driven to Wilma's, got there near dusk, killed her, then driven back, got to the Kingdome around eight, eight-thirty. Made your call to Harold."

"I was at the game."

"But you've got no way to prove when."

"I was."

"But that's not all, Mark. Not by any stretch. You know that copse of trees across the street from Wilma's? That little side road off Weaver? Guy was parked there that day. Heard the gunshot. Saw a man leaving in a truck a few minutes after that. A white Chevy S-10. Late model."

Pruitt thought about adding the Mariners bumper sticker detail—in for a dime, in for a dollar as far as the lies were concerned—but felt it stretched his already thin credulity too far.

"Somebody just waltz up with that story? Some hobo?"

Pruitt chuckled. "A hobo. That's funny, man. I like it, but, no. We had to do some digging."

"Digging?"

On the pad, Pruitt wrote *Dirt*. "That meth bust over in Centralia? You must have read about it."

"Yeah. I dunno. Maybe."

"That's why we're here. I'm going to have you do a lineup for us today."

"What? A lineup? What for?"

"We'd appreciate it." He wrote *In a row*. "If you don't mind."

"I do mind." He looked around as if he'd lost something. "Maybe I need to get a lawyer. I don't like what you're doing here."

"Getting a lawyer is your prerogative. But the lineup will happen with or without a lawyer."

Gillespie was aching to read what had been written down on the legal pad. His eyes kept darting toward it whenever Pruitt tipped it a little. Finally, he said, "I don't believe you've got that witness."

Pruitt wrote *We'll see*. "Well, he may not be what most people consider a stand-up citizen . . . in fact, he was waiting to rob the place."

"Wilma's?"

"He was after Wilma's computer. You didn't see it that night when you left, did you? The computer?"

Mark opened his mouth, but then closed it again. "I knew she had a computer. That's all I knew. I wasn't there that night, so I wouldn't know anything about it. How could I?"

"He described your truck." Pruitt wrote *Chevy*. "But more importantly, he saw you plain as day. Just dusk, remember? Three-quarter moon?"

"No. I don't remember any of what you're saying. Why would I? I wasn't there."

Pruitt tapped his front tooth with the pen a couple of times. The last two denials, Gillespie was working hard to will his eyes to stay on his interrogator and not go darting off to the right. Among the other preparations Wilma's husband had made, he'd read somewhere that liars' eyes darted right—and he was fighting it.

"The only point I'm making, Mark, is it was still early enough that the eyewitness got a good look at your face. He didn't know who you were, or why you were there, and he didn't care, really."

Gillespie drew his mouth into a tight line. "Why didn't he come forward before now?"

"Like I told you, the guy's a criminal. No way was he coming forward." Pruitt wrote *From the grave*. He looked up. "But then all these months pass and guess what? He gets busted as part of that methamphetamine ring. Over in Lewis County? Our department was part of that, you know." Pruitt looked at Gillespie earnestly. Just two buds talking. "You read about it, didn't you? Pretty big deal and all. We were pretty proud of ourselves—our part in it—even if I have to say so myself."

"It was in the paper."

"So you did read about it. And it's as simple as that. We got four or five guys behind bars going down for dealing. One of them brought this to us. Looking to knock a few years off his sentence by cooperating with law enforcement."

Gillespie crossed his arms. "Jury would never believe a guy like that. A criminal."

Pruitt wrote *Jury wants your ass*. "That's a legitimate point, Mark. But we feel pretty comfortable with him. He was involved in a criminal conspiracy, to be sure, but he's also a vet, a decorated guy. Vietnam. As far as his credibility, he's going to clean up real good. We're going to get him a professional hair cut—maybe Super Cuts over there in Riverton, at the mall—and get him in a suit. A really nice suit, even if the county has to pay for it. Men's Warehouse has good deals, probably won't cost us as much as we think. We're going to get him talking about paying back his debt to society—a society he's served once already, with distinction. He's going to talk about his rehabilitation, how he's going to get off the meth, find Jesus.

"Oh, he's gonna have a great story to tell. How he's had this transcendental experience? How he's ready to get back on the straight and narrow? One of those jailhouse conversions, you see. A born-again decent guy. A born-again war hero."

Gillespie said nothing. Neither would he look at Pruitt. A flush had come to his cheeks.

"So let's get to that lineup, what do you say? You can call a lawyer, if you want. We've got no problem with that. But you will do the lineup. Today, next week. Whenever. The witness isn't going anywhere, that's for sure."

Uncrossing his arms, Gillespie said, "What's the guy's name?"

Pruitt looked down at the pad and tapped it with the nib of his pen as if the name was written there. "That's not something I really need to share with you, Mark. For his protection, you see."

"His protection?"

"Well, you know, you might try to have him killed. Something like that."

Gillespie's eyes grew wide. "What? I thought you said he was in jail?"

Pruitt paused a moment. "Okay, I guess you're right. He's safe and secure." Pruitt then gave him the name of one of the other suspects arrested at the Conley bust, whose name had appeared in the paper. He couldn't tell if Gillespie recognized the name or not. So far, his poker face waxed and waned. The tells were there, but which was which was hard to decipher.

"But you haven't got a weapon." He held up his hands for emphasis. A broad gesture, unlike anything Pruitt had seen from him before. "Got to have a weapon for a conviction."

Pruitt smiled at him. "We've got the weapon. You know that."

"How would I know that?"

"Because you left it there for us to find."

Gillespie waved the notion off with a second exaggerated sweep of his hand. "Any fingerprints on it?"

"You know there aren't." Pruitt leveled his gaze on him. "You did your homework, man. That much we know."

"Homework? What are you talking about?"

"I'm talking about that little book you bought. What was it called again? *Death Dealer's Manual*? Something like that?"

"I don't have a book like that."

Pruitt said, "No, of course not. I'm sure you don't have it *anymore*. But you bought one." Pruitt slipped a piece of paper from his shirt pocket. "Bought it from a little publishing outfit out there in Colorado. Paid by check. Check number 1542." He snapped his fingers. "Oh, you'll like this. We bought a copy for ourselves. Good stuff in there, man. You know, like how to pull off an assassination?"

Gillespie got ruminative, head lowered. Pruitt waited him out, pretending he was writing more stuff down on his pad, like he was keeping track of the interview for later transcription.

When Wilma's ex-husband looked up again, Pruitt could see that the resolve he'd been showing up to now was beginning to ebb. "Gun can't be traced to me. This book you say I bought, even if I did buy it, it's circumstantial. Just a book. For entertainment purposes."

"Circumstantial. Yes, that's true. Oh!" Again, he snapped his fingers. "Speaking of circumstantial. Oh, man, you're going to love this." Again, he leveled his gaze at Gillespie. "Back when we had that warrant for your house? You remember?"

Gillespie shrugged. "Yeah, whatever."

"The one thing I thought was odd was you having those baby wipes in your bathroom."

The corner of Gillespie's eyes wrinkled. The thin line of his lips toying with the idea of a smile. "What're you tryin' to insult me? Because of my fuckin' hygiene? That's bullshit."

Profane language now. From a man Pruitt had never heard use an expletive stronger than darn. "Exactly. That's what my deputy said, too. Just a hygiene thing. Talking about her dad, you see. But I still thought it was odd, so we went ahead and collected a sample of them. Four sheets to be exact. You remember? I had you sign that form."

"Baby wipes?"

"Yeah. Of all things. And you know what? That stuff has what they call a chemical signature."

From his other pocket he pulled out the chemical analysis printout, a copy he'd folded up. Now he unfolded it on the table, turned it toward Gillespie and pushed it to him. "And guess where we found traces of that same chemical signature?"

Gillespie remained silent, his gaze fixed seemingly on the report in front of him. But something was eating him inside. There was twitching around his jaw, and he was perceptively shrinking into his chair.

Pruitt raised an eyebrow. "On the gun that killed Wilma."

Yen had told him to use the phrase chemical signature. "Sounds high-tech," he'd said. "Scary to guilty man."

Pruitt had agreed. Scary, indeed.

Gillespie looked to be getting ready to respond, but Pruitt suddenly didn't want that. It was time to cut off his denials before they came out of his mouth. "So, Mark. To answer your question: yes, our case is going to be circumstantial. But also quite compelling. I mean, you followed those directions from that book to the letter. Including wiping the gun down after you used it with one of those baby wipes. But that also gives us one more way to connect all the dots. We've got your motive, got you with the expertise, got you at the scene . . . "

"Motive?" His worry lines had suddenly disappeared. He sat back up again. "What motive?"

Pruitt spread his hands. "The oldest motive in the book, Mark. Jealous husband. You know that song: 'Hey, Joe'? And that line 'where you going with that gun in your hand?' That's you, Mark. You're our Joe. 'Going to shoot your old lady because you caught her messin' round with another man.' Good criminy, Mark, you shot your baby down by the river. You're a walking cliché. You know as well as I do that everybody knows you did this. You think just because we can't trace the gun to you they're going to care? Believe me, they won't. Everybody loved Wilma. Everybody in the county wants somebody to pay. And everybody knows it's you that did it. Just like everybody knew Wilma and Dan were having an affair. Everybody knew it and, guess what, it was true. We've got enough circumstantial to give a jury the rope they need to hang you. Which is what they still do in this state, in case you didn't know. And from what I've been lead to understand, it's no picnic, dying like that."

Gillespie had lowered his head, staring, ostensibly, at the printout of the chemical analysis Pruitt had handed him. "I got an alibi."

"The jury's gonna see right through it, Mark. The reality is, they're going to be very suspicious that you made such a stink about having that alibi. Playing Harold with that 'I've got shopping to do' story, knowing he'd never show up at that game on his own. Buying that phone when you did. Holding it up for Harold to hear. You'd never done that before, you never did it again. You only did it on the day Wilma was killed. It's going to look too pat. Too easy. Too preposterous."

"It wasn't what I meant to do."

Pruitt waited a moment. He almost said, *You take an untraceable gun out to her house, you march her down a path to the river, you kneel her down and shoot her in the back of the head, then through the heart, and it wasn't what you'd meant to do?* But he checked his emotions, tamped them down, lowered his voice back to two-buds-talking again. "I know you're not much of a drinker, Mark, but did you have a couple pops that day?" Trying to give him an excuse, keep him talking.

Gillespie nodded. "On the drive down. To Nalpe. I had a couple of those little airplane bottles." His rosacea had flushed his cheeks. "I didn't feel like myself."

"It's understandable, man. You were upset."

Gillespie's already ruddy complexion practically glowed. "I haven't touched a drop since. I got mad. I wanted to scare her. It just got out of control."

He squeezed his eyes together. "I didn't know I loved her that much. I didn't know until I got there."

Again, Pruitt had to stop himself from getting in the man's face. *Loved her?* But he could not. Even though Gillespie was in the throes of confession, there was still a long ways to go here.

He also knew blaming the alcohol was a crock. Maybe if he hadn't planned everything out so carefully it might have served as a mitigating circumstance, but he was speaking to the jury right now, trying to explain to them something that he probably couldn't explain to himself. Which was exactly the mindset Pruitt wanted him in.

"Had to be pretty emotional out there, man. I'm not saying one way or another. But it's time to get it down on paper." Pruitt ripped off the top sheet of the pad he'd been writing and doodling on, folded it and stuck it in his pocket. He collected the photocopy of Gillespie's check to the Colorado publisher and the printout of the chemical analysis and placed them off to the side. Then he passed the pad that he'd been pretending to write important things on, and the pen he'd been pretending to write them with, to Gillespie. "Put everything down here. All the details you can remember. Okay?"

"I want a deal first."

Pruitt pursed his lips, as if he were thinking it over, but what he was really considering was Gillespie's coldness. It was sociopathic. Seconds before he was talking of love, then suddenly acting the lawyer, dispassionate, calculating. Who would have known.

Yet while disturbing, asking for a deal was good. Pruitt said, "No problem. We take the death penalty off the table."

Gillespie thought for a moment. "I want the possibility of parole."

Pruitt preferred that he rot in hell, but he hadn't clinched this yet. "After a reasonable amount of time? Yeah, we can do that."

"I want it in writing."

"No problem. I'm going to go to my office and get it down officially. While I'm doing that, you do your part. Then we'll each have what we need."

"I'm not writing anything without that document first."

"Mark," Pruitt said kindly. "Just don't sign it. Without your signature, it's just a story on paper. You write, I'll write. We'll get back together here in a few minutes and read before we do anything else. We won't sign anything until you're satisfied."

•••

Pruitt called Deputy Jones into the interrogation room and left her with Gillespie, already with his head down, intent on his story. She looked at Pruitt expectantly, but he just exited.

He walked directly to his office, not slowing as he said to his office manager, "Joyce, follow me, would you?"

Once the door was closed, he said, "Write down on official letterhead that for confessing to the murder of his wife, Wilma Gillespie, Mark Gillespie will be spared the death penalty. And also that we won't oppose parole, after a reasonable amount of time."

The request took her a moment to digest. "He confessed?"

"He's in the process. I need the letter right away."

"Don't we need Carl's okay on this?"

"I'm not worried about that."

"Wow," she said, and began to leave.

"And, Joyce?"

She looked at him. "Make two copies, would you?"

•••

A couple of minutes later Ing Yen knocked. "Go okay?"

Pruitt was jotting down some notes, but put his pen down. "I think it went well."

"He buy it?"

"He's writing up a confession."

Yen assessed him. "You don't look good about it."

"I'm good with it as far as we've gone."

"You want more than confession?"

"Yeah. We need something hard. Something irrefutable."

"You got something in mind?"

"There's one last play, and we gotta have it. If it works, we've got him. If it doesn't, it turns into a lawyer's battle. If Mark gets a good one, he might walk."

•••

About fifteen minutes later, Yen was back knocking on his door. It was the longest fifteen minutes of Pruitt's life.

"Raphe says he's ready."

Pruitt and Jones exchanged positions again. Pruitt in, Jones out. Again, she scanned his face for answers; again, he ignored her. The last thing he needed now was putting Gillespie on guard, thinking there was a conspiracy against him. Which, obviously, there was.

"All right, Mark, lemme see what you got."

"You'll just keep it."

"Have you signed it yet?"

"No."

"Like I told you, with no signature, it's just a story on paper. Look, here's my end of the bargain." He handed Gillespie the two copies of the agreement Joyce had typed up. "You read what I've written, I read what you've written. Once we're both happy, then we sign."

For a full minute or so, both quietly read.

Gillespie finally handed the letter back. "Okay."

Pruitt, however, placed the confession back in front of Gillespie. Handed him back the pen. "You forgot the make and model of the .22."

Gillespie said, "Oh," then wrote that down, too. A Ruger MKIII 4. The short barrel model. The exact model they had in custody.

"You didn't happen to memorize the serial number before you ground it off, did you?"

"No. Why bother?"

"Fair enough. Where did you buy it?"

"What difference does that make?"

"There's a state task force looking into where the guns used in homicides are coming from. See if there's any sort of trend. Correlations. You know . . . it's statistical."

Gillespie sighed and wrote down the name of the gun dealer in east Pierce County, the one who had been unable to identify him. "But I didn't buy it at his store. I bought it at a gun show," he said. "If I'd bought it at the store, it was traceable."

Pruitt said, "Smart," but was practically jumping out of his skin. Yes, Gillespie had purchased the gun at a show, but he'd bought it from a licensed dealer. He might have thought the gun show "loophole" had secreted his transaction, but it wasn't the licensed dealers who kept no records, but rather the private sellers. The dealer had played along with Gillespie, not questioning the use of the phony name, James Hendricks. Wrote the receipt and delivered it with a wink. As soon as he was done here, Pruitt would call his counterpart in Pierce County. Now that they had something solid, they could lean on the gun dealer more effectively.

When Gillespie was done adding the information to his confession, Pruitt said, "Now we'll both sign and date our documents."

"I keep mine? That says the death penalty's off the table? That I'm going to get parole?"

"Absolutely. Make sure to show it to your lawyer. First thing."

When the signing was finished, Pruitt took the confession in his hand. "Thanks."

He turned to Raphe Jones, who had been standing silently at attention by the door. "Officer Jones, please arrest Mr. Gillespie on the charge of murdering his wife, Wilma Gillespie, in the first degree."

CHAPTER THIRTY-SIX

PRUITT WAS ALONE in the interrogation room. He'd stood, meaning to leave, then sat down again. Near the end of the interview, some twitching had begun in his upper back. It was twitching again now. He rotated his neck and pulled back with his trapeziuses, trying to get it to stop. It took a minute, but it finally subsided.

Sitting in front of someone so cold felt like standing before the gates of hell. Icy hot. Unfathomable. Yet his urge to hate Mark Gillespie had been ameliorated by the interrogation game. Maybe the hatred would return, maybe not. Right now nothing mattered as much as having won. In an interview that could have gone south at any second, it felt good that his training had come back to him. When you used such techniques as infrequently as they did in a small county, it was especially unnerving when you did. He was pleased with himself, and with his team, but mostly he was glad to finally have the killer arrested and behind bars.

He thought about leaving the room, but the silence and sickly lighting comforted him in an odd way he couldn't have explained. He thought of Wilma, tried to bring her back to life in his mind, see her as if she were standing there at the interrogation room door.

But he couldn't. What he remembered instead was first seeing Wilma's body at the crime scene and how he'd thought of Saint Stephen. The slope into the river, the suds-cleansed shore. The primeval ooze from whence our not-really-so-distant ancestors had pulled themselves. The confluence of water, mud, flora, and fauna creating that tangy smell that repelled and enticed in equal measures. Wilma, like the saint, had indeed known something others did not want her to know about or speak of, but that was not what had gotten her killed. Just a cold man unable to let go and move on. Stagger Lee, Diamond Dupree, Joe—the same old cast of characters, a single archetype. There seemed to be an endless supply of them. Why? Was it biology? Society?

As a cop, Pruitt understood that where the Mark Gillespies of the world came from ultimately wasn't his bailiwick. His job was getting them off the street—or better yet, stopping them before they acted, hard as that was to do. Yet such clarity wasn't much comfort, just the only comfort he had.

Ladyfinger dipped in moonlight, Pruitt thought. *Writing "What for?" across the morning sky.* What for, indeed. And then he thought of her bracelet, the one with the Christian cross, Star of David, and Islamic crescent. And he could see her wrist. And then he could see her face, laughing. She was at work at Elkhorn PD, at her desk. He'd come in to see Dan and said something funny to her. She had a deep laugh. A beautiful smile.

The interrogation room door opened. It was Joyce. "Sheriff, the Prosecutor's on the line. He sounds a little miffed."

Pruitt remained seated. He was glad Joyce was at his back. He didn't need to wipe away the tears. "Tell him I'll call him back after lunch."

Epilogue One

ABOUT TWO WEEKS later, Pruitt sat in Bill Logan's backyard with Angela. Bill was in the house whipping up some iced coffee slushies. ("Ice," Bill had explained, "and coffee, a little sugar and heavy cream—throw it all in a blender." Apparently his new life with Angela included the acquisition of culinary skills.)

Angela was wearing unremarkable jeans and her Doc Martens, and a wool, plaid shirt, the kind favored by both grunge rockers and local loggers. She had her nose ring in. Before Bill had gone off to make the slushies, Pruitt noted he was wearing one of his new collection of stylish western shirts, this one blue, and also jeans. Boots, too. Frye's. Pruitt almost asked him where he got them; frankly, he coveted a pair for himself. The psychological effect of their wardrobes, if not intentional, was very real. Angela and Bill were a couple. Compromises had been reached that were comfortable for each to make. Angela down-scaling some, Bill up-scaling some. She wasn't asking him to get a tattoo; he wasn't asking her not to. Amazing.

Pruitt had stopped by to bring them up-to-date on Mark Gillespie's legal proceedings. He first stated it in the simplest terms: "He's going down."

Angela, basking in the early evening sun, said. "Glad it worked out, Gav." Then she met his eyes and winked at him. "You won't need me to come to the rescue this time."

It was the first time Angela had directed a comment at Pruitt that hinted at last fall's events, and Pruitt took her chiding with the grain of salt it was meant to come with. "Getting that gun receipt sealed the deal."

"He's not backtracking, is he? Trying to wiggle out of the confession?"

"Well, I suppose he could argue something to mitigate the effect it would have on a jury—coerced, whatever—but it won't go away. Too late for that."

"Is he going to plead out?"

"Remains to be seen. But his attorney's already called the prosecutor. Blathering on about how we lied and entrapped him, etcetera, etcetera."

"You guys cool on that?"

"It's bluster. We did nothing illegal. Moved all of our circumstantial from weak to damning. That gun dealer in east Pierce County picked Mark's photo out of an array." Pruitt smiled. "I shouldn't be telling you this, so please keep it to yourself, but they had a Pierce County detective and an ATF agent standing there. Just daring him to mess with them."

"Is the gun dealer facing charges?"

"Well, he obviously didn't ask to see Mark's ID. So technically, yeah, he did break the law. And believe me, the ATF agent being there sent that message loud and clear: stonewall us and expect your books to get scoured. But he cooperated, helped put a guilty man behind bars. He gets brownie points with law enforcement. A win-win for all of us."

"He almost got away with it."

Pruitt shrugged. "True enough."

"If your ploy hadn't worked."

"I just played to his guilt."

"He's in for life?"

"I think what the defense is really trying to do is negotiate the parole part of the deal."

"He's not going to get parole, is he?"

"Yes, he will. If he outlives the minimum twenty-five years he'll get."

"Puts him at what, pushing seventy?"

"Yeah, about that."

Angela laid her head back and gazed at the blue sky above her. "I hope he gets shanked in the laundry room."

Pruitt let a beat pass. "That doesn't surprise me."

"It doesn't surprise you I'd think that, or it wouldn't surprise you if he got shanked?"

When he didn't answer, she looked at him. "You think I'm being too harsh?"

"I didn't say that."

She gazed at the sky again. "Sometimes I say things other people only think."

Pruitt smiled. There was nobody he knew, or probably would ever know, who was quite like his dear friend, Angela.

Then Bill was calling from the back stoop: "Man, these look good! You want me add a little Amaretto?"

Epilogue Two

THEY'D RUN OUT of ice chips, but Pruitt didn't want to leave Molly's side. "Go," she told him. "Those are helping."

"But we're right in the middle of things."

"Contractions are about five minutes apart. Go."

So he hustled out to the ice machine, down the hall near the nurse's station. It looked like the same machines you found in hotels, except it dispensed chips not cubes. The plastic bucket, too, looked like the kind you'd find in a hotel.

Molly's water had broke around dawn. They'd called the hospital and were told to gather up their stuff and come on over. A curious attitude, somewhere between laissez-faire and calming. Don't worry. Just proceed. Pruitt realized it was one they also used in law enforcement, when appropriate. About nine they found themselves walking into the birthing center under a clear, crisp sky, not a cloud to be seen. Just walking across the asphalt parking lot like any number of other people on their way in or on their way out, going to work, finished with appointments. Whatever. No big deal.

Pruitt said, "This isn't the way I pictured it would be."

"Me, neither. I was thinking a dark and stormy night. All that stuff."

Pruitt chuckled. *"Just like any other day that's ever been."*

Molly took his arm. "I know that song. 'Black Peter.' But it's sad."

"Sad song, but not a sad lyric."

"The first part of it," Molly said, "if I remember right, is *See here how everything leads up to this day.*"

Pruitt looked at her as they walked. "When did you start quoting the Dead?"

She smiled. "I've been picking up a few things."

Pruitt stopped her. Wrapped his arms around her. "Wow. I just love you, that's all."

•••

The ice bucket filled quickly, but rather than returning immediately to the birthing room, he thought he'd check in briefly with the rest of his family.

It was three in the afternoon now, and Olivia and Christopher were in the waiting room. Had been for an hour. A nurse had brought a message, but Pruitt hadn't wanted to leave Molly. Now, out in the hallway anyway, he thought he'd see how they were doing.

"Pop-cop!" Olivia said. "How's it going in there?"

"Good. I've got about two minutes before the next contraction."

"Well, give your granddaughter a kiss, then get back to business. We'll be waiting."

Pruitt pulled back the soft baby's blanket covering Fiona and planted a gentle kiss on her forehead, the stork bites fading but still slightly visible. Apparently it took a few weeks for them to go away, and it had only been a few days over two weeks since her birth. Little Fiona Michelle had come a bit early, but had arrived quite healthy. Then he planted another one on his daughter's forehead. "God, she's beautiful."

Sitting next to them, Christopher smiled. The day before, word had come that he was up for a job interview in nearby Riverton. Degree in hand, it looked like things were turning out well for him. Maybe for them both? The limerence of Fiona's arrival would wear off at some point. Pruitt hoped that the power of parenthood would give them the boost they needed to overcome their youth and inexperience. He gave his common-law-son-in-law's shoulder a quick grab.

"Gotta go, guys."

He got back to the birthing room in time to deliver an ice chip to Molly's lips a moment or two before the next contraction.

Gary McKinney is the author of the rock and roll novels *If You Want to Get to Heaven* and *Choosing*. *Darkness Bids the Dead Goodbye* is his second Gavin Pruitt, Deadhead County Sheriff, mystery, *Slipknot* being the first. He lives with his wife and children in Bellingham, Washington.